FIRE IN THE ANDES

U. S. Foreign Policy and Cocaine Politics in Bolivia and Peru

Sewall H. Menzel

University Press of America, Inc.
Lanham • New York • London

Copyright © 1996 by
University Press of America,® Inc.
4720 Boston Way
Lanham, Maryland 20706

12 Hid's Copse Rd.
Cummor Hill, Oxford OX2 9JJ

All rights reserved
Printed in the United States of America
British Library Cataloging in Publication Information Available

First paperback edition published in 1998.

Library of Congress Cataloging-in-Publication Data

Menzel, Sewall H. (Sewall Hamm).
Fire in the Andes : U.S. foreign policy and cocaine politics in Bolivia
and Peru / Sewall H. Menzel.
p.   cm.
1. Narotics, Control of—United States. 2. Narotics, Control of—
Bolivia. 3. Narcotics, Control of—Peru. 4. Narcotics, Control of—
International cooperation. 5. Drug Traffic—Boliva. 6. Drug
industry—Peru. 7. Cocaine industry—Boliva. 8. Cocaine
industry—Peru. 9. United States—Foreign relations—Boliva. 10.
United States—Foreign relations—Peru. I. Title.
HV5825.M377   1996   363.4'5'098—DC20   96-34246 CIP

ISBN 0-7618-0507-9 (cloth: alk. ppr.)
ISBN 0-7618-1001-3 (pbk: alk. ppr.)

∞™ The paper used in this publication meets the minimum
requirements of American National Standard for information
Sciences—Permanence of Paper for Printed Library Materials,
ANSI Z39.48—1984

To the DEA field agents who place their lives on the line every day - unsung heroes in a most difficult endeavor.

Contents

Introduction	....	vii
Chapter I	Bolivia's Eradication Quagmire and Operation Blast Furnace	1
Chapter II	Searching for Solutions	23
Chapter III	The Andean Initiative	43
Chapter IV	Bolivia in the 1990s	69
Chapter V	Observations and Conclusions - Bolivia	97
Chapter VI	U.S. Anti-Drug Efforts in Peru - The 1980s	115
Chapter VII	George Bush and Alberto Fujimori	151
Chapter VIII	Fujimori Reigns Supreme	175
Chapter IX	Observations and Conclusions in Regard to Peru	201
Chapter X	Final Observations, Lessons Learned and Conclusions	217
Appendixes	....	235

Contents

Bibliography 247

Index 273

Author Biographical Sketch 281

Introduction

The US anti-drug policy in the Andean countries of Bolivia and Peru has evolved considerably since the early to mid-1980s when it first became a paramount issue on the National Security Council agenda. Perceptions of a threat to American society were highlighted and sharpened by reports of thousands of drug related deaths, an ever increasing level of cocaine addicts and the inability of prisons and rehabilitation centers to handle the social load. The considerable drain on national health care resources as well as the increasing number of American drug user casualties confirmed for many that here was a social threat with international dimensions. Towards the end of the decade in September of 1989, President George Bush stated that illicit drugs were the "greatest threat facing our nation today." (ONDCP 1993:1) Because countering international cocaine trafficking became a key part of the national security strategy of the United States for bringing about stability in Latin America and securing US interests therein, each of the aforementioned countries has been offered or received substantial US financing, equipment, training, advisors and even direct US involvement. All this was designed to help resolve their respective narcotrafficking problems as well as those of the US. Policies, programs, strategies and a variety of operations costing billions of dollars have been the result. By the mid-1990s, Bolivia and Peru had become the primary focus of the US anti-drug eradication policy for

Latin America. It is for this reason that this study of these Andean source countries derives its importance.

After an uneven beginning in its own anti-drug programs in Bolivia, from 1987 to 1989 the Reagan administration requested and Congress approved over $350 million in assistance for the Andean countries. The goal of this effort was not only to counter the production and trafficking in cocaine but also to buttress those countries own respective efforts. Several years after the initiation of the Reagan program, US government studies indicated that thousands of additional metric tons of cocaine had been produced and were being transshipped for sale into the continental USA. The response was a Bush Administration, five-year $2.2 billion program called the Andean Initiative which was focused on Bolivia, Peru and Colombia. Despite this additional program and other supportive efforts to combat cocaine and heroin narcotrafficking through eradication, interdiction and the targeting of the leaders of the drug trafficking organizations (cartels), coca production continued to increase, contributing in its way to an additional ten-thousand drug related deaths, but also bringing into question the US anti-drug policy in the Andes. The declarations of Cartagena and San Antonio as well as the operations named *Blast Furnace, Snowcap, Ghost Zone* and *Support Justice*, among others, are tribute to the determined efforts of the US and Andean governments to disrupt or otherwise halt narcotrafficking at its sources - a supply sided approach to solving the problem.

Using a comparative case study approach, this book describes, analyzes and explains the US anti-drug policy and its related initiatives in Bolivia and Peru. The focus of the study is on the US anti-drug policy as conceived in Washington, D.C. and implemented in the Andes. How this policy effort came about in terms of the Andean countries involved, where it has gone and where it appears to be going for better or worse in the 1990s are central interests in this comparative analysis of US drug policy implementation. Each country is specifically analyzed in terms of its impact on the respective US anti-drug policy in play. In addition, a brief examination of the US government's perception of the drug threat and the related policies which emanated from this are presented. Finally, appropriate observations, lessons learned and conclusions concerning the case studies are rendered.

The central thesis of this study is that even if the White House's anti-drug policy for the Andean region is considered successful, its *greater success* will be relative and limited over the long term and the Andean

Introduction

drug trade will continue to flourish. There are simply too many complicating factors, including high international demand, which undermine the ability of the supply side anti-drug strategy and its implementing efforts to confront the narcotraffickers decisively within the source countries. The US government has given the supply side control effort in the Andes its best shot. Albeit a best shot, it has neither resolved the trafficking problem nor created the desired political and economic stability throughout the region. The winning of some battles does not necessarily win a war, and, as a respected US government report stated: "There appears to be a loss for every gain in the drug war...." (DOS INM 1993b: 1)

When statistics are considered, the *Andean Strategy*, which for the best part of five years has been the center piece of the US international supply control efforts that were originally meant to reduce the amount of illicit drugs entering the United States by 15 percent over two years and by 60 percent over ten years, has not revealed a great deal of promise for success. Official US estimates show a 175 percent increase in the cocaine supply alone from 1988 to 1991 or from 400 metric tons to about 1,100 metric tons respectively. This fact has not been fully comprehended by the administration of President Bill Clinton which has promulgated another anti-drug policy approach in an effort to salvage the situation with an alternate set of "new" strategies and yet another *"drug czar"*, now with cabinet level status.

Related questions which require answers in light of the above are:
1. Is targeting source countries in the Andes through a supply oriented strategy viable?
2. Is there a conflict of interest or contradiction between the US objectives of the so-called *war on drugs* and its traditional interests in fomenting democracy and political-economic stability in the region?

Other issues which also need to be addressed in relation to the above are:
1. The *soundness* of the policy and its play out as a national security strategy.
2. The *effectiveness* of US anti-drug policy leadership in the region.
3. The *adequacy* of the resources committed in light of the alleged national security implications of narco-trafficking.
4. The *cooperation* of host nations with the US policy.

5. *Single issue* foreign policy dominance.
6. Evaluation *criteria* to determine effectiveness of the policy.

The above are part and parcel of the discussion and analysis and serve as additional indicators for evaluation.

Some of the more relevant types of data, indicating US anti-drug policy successes or failures in the Andes, are based in terms of the main on US government reports and documents. The reader should note carefully the levels of coca leaf production which may be in metric tons or total hectares (one hectare is equivalent to 2.5 acres) under cultivation and the quantities of cocaine and other drugs produced. Other indicators worthy of interest are the number of farmers who switch from coca to alternate crops and the quantity of hectares of coca eradicated. This latter category should be compared to the total amount of hectares still in production. At the same time the variation in coca leaf prices may indicate positive or negative trends. Nonetheless, the bottom line or principal criteria in this study to determine whether the US anti-drug policy in the Andean region has worked is the *amount of cocaine reaching the US* and the variation in its prices on the street. A rise in prices indicates a scarcity of cocaine coming into the US and a lowering of prices indicates a ready availability of cocaine or even a saturation of the market. Here too the size of the user population is an indicator of drug policy success or failure, although this may reflect domestic US demand reduction policies in play.

When the effort to control domestic drug usage in the United States was extended to the exterior and became part of the US foreign policy menu, this introduced a new dimension of political intervention in the US relations with most of the nations of Latin America. The outcomes of this process, their repercussions and continuing interaction as influenced by the internal social, economic, political and security conditions and related actors within each country in the Andean region do have an impact on the success or failure of the US policy in play. In addition, non-state actors, interest groups and social movements all play a part and interact with the state actors and the conditions present. As such, narcotrafficking operations in general and their respective markets impact on both the individual and state actors. Latent or real antigovernment insurgencies, such as those in Peru, as well as economic exigencies have influenced each state's respective reaction to narcotrafficking. Other factors involving Venezuela, Brazil, Ecuador,

Introduction

Chile, Paraguay and Argentina are addressed in this study as the traffickers attempted to circumvent US policy through trans-national operations.

In preparing this case study, I first researched and read as much as I could about the US anti-drug policy and its implementation, drawing in part on my own ten years experience in Bolivia, Peru and the region during the 1980s. I then travelled to Bolivia, Peru, Colombia, Panama and Washington, D.C. to conduct further research and interviews. In so doing I was impressed by the variety and number of government reports and studies, such as those put out by the General Accounting Office (GAO) and the US Congress. They are often unvarnished and critical in their approach which helped to surface a number of countervailing factors in play. In addition I found that interviews with participating actors, as well as other keen observers of their respective national scenes, such as members of academia and journalists, were quite useful. No one primary source was overwhelmingly more useful than any other. All melded together and, in conjunction with secondary sources such as books, magazines, and newspapers, made the picture more complete and rendered the inter-play between the various actors and factors impacting on US anti-drug policy implementation that much more discernable and understandable. Often most revealing were the myriad of diverse reactions to my interviews by members of the US Country Teams in Bolivia, Peru and Colombia. Attitudes towards and opinions on the US anti-drug policy ran the gamut from dismay and apparent hopelessness to overwhelming confidence in success and that all was going well.

During the interview process, I found that some persons, working for the US and foreign governments in particular, were often guarded and circumspect for fear they would reveal too much information to me and be duly chastised or punished by their respective offices. Others were often extremely forthright and open and only desired that their perceptions and the *facts* be known. Here a "*damn the torpedoes*" attitude prevailed. So as not to place in undue jeopardy and to accede to the personal desires of those who wished to retain their anonymity, I have accordingly coded for identification some interviews of interest for this study. For example, an interview with a knowledgeable or highly placed DEA official in Bolivia (BL) and Peru (PE) would be referenced as: (Interview DEA: BL). Another example is a key member of a Country Team's (CT) staff, which would be referenced as: (Interview CT: PE). In order to simplify and maintain continuity for the reader, I have also coded references to US Embassy cable traffic for Bolivia and Peru. An example would be: US Embassy (USE) Bolivia (BL) coded as *USE-BL Cable* etc.

It should be remembered that this is a case study and not a history. As such it seeks to illuminate the US anti-drug policy in play, indicating its relative merits, successes and failures by examining enough of the nuts and bolts or events and processes which *make or break* the policy as it has come to fruition via its implementation process. Readers knowledgeable in the field may find that I have not included *all* the information available or that *something* has been left out. I can accept this as my premise is to demonstrate what can happen and why to a foreign policy initiative in the reality of the international world, no matter how well intentioned or motivated the perpetrators of the policy were and still are today.

I have organized these comparative case studies using a geographical and chronological approach as opposed to a thematic approach, starting with Bolivia in the south and then Peru to the north. It is in the actual play out of the anti-drug policy within the Andean countries, that most of the relevant lessons are to be gleaned. The general analysis is followed by conclusions which will bring out the lessons learned from both a regional and a country-specific perspective.

Bolivia was selected as the lead section of this study due to its status as being the one country in the mid-1980s which most fully opened its doors to the US anti-drug policy and allowed it almost free play, including the actual intervention of a US military force. In doing so it became the subject of a veritable blitzkrieg of militant anti-drug activity involving the first direct application of US military forces on an antidrug mission inside a Latin American country. This offered a new dynamic to the *war on drugs* that saw Bolivia become the test bed for a wide ranging US anti-drug policy that continued into the 1990s.

Peru was selected as the next focus for the case study as it is not only in a logical geographical progression northward from Bolivia but also because it contrasts significantly in terms of the relative success of the latter for US anti-drug policy. Whereas Bolivia is deceptively simple as a problem to be resolved by US foreign policy strategies, Peru is far more complex, involving a deeply rooted and vicious insurgency movement and an intransigent, dire economic condition which continues to be very difficult to resolve. These have produced serious consequences which have impacted on the US anti-drug policy in that

Introduction

country.

Because US anti-drug policy is generally formulated in Washington, D.C., either at the White House itself or at one of its agencies or departments, I believe it could be best understood by reflecting on US government policy decisions and actions in the context of knowing what transpired in Bolivia and Peru. The US Southern Command in Panama, because of its overarching regional prominence in promoting and implementing various aspects of the policy in terms of the operations and logistics involved, is included as part of this analysis. It is out of this regional policy perspective that the concluding chapter has evolved and serves as the basis for the conclusions and lessons learned.

While many specific anti-drug "battles" involving the capture or dismantling of entire drug cartels and prominent traffickers have been won, the drug war in general continues to be lost. This is not because of the amount of effort expended, which is considerable, but because of an improper focus on the key center of gravity of the narcotrafficking supply and demand relationship. More than anything else it is a lack of complete understanding of what underlies the drug issue - intense and continuing international demand from both the United States and Europe - which has stymied the US anti-drug policy implementation effort. This may be very discomforting to the reader, yet, when all is said and done, one should come to the conclusion, as I have done, that the US anti-drug policy in the Andes is indeed focused on the wrong center of gravity and for this reason cannot produce decisive or long lasting results.

Acknowledgements

The inspiration for this work emanated out of a lecture series on narcotrafficking in the Americas by Professor Bruce M. Bagley of the Graduate School of International Studies, University of Miami (Coral Gables) and my own endeavors while working in Bolivia and Peru during the 1980s.

I wish to thank Ambassador Ambler H. Moss, Jr., Director of the University of Miami's North-South Center, Professors Bruce M. Bagley, Enrique Baloyra and Alexander H. McIntire, Jr. of the University of Miami and Professor Eduardo A. Gamarra, Director of the Florida International University's Latin American and Caribbean Center, who read the original manuscript. They offered advice and numerous insights which enhanced my own research efforts and the writing of this work. A special thanks also goes to Aldo Regalado of the University of Miami's Richter Library Staff who greatly facilitated the production of this book.

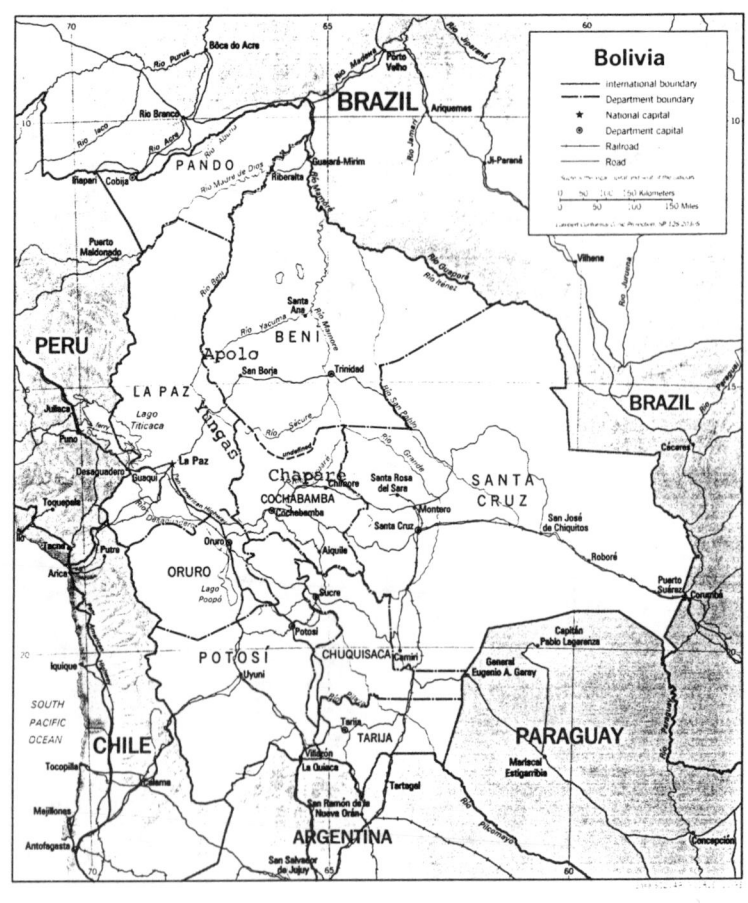

Chapter 1

Bolivia's Eradication Quagmire and Operation Blast Furnace

Over the last decade Bolivia has become infamous as one of the *big two, along with Peru,* of the illicit coca-cocaine producing and narcotrafficking nations in South America's Andean region. Producing about one-third of the region's coca leaves which are converted into cocaine, it has since the 1970's, assumed an even more important position and focus in US-Latin American relations and has constituted a critical part of not only the issues and US national security interests involving Latin America but also the US anti-drug policy in the Andes. For this reason the effects of the various actors and factors involving the social, economic, political and even security aspects of the Bolivian ambience on the US anti-drug policy take on considerable significance.

The social-economic situation of Bolivia's population of roughly 7 million (World Bank 1992: 137) characterize the nation as one of the poorest in South America, including one of the lowest life expectancies and highest infant mortality rates in the region. In the early to mid-1980s, with the tin metals and natural gas markets in a precipitous decline, its economy virtually collapsed with the GNP falling 20 percent and per capita income declining 30 percent, as 20 thousand tin miners were laid off in late 1985 due to the closing down of state run mines. (Youngers 1991: 10)

Unemployment doubled to 20 percent of Bolivia's 1.7 million person labor force. Exports fell some 25 percent between 1984 and 1985 and inflation literally spiralled out of control, reaching an astronomical 24,000 percent in 1985. (House 1990c: 67; and Andreas and Sharpe

1992: 75) In 1985 it was known to the author, then on station in Bolivia, that per capita income for the poorest 20 percent of the population often ran as little as from $60 to $160 annually, exacerbating the social economic condition. (Economist 1989: 10)

Offsetting this relatively dire situation was the coca-cocaine industry which provided jobs for over a quarter of a million people. Towards the end of the 1980s coca was credited with supporting upwards of half a million jobs and generating some $600 million in badly needed foreign exchange, equal in value to all other legal exports combined. (Youngers 1991: 10) In this situation the coca farmers could harvest up to four and even sometimes five crops a year and earn roughly up to $5,000 per hectare (one hectare is equivalent to approximately 2.5 acres) or an income five times greater than that earned from rice and ten times greater than that of corn, providing for many for the first time in their lives a reasonable standard of living for themselves and their families. (Craig 1990: 317; Dunkerly 1984: 312; and Baldivieso 1992) Essentially, Bolivia had moved from an economy of tin to an economy of coca. A World Bank analysis indicated that the illicit coca-based drug trade in Bolivia was growing at an annual rate of 35 percent since 1980. (House 1990c: 45)

The coca bush in Bolivia has been cultivated for over two thousand years. Whether its leaves are used as a mild stimulant to combat cold and fatigue, as an appetite suppressant to dull hunger or as a sign of social acceptance and friendship, it is part and parcel of the traditional Indian culture and mystique, involving religious concepts of *Pacha Mama* (Mother Earth) and even sun gods going back to pre-Incan times. (Alcaraz 1989: 126-127) Whether chewed at weddings, celebrating births or just being sociable among friends, it is from the Indians' point of view an essential, if not vital, mainstay or factor in their life style and livelihood. (Dunkerley 1984: 310; MacDonald 1989: 5; and Baldivieso 1992) The above are all factors which should be seriously taken into account and serve as a backdrop to better understand the US-Bolivian anti-drug policy relationship.

Four basic steps are used in the Bolivian (also Peruvian and Colombian) coca-cocaine production process (see also Appendices A-1 and A-2 for greater detail):

1. Coca bushes are planted and after about eighteen months reach maturity, producing on the average two to four crops per year over a cycle of about two decades. (Tokatlian and Bagley 1990: 312)
2. The freshly picked leaves (*Erythroxylum* coca) are then bundled

and transported to the coca paste maker who places the leaves in a plastic sheet, adds kerosene and diluted sulfuric acid, and together crushes them through a process of stomping in what is called a maturation pit to produce a paste-like substance.
3. Alcohol is then added to the paste to bring the alkaloids to the surface, allowing the remaining syrup to be syphoned off and left to solidify into what is called cocaine sulphate paste (also called *base*). While this paste (base) can be exported at this stage, it is more often passed on to a final stage.
4. During this final stage at a laboratory complex, the cocaine base is further washed in ether or acetone and dried under intense heat from lamps to produce the chlorohydrate of cocaine, often called HCl. (MacDonald 1989: 5)

The Chapare, Yungas, and Apolo areas, otherwise vast subtropical rain forests of about 30,000 square kilometers or about the size of Vermont, form one gigantic swath through central Bolivia and constitute the principal coca growing regions. The Chapare reportedly grows 70 percent of the coca, with the Yungas and Apolo regions growing about 30 percent. (DOS INM 1996: 65 and Lee 1991: 22) Yet it was and still is today the well organized trafficking organizations from Colombia that spurred on and pursued the development of expanded sources of high grade coca in Bolivia. Under their tutelage, the Chapare region changed from being a marginal producer of agricultural products into a sustained position of producing as much as 80 percent of the total Bolivian agricultural output. (USAID 1986: E-1)

Although the Bolivian government had finally ratified in 1976 the Single Convention for Narcotics Control (first promulgated in 1961), under which it agreed to control the legal manufacture and distribution of coca products by the end of the decade, limit their use to medical purposes and to suppress illicit trafficking, the family of then Bolivian President, Hugo Banzer Suarez, was itself involved during the 1970s in narcotrafficking. (USAID 1986: E-1) To this effect his own government had provided state bank loans to the early developing cocaine industry. Money ostensibly borrowed for agricultural ventures was directed to construct a drug production apparatus which was further linked to drug trafficking cartels principally operating out of Colombia. Since the quantity of hectares (ha) grown is an indicator of narcotrafficking, that the quantity of coca in production in the Chapare region of Bolivia virtually doubled during the Banzer regime (1972-1978) from about 2,700 ha to 6,000 ha over a six year period indicates the true nature of the situation. (Alcaraz 1989: 47)

One of the issues of concern to American voters on the eve of the 1980 presidential election was the evolving domestic problem of ever-increasing drug usage. Prior to 1980 it was estimated that as little as 20 metric tons (mt) of cocaine from Bolivia and Peru were sufficient to supply US demand. (Walker 1989: 197) As the newly elected President, Ronald Reagan, took office, both the number of cocaine users and their supply was steadily increasing. The Department of Health and Human Services reported that some 40 percent of the national population between the ages of 18 and 25 were using drugs. About ten percent of the adult population age 26 and older or some 20 million people were also using drugs. (NIDA 1990-1991: 21) Over time the US Congress became more and more aware of the involvement of the Andean countries in the international cocaine trade. A series of debates took place among its members over what should be done to deal with the drug problem. At this time, the Drug Enforcement Administration's own overseas policy was to encourage local governments in the source countries to pull up or eradicate coca bushes. (Interview DEA 1993)

President Reagan was concerned over the drug issue and it became readily apparent that local law enforcement officials needed help in dealing with the problem. In 1981 Senator Sam Nunn (D-GA) and a number of his colleagues declared the need for a fuller government involvement in the anti-drug effort. To this end they were able to modify the Posse Comitatus Act of 1878 against the involvement of US military in civilian law enforcement functions by attaching an amending bill to the 1982 Defense Authorization Act, which would allow the US armed forces to share drug-related intelligence derived from military sources with civilian offices. The military was also allowed to both operate and lend equipment in support of the Department of Justice's Drug Enforcement Administration (DEA), as well as allow the latter to use military facilities when and where needed. Nonetheless, the US military was prohibited from direct involvement in searches or arrests of civilians. Likewise, any assistance which would adversely affect military preparedness was also prohibited (Title 10 United States Code, Sections 371-375). Exemptions were also made in 1981 by Congress to the 1973 Foreign Assistance Act, allowing the military, as well as the DEA and the Federal Bureau of Investigation (FBI) to conduct police training in support of the US anti-drug policy. It was on this basis that a concerned Reagan administration and Congress initially pursued the anti-drug issue. (House 1990: 9-10; GAO 1992b: 2-3; and Bagley 1991: 3-4)

Nonetheless, it was not until the 1980-81 dictatorship of Army General Luis Garcia Meza that the Bolivian government was singled out for its conspicuous connections to the drug trade. With the financial assistance of Issac Chavarria, the principal head of narcotrafficking in Bolivia, Garcia Meza overthrew the constitutional presidency of Lydia Gueiler Tejada. Chavarria, then working with the cocaine cartels of Medellin and Cali, was made Minister of Government. (Nuevo Herald: 29 Jan 94) There was now a virtual symbiosis of the narcotrafficker and state government working together to foster, protect and engage in the illegal drug trade effort. (Lee 1991: 119) In a machiavellian manner the regime placated the US Drug Enforcement Administration (DEA) office at the US Embassy (*Country Team*) in La Paz by persecuting narcotrafficking competition, all the while protecting its own interests. US sponsored coca eradication and crop substitution efforts, important features of the US foreign policy in Bolivia even then, were gradually suspended as they more and more came into conflict with Garcia Meza's *narco-politics*. Objecting DEA agents in the country were declared *persona non grata* by the Bolivian government. In response the US refused to recognize the regime and suspended much of its $127 million in assistance and aid programs. On this note the Garcia Meza government also declared the US Ambassador to Bolivia, Marvin Weisman, persona non grata. As time went on the US then reacted further by pressuring the International Monetary Fund (IMF) and the World Bank, as well as other countries, to isolate Bolivia by cutting off all forms of financial support. (Malloy and Gamarra 1988: 148 and MacDonald 1989: 79)

During this time a tightly-knit, family tied, Bolivian agro-industrial elite of several dozen families operating out of the Beni and Santa Cruz regions, including such personalities as cattle rancher Roberto Suarez Gomez, promoted and coordinated most of the narcotrafficking operations; all the while supported by the unqualified state backing and patronage of Garcia Meza and his military cronies. (Corr 1985; El Nuevo Herald: 29 Jan 94) This is not to say that the impact of narcotrafficking on Bolivia was negative. Hospitals, roads, schools, and even low income housing and other basic services were for the first time made available to some segments of the local population in the Cochabamba, Santa Cruz and Beni Departments as part of a natural infrastructure buildup derived from narcotrafficker proceeds. The national government did not have the resources to compete, and the otherwise poor population did not ignore the apparent economic benefits accruing to itself and the region in general. (MacDonald 1989: 73)

Yet, like so many other similar dictatorships, the Bolivian military ultimately found its own institution pulling against itself with petty jealousies, internal feuding and intrigue becoming dominant as contending interests vied for the spoils of the drug trade. In addition, the Bolivian military fell victim to its own corruption and incompetence at running the economy. (Dunkerley 1984: 321-323) As the economy declined, pressures grew for a change of government. Officers within the institution responded with a *golpe* (*coup*) which eventually succeeded in placing General Celso Torrelio in power as the new president. He attempted to end Bolivia's international isolation by favorably influencing the US through announced intentions of reintroducing the democratic process and combating the illegal cocaine drug trade. (Corr 1985)

In February of 1982 President Ronald Reagan, cognizant of the escalating drug usage and its effects on the health of significant portions of the US population, declared war on drugs both at home and abroad. The US government's focuses were to be on drug abuse and illegal drug dealing within the continental USA, and production, refining and trafficking overseas in the source countries. To this end expenditures within the federal government over the next seven years of the Reagan administration were increased substantially to about $4.3 billion by 1988. To promote his initiative Reagan made use of national television to dramatize his perspective and to galvanize support for his mobilization of federal resources to fight the war on drugs. The US Congress supported the Reagan initiative with anti-drug legislation to enhance law enforcement programs in foreign source and transit countries and over time would authorize a greater involvement in the drug war. The President's spouse, Nancy Reagan, launched her own "Just Say No!" campaign in an effort to educate and indoctrinate the American public and its youth about the dangers of drug usage and abuse. (Callahan 1993)

Over time, more information became known about the international aspect of cocaine trafficking which emanated from Bolivia and Peru. It was supposed by Reagan and others within his administration that the supply of cocaine was exacerbating the domestic drug problem within the US. If the supply could be reduced significantly or even stopped, then fewer people would be involved in drug usage, or so the reasoning went. Eradication of coca could be easily measured and quantified in terms of how many hectares of plants had been destroyed. Over time it became the principal yardstick by which the US Congress and other government offices would measure the progress of the Andean anti-drug policy effort. All government agencies were expected to assist in their own way in addressing the drug issue. US Embassies in the Andes were urged to further develop coca eradication and other suitable drug control programs which had been initiated in the 1970s under the administrations of Presidents Richard Nixon and James E. Carter. (Interview NSC: 1993)

The Reagan administration, to better address the drug issue, wanted to develop and coordinate anti-drug policy in a coherent manner as part of an integrated national strategy. The Congress assisted by creating the National Drug Policy Board (NDPB) which was chaired by the Attorney General, Edwin Meese III, and was comprised of the heads of some 15 US government departments and agencies. This was acceptable to President Reagan who opposed the concept of a drug czar or a single dominating agency whose all-encompassing powers would eclipse all other agencies as it formulated general anti-drug policy and directed all drug related federal operations of the several dozen agencies involved to one degree or another in federal anti-drug efforts. (GAO 1988a: 15; and Van Wert 1988: 6) The NDPB, while establishing nine lead agencies to review issues and make recommendations for formulating the anti-drug policy, looked to the Department of State's Bureau of International Narcotics Matters (INM) to chair the International Standing Committee (ISC) which made policy program recommendations involving the Andean countries. (Van Wert 1988: 6-7)

The Department of State (DOS) never really accepted the NDPB's involvement in overseas anti-drug issues and asserted its prerogative to represent the US government's international anti-drug position, using Section 400 of the Foreign Assistance Act legislation as its own justification as to why it should be in charge of all international narcotics matters. Also irritating to the DOS was Meese's tendency to blend together foreign and domestic anti-drug policy issues. (Interview NSC 1993) The basic problem with the NDPB, however, was that it did not have the legal authority by statute to require other government agencies to redirect their plans and programs in support of anti-drug activities and perceived priorities or, even if they did, to coordinate the various diverse efforts toward a common goal. The NDPB strategy consisted of nothing more than a generally disjointed compilation of plans and ideas submitted by separate US government departments and law enforcement agencies. In addition it was difficult to develop budgeting priorities because the NDPB also did not have the information required to determine which anti-drug initiatives merited priority attention. As a result US anti-drug policies were frequently fragmented and uncoordinated. (House 1990; 1; and GAO 1988a: 15)

After Bolivia expelled a known narcotrafficker (Alfredo Gutierrez) in 1982, the administration of US President Ronald Reagan responded favorably by relinquishing its sanctions and dispatching Ambassador Edwin Corr to La Paz as its representative. Recognizing that national security interests are often best served through the consolidation of democratic regimes, Corr was charged with working towards achieving four major US policy goals in Bolivia:
1. Asserting Bolivian and US control over cocaine production and trade.
2. Reinstitution of formal democracy.
3. Stabilizing and reactivating the Bolivian economy.
4. Enhancing the organization and political activities of the private sector. (Malloy and Gamarra 1988: 150; and Gamarra 1990)

Although no one goal was allegedly any more important than any other, the democratic process was seen by the US as the only real solid foundation on which a viable anti-drug policy could be built. It was felt that the *high moral ground* which democratic governments generally represented would constitute the necessary imperative for an anti-drug policy to come to fruition in a successful manner. On this basis the goal was most often discussed and emphasized. (Corr 1985)

To a considerable degree Corr's influence prodded the Bolivian political system forward in 1982 and succeeded in fostering a transition to democratic rule with Hernan Siles Zuazo elected as president. In the face of coca grower mobilization and fearing a militant confrontation, Siles on at least two occasions had to amend his strong legal position of reasserting the Bolivian government's control over coca and reinstate by decree a modified position, tolerating the *free marketing* of coca. (Healy 1988: 112) At the same time, Siles was also pressured into renewing the US Department of State's (DOS) coca eradication and crop substitution programs. This came to fruition in 1983, whereby the US promised Bolivia a drug control program ($30 million) and an aid package ($58 million) if the latter eradicated 4,000 ha of illegal coca bushes by 1985. As the US was threatening to cut off aid if eradication was not entered into, Siles invoked a decree mandating the eradication the eradication of 4,000 ha of coca crops by 1985. (GAO 1987: 3-4 and Healy 1988: 111)

The US provided $4 million to form, train and equip a several hundred man *Unidad Movil Policial Para Areas Rurales* (UMOPAR - Rural Area Mobile Police Unit) to patrol the coca growing zones. To this was added a thirty member special detective squad to assist Bolivia in bringing narcotraffickers to trial. (DA 1991: 261) Since Bolivia had an infamous history for more than a century of coups and changes of government averaging about one per year, it became a top priority for the US to strengthen the new democratic initiative now in play and to sustain it for as long as possible so as to provide continuity for future US policy initiatives. Promised US economic and military aid increased accordingly from $20 million in 1982 to 78 million by 1984 (due to human rights opposition in the US Congress, only about $5 million was actually dispersed). (Malloy and Gamarra 1988: 176; and Corr 1985) While all this sounded promising, between 1982 and 1985 the actual total number of hectares of coca under cultivation doubled to about 35,000 ha. (DA 1991: 209)

The US anti-drug policy and program for Bolivia during the Siles Zuazo administration was largely based on an Agency for International Development (AID) narcotics control strategy which evolved out of its initial mid-1970s studies on the feasibility of a coca crop substitution program. Initiated in 1983, the *Chapare Regional Development Project* (CRDP) represented the first AID development project in the primary coca-growing region of Bolivia. Its goal was to reduce in a phased manner some 20,000 ha of coca over a five-year period. This project was begun in the face of an ever greater production which had seen coca increase by 78 percent from 1977 to 1981, despite a $1.9 million AID effort (*Agricultural Development in the Coca Zones Project -* ADCZP) which, because it was ill-defined and not properly thought through, turned out to be an abject failure. (USAID: E 4-5) The AID project area consisted of 422,000 ha whose erosion, excessive moisture due to seasonal flooding, rapid loss of fertility due to leaching, soil acidity and a lack of organic matter were apparently conducive to no other agriculturally lucrative crops except coca, which thrived in this climate, and to a lesser extent rice. Since the coca farmers were acknowledged as having improved their standard of living relative to the rest of the majority of the population through production of the perceived sacred and traditional coca leaves, they themselves did not deem coca cultivation to be an illegal activity but instead saw it as both socially acceptable and financially fruitful activity. Considering that no other viable alternative crop appeared suitable for the Chapare region, an AID study concluded that success for a US crop substitution project at that time remained "a very distant goal." (USAID 1986: E-7). The study further concluded:

> The evidence suggests that coca is the cash crop of choice because labor requirements are minimal and the plant can be harvested three to four times a year, thus providing the family with a continuous flow of income. Although cacao may in some cases yield a net profit per acre that is higher than that yielded by coca, the former is much more labor intensive. Because labor is the limiting factor to increased family income, coca therefore remains the preferred crop. (USAID 1986: 26)

In its turn, the US Congress, then monitoring Bolivia's compliance with the 1983 eradication agreement in which the latter had promised to eradicate 4,000 ha over a three year period in return for a $14.2 million US aid package, came to the conclusion that the Bolivian government was failing to comply with the US stipulated goals. It thus threatened to invoke the 1985 Foreign Assistance Act which limited aid to countries that engaged in drug trafficking. Yet limiting aid would tend to undermine the US objective of assisting in the consolidation and strengthening of Bolivian democratic institutions, which were deemed critical to fight drug trafficking. Nonetheless, this would ultimately take place in 1986 when Washington announced the suspension of $7.1 million in aid, despite President Siles' May, 1985 decree calling for extensive drug enforcement programs. (DA 1991: 209-210)

Ambassador Corr, having completed his tour in Bolivia, left in August of 1985, having seen a successful Bolivian national election take place with the democratically elected incumbent replaced by another, Dr. Victor Paz Estenssoro. Ambassador Edward Rowell replaced Corr. For President Paz Estenssoro the national economic situation he inherited was a disaster. In October the bottom fell out of the international tin market and the London Metals Exchange terminated all trading in tin, Bolivia's principal foreign exchange earner. With the mining and industrial sectors no longer able to sustain a major segment of the population (the miners), only coca production appeared to be a viable alternative for many of the now unemployed. The national debt was $3.7 billion and well beyond the capability of the government itself to service. To obtain urgently needed financial aid and loans, the government would somehow have to overcome the coca production/drug trade obstacle and thus cement better relations with the international community, especially the US. (MacDonald 1989: 77-78)

Paz Estenssoro did begin a drastic economic stabilization and austerity program (*Nueva Politica Economica* - NPE) in August 1985 which was to see Bolivia into the 1990s. He devalued the currency, cut government subsidies, froze wages, and put up for sale non-productive state owned enterprises, including a number of the tin mines. In addition to these measures, Paz and his economic advisors, many of whom came from an alliance of Paz's *Movimiento Nacionalista Revolucionario* (MNR - National Revolutionary Movement) party and former President Banzer's *Accion Democratica y Nacionalista* (ADN - National and Democratic Action) party, saw the need to further stabilize the economy and cushion the shocks of the new economic policy in play. To enhance the process, Paz allowed a tax amnesty on all repatriated capital, relaxed disclosure requirements from the Central Bank, and prohibited official investigation into the origin of outside wealth brought into the country. As such he was exploiting to a significant degree and bringing into play to stimulate the economy those narcotrafficker profits remaining outside the country. In this manner he increased Bolivia's foreign exchange reserves and raised short term deposits from $28 million to $228 million by early 1987. (Andreas and Sharpe 1992: 75-76) The narcotraffickers now had the option of laundering their money via investment inside Bolivia, as well as outside of it. Nonetheless, despite loans being renegotiated, credit lent and prices stabilized, unemployment went up as the government divested itself of all its previously unprofitable, nationally controlled enterprises. Most importantly included in this effort were the tin mines, involving upwards of 25,000 miners, most of whom now no longer had any work and found their traditional high-Andean life style seriously threatened. (Tokatlian and Bagley 1990: 319) There was at this time a world-wide recession and this did not help Dr Paz's own programs for economic recovery.

Ambassador Rowell intended to work closely with Paz's government to overcome both Bolivia's economic crisis and the still flourishing drug trade. As mentioned, the Paz Estenssoro government had agreed with the US interest in developing an anti-drug policy which authorized only *traditional* or a limited production of legal coca in the Yungas and advocated voluntary destruction of the other, illegal coca bushes, followed by a forced eradication, as required, in the remaining areas which included the Chapare, Yapacani and some parts of the Yungas. (Tokatlian and Bagley 1990: 320) The previous Siles government had promulgated (May 1985) a narcotics law which laid out the legal basis for implementing any and all new bilateral agreements with the US in this regard. This also became the basis on which the Paz Estenssoro government would also initially work. The Bolivian government's Coca Reduction Directorate (DIRECO) was reorganized and a system of licensing for legal coca crops as well as the eradication of illegal coca crops was established. Yet it would not be until that September that the eradication program was actually begun. (USAID 1986: E-3 and E-6)

While the raging inflation of 1985 was gradually brought under control by 1986 (50 percent), the US congressionally mandated eradication program appeared to be going nowhere for as many or more coca bushes were being planted for every one cut or pulled up and destroyed. Often they would disappear and then be rediscovered in other newly planted coca plots. The DEA directed UMOPAR, assisted by DIRECO personnel, was attempting to force the issue and confront directly the then estimated 250 thousand coca farmers and their families in the Chapare region. This only inflamed the passion of the farmers who saw their livelihood and families being threatened by the US supported UMOPAR's high pressure, raid style tactics. For every primitive coca paste maturation pit or paste laboratory that was forcibly destroyed, another could be quickly reconstructed in its place in less than an hour. Roughly 5,000 of the paste laboratories were operating in the Chapare region or about one for every eight coca-growing families. (Lee 1989: 31) Thought had been given to involving the military, but the 1984 employment of an Army infantry regiment (*Manchego Rangers*), attempting to accomplish the same thing during the Siles Administration, had fragmented in the face of narcotrafficker bribes which promptly bought off the regiment's key officers, leaving the coca farmers and the narcotraffickers relatively free to ply their respective trades. (Corr 1985)

Up to the mid-1980s the National Security Council (NSC) looked at the international narcotrafficking issue as merely peripheral and part of its Middle East focus concerning terrorism. This began to change as the intensifying domestic interest in the issue, along with a fear of international terrorism competed for attention at the highest levels of the Reagan administration. A 1985 household survey which had considerable impact on government leaders indicated that cocaine client admissions since the advent of the Reagan administration had doubled! (DHHS 1987: cover page) Over ten percent of the population or some 23 million persons over twelve years of age were now reported to be using drugs in some form each year. These were startling figures for an administration which had supposedly declared war on drugs two years earlier. Every month the situation appeared to be getting worse rather than better. As a result the decision was made to highlight the problem for the American people by elevating and presenting the government's concern as a national security issue. (Interview ONDCP

1: 1993)

Besides attracting public attention and support, it was expected that a national security emphasis would better focus the government's efforts and justify increased government spending, as well as an ever greater role for the military in the counter-drug effort. Both Reagan and the NSC thought that making the drug war a national security issue would both underscore the seriousness of the drug problem and send a signal to the international community that the US was very serious in its pursuit of the narcotrafficking scourge. The Andean countries would receive a special focus in order to deal with cocaine at its source. the source of the cocaine supplies, or the drug producing countries of Bolivia and Peru, were perceived as the root cause of the US drug problem. To this end, in the Fall of 1985, government agencies and Country Teams overseas were put on alert that dealing with drugs was now a national security imperative. (Interview ONDCP 1: 1993; GAO 1988a: 14 and author observation)

The US eradication program at this time in Bolivia was seen as ineffective and out of control. An informal Country Team study, known to the author in La Paz, calculated that it was costing the US government $1,000 for every coca bush actually eradicated. For Bolivia the overall gross national product had continued its early to mid-1980s trend, declining by 2 to 3 percent each year with an official unemployment rate rising from about 6 to 20 percent. During this time coca cultivation and the number of families engaged in it had tripled. (Lee 1988: 90) In October 1985 at a Country Team meeting attended by the author, it was announced that a successful anti-drug and coca eradication program in Bolivia was now considered in Washington to be a national security imperative! This was a significant shift in the intensity of US policy and the Country Team was now expected to focus for the most part on developing ideas to support the new imperative. As time went by and November came on, there were no new ideas being brought out over the approaches already in play. the DEA continued to insist that operations in the Chapare should continue, trying to arrest recalcitrant farmers and coca paste producers and shippers, all the while continuing the otherwise less than successful eradication effort. (Author recollection)

As frustration amongst the embassy's leadership mounted over the inability to articulate an effective anti-drug, action oriented policy, another Country Team meeting in November 1985 saw the Deputy Chief of Mission, Jeffery Biggs, inquire if there was anyone in the room who could contribute a new idea as to how to resolve the narcotrafficking situation in Bolivia. The author, as the Army-Navy Attache, having considered that the embassy was now operating under a national security imperative to do something about the drug problem in Bolivia, volunteered to examine the situation and attempt a solution. The Defense Attache Office (DAO) supported by the Country Team studied the problem in some detail. It was concluded that the current policy then in play, through its confrontation tactics with the coca farmers and the up to 5,000 paste laboratories estimated to be functioning (Lee 1989: 31), was placing the US in the incompatible position of potentially fostering a civil war in the Chapare and was further undermining the fragile democratic process in play, as well as the US anti-drug policy objectives.

The DAO study determined that, within the narcotrafficker system then operating inside Bolivia, there was one major focal point and two related adjuncts which, if addressed intensively on a sustained basis, could decisively collapse the narcotrafficker production system. If the system collapsed, it was theorized that the lack of a suitable market would drive the price per hundred weight of coca leaves below the DEA estimated minimum profit level of $30; thus rendering coca leaf production an unprofitable business for the coca farmer. This, in turn, would make it possible for the US and Bolivian governments to then place leverage on the coca farmers to desist from growing coca crops and transition into alternate crop substitutes sponsored by USAID, successfully accomplishing the US anti-drug strategy goal of gaining control over the illegal cocaine trade inside Bolivia. (Author recollection)

The strategy concept elaborated in the study was a highly militant approach which called for an airmobile force (the UMOPAR transported in US-piloted helicopters) to attack the narcotrafficker HCl cocaine laboratory system. In addition, the laboratory system, located principally in the Santa Cruz, Beni and Pando Departments, was to be sealed off from cargos of coca paste flowing in via selected rivers and roads coming out of the Chapare and Yungas regions. This would necessitate the involvement of a mobile riverine force (UMOPAR elements transported in US supplied swift boats) and road checks at critical choke points. The third component involved a national aircraft flight registration program to be coordinated by the Bolivian civil aviation authority nationwide. This program was intended to be monitored by US aerial detection and intelligence gathering platforms and radars which would pinpoint and assist the Bolivian Air Force in the interception of narcotrafficker aircraft flying into and out of the laboratory sites. Suspect aircraft which refused to land for inspection could then be shot down by the Bolivian Air Force. This *triad* approach was considered to be well within the capability of the US to implement. (Menzel 1989: 26-27) Participation by the Bolivian military was to be kept at a minimum to reduce the possibility of corruption and place the interdiction emphasis on the Bolivian law enforcement elements (UMOPAR) wherever possible. The US would play both a guiding and supporting role, while the Bolivian police forces (UMOPAR) and the judicial system were to deal directly with the narcotraffickers and enforce the law.

The triad approach expected that a successful execution of any combination of its elements would close down the narcotraffickers HCl laboratories. This would force the coca farmer to become amenable to eradicating his crop and collecting the $2,000 per hectare that the US and Bolivian governments were offering as an incentive for switching to a selected alternate crop substitute. In this manner the US policy could meet its goals and avoid the confrontational situation with the farmers which at that time was leading to a perceived civil war between the local populace and the US supported Bolivian police forces.

The DAO study also indicated that a four to six month preparation phase should be undertaken to operationalize the concept and develop suitable, coordinated campaign and support plans involving the application of intelligence, logistical support and the actual operations themselves. It was thought at the time that anywhere from two dozen to several hundred narcotrafficker cocaine base and HCl laboratories were potentially operating throughout Bolivia. Intelligence data on the matter was skimpy and based in the main on unverified DEA agent reports which were known to be frequently unreliable. Where the laboratories were specifically located had to be found out in sufficient enough detail to enable the formulation of a logical campaign plan. It was reported to the author by the DEA sources that up to six narcotrafficker flights per day were going from Bolivia to Colombia and points north, carrying either cocaine paste or refined cocaine HCl. It was also noted that USAID, which was in charge of the crop substitution program, would need some months to gather the appropriate crop seedlings and supporting funds to develop its own side of the program. The DAO concept was studied and approved by Ambassador Rowell and the highest levels of the Country Team. (Author recollection) The US anti-drug policy for Bolivia was about to enter a new phase.

Obviously the US could not just bring into play any plan it desired unless it was approved not only by the host country but also by the DOS and the Washington community. In January of 1986, Ambassador Rowell approached President Paz Estenssoro in a private meeting and explained the concept in general terms. Dr. Paz, possibly feeling pressures not to jeopardize a forthcoming US aid program, approved whole heartedly the concept, exclaiming: "Mr. Ambassador, you can do anything you want to do!" He further stated that narcotrafficking was undermining the moral foundation of Bolivia and he wanted to stop it anyway he could. In this vein he also suggested that the actual plan to be executed be kept a secret until the moment it was executed. (Author recollection 1986) He knew all too well that narcotrafficker familial ties, as well as other political linkages to his government and the Bolivian Congress, ruled out further revelations of the concept's details. While President Paz did not make an issue of it, Bolivia was now a constitutional democracy and Bolivian congressional (Chamber of Deputies) approval was required to permit the presence of foreign military forces on national soil. The Country Team did not raise the issue which was to have some political repercussions later on.

From a Country Team perspective, President Paz was quite correct in his perception of the corrupting influence and penetration of narcotrafficking elements into his government at all levels. In 1985, when DEA and UMOPAR forces had attempted to raid paste laboratories using Bolivian Air Force helicopters, the Bolivian pilots had given excuses for several days as to why they could not conduct the missions. When the strikes were eventually mounted, the labs were found to have been abandoned - a mere day or so earlier! (Abbott 1988: 106) President Paz concluded by saying he would control the political situation, allowing the plan to come to fruition whenever the US decided to execute it. This was reasonable to Ambassador Rowell as President Paz Estenssoro was a veteran of Bolivian politics, having served as President in the 1950s, and was still viewed by Bolivians in general as the hero of the 1952 revolution which resulted in major land reforms in favor of the majority of the peasant population. Having made this coordination, the Country Team's strategy concept was then cabled to Washington for further analysis and hoped for further rapid approval and appropriate support during the next few months.

Some months passed and there appeared to be neither an interest nor even a response to the concept by the Washington community. Not one DOS official or other US government representative came to Bolivia to discuss the merits of the concept, its coordination with other US policy efforts in the region, or the support required for its execution. A single exception during this time was the visit to Bolivia of General John Galvin, the Commander in Chief (CINC) of the US Southern Command (SOUTHCOM) in Panama, who was briefed by the Country Team. He appeared unperturbed that there was a national security imperative in play. As it was, he was more interested in maintaining SOUTHCOM's then current focus on the Central American war effort, involving the US openly in El Salvador and Honduras and more clandestinely in Nicaragua. The last thing he wanted was a distraction to the south which would siphon off his limited assets, then supporting operations in Central America, to support competing requirements in the Andean Ridge. (Author recollection)

During this time the government of Paz Estenssoro did formally charge in its Congress the nefarious Garcia Meza, as well as fifty-five of is former colleagues, with various crimes, involving sedition, armed uprising, treason, murder, fraud and drug trafficking. (DA 1991: 256) For the Country Team this was a good sign and was interpreted to mean that the Paz government was in full accord with the US anti-drug policy. In Washington, President Reagan formally declared that drug trafficking constituted a national security threat to the US and issued his National Security Decision Directive (NSDD) 221 on 11 April 1986 to that effect. As such, US military participation was to be guided by three principles:

1. Host governments had to invite US forces;
2. US civilian agencies (DOS and DEA) were to coordinate the effort of US forces; and
3. US forces were to be limited to support functions. (Bagley 1991: 5)

At about this same time in April, in contravention of the Bolivian Constitution (Article 59) and without congressional approval, President Paz Estenssoro in a note to Ambassador Rowell quietly *invited* the US to support the Bolivian anti-drug effort. Nonetheless, it was not until late June that the Country Team received a response from Washington to its strategy concept cable sent out in January. In this case Ambassador Rowell was unexpectedly told by the DOS that a 160 person US Army task force (Task Force Janus), initially commanded by Major-General James Taylor, including six high performance UH-60 helicopters, would arrive within two weeks to begin operations against the narcotrafficker laboratories. With this short notice, the operation known as *Blast Furnace* began with the arrival of US Air Force C-5A cargo transports, bringing in the helicopters and related support packages of personnel and equipment to the Santa Cruz airport. Any element of surprise originally called for in the Country Team's strategy concept was lost as scores of small narcotrafficker aircraft and up to 800 persons fled Bolivia in a panic. (Menzel 1989: 28; and Abbott 1988: 103) This was viewed as a significant setback initially as a clandestine insertion and surprise application of the UMOPAR against the laboratories would most likely have captured some narcotraffickers who, in turn, could have provided valuable information on narcotrafficker systems and linkages which would have been useful in subsequent operations. This shortsightedness and the failure to plan for the mass exodus of narcotraffickers from Bolivia to other parts of Latin America are indicative of the experimental nature and the auspices under which Blast Furnace was actually undertaken by the US government.

Operation Blast Furnace, which lasted from early July until November of 1986, was initially characterized by a dire lack of timely and complete intelligence on the whereabouts of the laboratories. Task Force Janus, reacting to the intelligence information developed over those months, ultimately did reconnoitre upwards of several hundred potential laboratory targets, but rapidly reduced the list of lucrative targets to about fifty that offered the promise of successfully encountering a narcotrafficker-run laboratory in operation. Also inhibiting operations were the disagreements which developed on the part of DEA, DOS and the US Army personnel over which laboratory targets should be hit and when. This frequently led to delays in conducting operations against priority targets as the Task Force's leadership tried to placate the several agencies involved in terms of exploiting their respective sources of information. The UMOPAR's leaders and personnel were not fully trusted by the US personnel because of the possibility of narcotrafficker corruption, compromising the anti-drug operations. As a result, the UMOPAR was only notified of a pending mission an hour or so before the helicopter strike force actually took off to attack the target. Although twenty-two cocaine laboratories were eventually discovered, no cocaine of any significance was seized and no important arrests were made as a result of Blast Furnace. (Author recollection)

Ironically, the largest laboratory discovered was not due to the efforts of Operation Blast Furnace's Task Force Janus at all, but due to the misfortune of one Dr. Noel Kempff, Bolivia's leading botanist, who was murdered by gunmen after his aircraft landed by accident at a major narcotrafficker cocaine production facility hidden in the Beni's Huanchaca rain-forest and national botanical preserve. This facility was stocked with approximately one thousand barrels (55 gallon drums) of precursor chemicals including ether, acetone and hydrochloric acid and was awaiting the delivery of a batch of coca paste to be further refined into cocaine. (Author recollection) As fortune would have it, this laboratory had been designated as *Target 157* by Task Force Janus but not yet reconnoitered and verified for possible attack. (Abbott 1988: 105)

As the news spread as to what had happened at Huanchaca, the Bolivian Air Force's leadership reacted by attempting an aerial counterattack against the laboratory site but to no avail. The target could neither be located nor could the actual attack aircraft be assembled, armed and fueled on the short notice necessary to be effective. In the meantime scores of thousands of people, principally in the Santa Cruz Department, conducted protest marches against the narcotraffickers over the murder of the Noel Kempff. This massive, spontaneous outpouring of antagonism against the narcotraffickers had never been seen before in Bolivia. Nonetheless, because of the experimental nature of Blast Furnace, no thought had been given in Washington or SOUTHCOM to the possibility of having a psychological operations detachment on hand to support the operation and, in this case, exploit the sympathies of the for the moment visibly and highly aroused population. After a few weeks the passions of the people subsided and life went on as normal. (Author recollection)

After some days had passed from the initial report of Dr. Kempff's murder, Task Force Janus was able to mount an operation against the laboratory at Target 157. The invading UMOPAR force encountered the thousand barrels of chemicals and the lab's processing equipment. The guards and those narcotrafficker processing personnel at the laboratory had vanished. At this point in time, the facility and its chemical contents became a matter of considerable dispute reaching the level of the Bolivian Ministry of Interior. What should have been a simple demolition exercise in the remote outback of Bolivia, now became an ecology issue fueled by the fear that a massive fire ball created by the burning chemicals might get out of control and adversely affect the area's ecology forever. (Author recollection)

While this was hotly debated within the Bolivian government, which also accused the DEA of narcotrafficker complicity and footdragging in responding to the Huanchaca murders, a SOUTHCOM demolition team (*Explosive Ordinance Disposal - EOD* team) was flown down to Bolivia from Panama to prepare the laboratory site for destruction. About a month later the EOD team went to check the condition of its demolitions in place and found that about half of the thousand barrels of chemicals had now been removed by the narcotraffickers to some other undisclosed site. Some weeks later Task Force Janus departed Bolivia along with the demolition team. The remaining five hundred barrels at the site were never destroyed, although the team leader had assured Ambassador Rowell that a safe, self-contained destruction of the chemicals could have been accomplished. (Abbott 1988: 106; and author recollection) Some years later in April of 1992, the former Minister of the Interior, Fernando Barthelemy, was officially cited in a Bolivian legislative commission report which stated that he had protected and covered for the narcotraffickers, including those involved in the Huanchaca matter, involving the death of Noel Kempff. (Nuevo Herald: 19 Apr 92)

As the original Country Team strategy concept had envisioned, the Blast Furnace operations did in the main bring about a collapse of the narcotrafficking system. (GAO 1987: 5) With the temporary shutdown of most, if not all of the laboratories, coca leaves and crude paste had no buyers and the price of coca leaves dropped to about $14 to $25 per hundred weight or well under the estimated profit, break even point of about $30 for the coca grower. Initially, the coca farmers placed no special blame on anyone in particular - what had happened with the Blast Furnace was considered "an act of God." Yet, this would change over time. (Fishel 1991: 64)

As a result of Blast Furnace, while some farmers decided to wait and see what would happen, other farmers from at least five coca-growing villages sought assistance from USAID in developing alternate crops. While this was all good and well from the US point of view, the fact that the interdiction campaign was not sustained from the dry season ending in October of 1986 throughout the ensuing rainy season to mid-1987 meant that the narcotraffickers could rapidly reconstitute their operations and linkages to the coca growing community, negating USAID's efforts to implement a viable and lasting crop substitution program. As it was, with the brief notice given for the execution of Blast Furnace, USAID did not have enough resources to satisfy the request from the erstwhile coca farmers. (Gamarra, 1991: 9) Washington decision makers had not studied the Country Team's strategy concept carefully and had only implemented a portion of it, omitting the riverine/road check point, aerial cap and AID portions, leaving the field as it were once again in the hands of the narcotraffickers. The consequences of this myopic execution of a comprehensive strategy concept tended to considerably undermine and even confuse US anti-drug implementation efforts in Bolivia during both the short and long terms. As it was, by the end of the four month operation, the price of 100 pounds of coca leaves gradually rose above the average cost of production ($30), as calculated by DEA, to levels running from $60 to $88 or about what they were prior to Blast Furnace. (GAO 1988c: 52)

One of the first impacts of Blast Furnace on the Bolivian national scene was political as both pro-narcotrafficker and pro-sovereignty biased government officials and representatives protested vehemently the introduction of US military forces into Bolivia without a formal Bolivian congressional grant of approval - a clear violation of the Bolivian Constitution. This attitude contrasted noticeably, however, with the routinely approved joint and combined SOUTHCOM-Bolivian military training excersises, lasting a month, which had only been approved that past April. The widespread controversy over Blast Furnace's US participation did place President Paz Estenssoro under considerable pressure even to the point of possible censure and even a toppling of his democratically elected administration which would have seriously imperiled the US anti-drug policy for Bolivia. Paz had entered into a political pact (*Pacto por la Democracia*) between his party and the ADN, as well as others, which enabled him to rule. Through the pact, Paz had crafted a coalition with a two-thirds majority (20 of 27 members of the Chamber of Deputies) in his favor. This pact was shaken considerably when Paz failed to take into his confidence Banzer and other political leaders before making a decision to allow US forces to enter the country. Nonetheless, as Ambassador Rowell had anticipated, Dr. Paz was ultimately able to weather the political storm due to his close, multi-party ties and pacts. In August, the Chamber of Deputies (Congress) in a face-saving gesture and after the fact did approve Blast Furnace. (Gammara, 1992; and Bagley 1991: 12)

The second impact was the eventual galvanizing to action of the highly organized *Central Obrera Boliviana* (COB - Bolivian Labor Federation) which mobilized coca farmers, workers and peasants in the Chapare and Yungas regions to demonstrate, contending that their livelihood was now being threatened. This action tended to both coerce and submerge to some degree those coca farmers actually interested in making the transition into USAID's crop substitution program. (DA 1991: 265) Groups, such as the *Federacion Especial Campesina del Tropico Cochabambino* (Special Peasant Federation of the Cochabamba Tropics), began a deliberate campaign to lobby the Bolivian Congress over their interests which they claimed were being thwarted by the US anti-drug policy and the UMOPAR's operations. (CEDIB 1992: 37, 69, 71 and 76) With the coca farmers now aroused and better organized than ever before as a virtual "coca lobby," the Country Team found itself no better off than before. The traffickers had been alerted to the more militant dynamics of the US anti-drug policy and were preparing accordingly. In the meantime the US was looking for other solutions.

Chapter 2

Searching for Solutions

The promoters and critics of the Reagan policy, both Democrats and Republicans, wanted to see an all-out escalation of the drug war effort with ever harsher US laws against drug consumption and narcotrafficking, an increasingly larger employment of US resources in the form of weapons, equipment and even fire power to defeat the traffickers, and tougher international law enforcement and interdiction programs as part of an intensified diplomatic pressure on the Andean source and transit countries' governments. (Bagley 1988: 193) This was forthcoming in the October 1986 Anti-Drug Abuse Act authorized by Congress which allocated some $3.9 billion for FY 1987. Of these anti-drug monies, about three-quarters were earmarked for expanded supply sided enforcement, involving interdiction and eradication and crop substitution programs. In addition, other government offices pitched in to help out. The Agency for International Development (AID) transferred some of its funding to the Department of Justice to enable the latter to enhance the investigative capability of law enforcement agencies in the Andes and elsewhere (the International Criminal Investigative Training Assistance Program). The remaining amounts of anti-drug funding were dedicated to education, prevention, treatment and rehabilitation or the demand side. (Bagley 1988: 193-194; and GAO 1992b: 13)

Yet, just a few months after the passage of the 1986 anti-drug legislation, the severe fiscal deficit and the constraints of the Graham-Rudman budget reduction requirements caused the Reagan administration to cut approximately $1 billion from its anti-drug budget. To this end most cuts were made in the areas of education, treatment, rehabilitation and local law enforcement, which spared the international supply side focus and guaranteed its continued high priority and prominence in the US anti-drug policy. It was also reported at this time by the US media that the price of cocaine on the street had dropped from $35,000 to about $20,000 per kilogram, indicating that there was an abundance of cocaine available on the US consumer market. Also during this time, some 25 mt of cocaine HCl was captured in southern Florida alone, further indicating the escalating efforts of the traffickers to smuggle the drug into the US from the Andean region. (Miami Herald: 10 Feb 85; and Gugliotta and Leen 1989: 275) Drug usage had intensified and up to six million people in the US were now reported as using cocaine at least once a month and another quarter of a million were known as compulsive users or addicts who consumed the drug every day. (DEA 1987: 26)

Congressman Charles Rangel (D-NY) and Senators Alfonse D'Amato (R-NY) and Paula Hawkins (R-FL) repeatedly condemned or criticized the US government and President Reagan for not bringing a fuller range of US economic and political power to bear on foreign governments to force their more complete cooperation with the US anti-drug policy abroad. Hawkins won a 1986 Congressional decison to suspend US aid to Bolivia and Peru on the grounds of not achieving their US stipulated coca eradication goals for 1985. That a sanction such as this might be counter-productive in that country was largely ignored. (Bagley 1988: 192)

In early 1987 with the traffickers now reconstituting their laboratory systems, the US and Bolivian governments agreed in an exchange of notes to the *Principals of Narcotics Cooperation*, providing the framework for Bolivia's new three-year plan for coca control. Yet there were some reservations expressed by reviewing US government officials who cited corruption, public apathy, an inability to fund an extensive coca control program and an apparent lack of will power on the part of the Bolivian government to capture and imprison known narcotraffickers. (GAO 1987: 4-5) While the US would have preferred to see upwards of 5,000 ha eradicated, the Bolivian Ministry of Foreign Relations said it was prepared to attempt to eradicate only a minimum of 1,800 ha. (Bedregal 1987) Nonetheless, a $300 million joint plan was formulated whereby 70 percent of Bolivia's coca fields would be eradicated over three years and the coca farmers reimbursed $2,000 for each hectare of coca destroyed. Some 2,000 ha were actually eradicated during the course of the next year. (DA 1991: 257)

During this time the DEA and the UMOPAR began to refocus on the Chapare region and reengage the coca farmers in violation of the spirit of the Blast Furnace concept of non-confrontation with farmers at all costs. In April US Army Special Forces began intensive training of the UMOPAR as part of Operation Snowcap. This was one part of a three-year law enforcement campaign, involving DEA, the DOS's Bureau of International Narcotics Matters (INM), the US Border Patrol and Coast Guard, which were to provide advice, training and operational oversight of the UMOPAR forces in the field and significantly reduce the supply of cocaine coming out of Bolivia. (DOS-IG 1991: 19; and Westrate 1989) Because of the refocus on the Chapare after the departure of Task Force Janus, DEA-UMOPAR operations became much like they were prior to the initiation of Blast Furnace and were again of considerable concern to the Country Team. Due to the perceived lethargic, unimaginative, and less than successful operations on the part of the DEA-UMOPAR forces, an investigation was called for to determine if corruption within the Country Team in La Paz was involved. This was held in-house and produced inconclusive results with no apparent irregularities having been found. Nonetheless, dissension over the efficiency and focus of the anti-drug effort continued within the Country Team. (Hayes 1988 and Montalvo 1992)

A few months later in July, irate coca farmers virtually laid siege to a DEA camp at Chimore in the central Chapare region, forcing out some 25 DEA agents and causing a shutdown of the UMOPAR base. (DA 1991: 265) Chagrined by this turn of events, the DEA worked to strike back and reassert more UMOPAR control over the Chapare. By the end of 1987 it was reported that over a thousand paste making pits had been disrupted or destroyed within the region, indicating once again the confrontational nature of the US-Bolivian anti-drug policy. (GAO 1988c: 53) Fueling much of the coca farmers' hostility was the perceived threat to their livelihood through the eradication of a traditionally essential crop and the inability of the state to provide similarly lucrative cash-crop alternatives to coca-leaf farming. The coca farmers, in their own interest and at the behest of the trafficker buyers, resorted to organized action at the grass roots level, forming regional federations similar to US labor unions in the Yungas and Chapare areas. An outgrowth of Paz Estenssoro's own 1953 national agrarian reform program, the unions (called "sindicatos"), numbering well over 150 and linked to five large federations by some thirty centrales, were formed. (Healy 1991: 89-90; and Gamarra 1990) Democratically linked to their respective federations via their elected delegates, the coca farmers became a formidable lobby in Bolivian politics, involving up to 20 percent of the national work force. Their influence was considerable and via a strong lobbying effort they were able to force the passage of a Bolivian Congressional prohibition ("Ley de Regimen") against the use of chemical herbicides to eradicate coca (Lee 1988: 93 and 93; and Healy 1991: 91), significantly eliminating a potentially cheap and effective option for the US anti-drug policy in Bolivia. Ignored by the federations in this ecological issue was the environmental damage being caused over time by the dumping of coca-leaf processing and precursor chemicals by the traffickers into the rivers and streams of the region, as well as the leaching of the soil itself from intensified growing of coca bushes which could ultimately lead to a desertification of the Chapare. (Healy 1991: 96)

By this time, despite the US effort, coca and cocaine production was generating an estimated $1.5 billion or an equivalent of up to 30 percent of the Bolivian GNP. Of this amount about $600 million reportedly remained in country, bolstering the otherwise weak economy. Some 300 thousand people in the Chapare and Yungas regions were now considered by the Country Team as dependent on coca for their livelihood. (House 1990b: 67) This was estimated at about 20 percent of the adult working population. When droughts, frosts and other natural calamities combined with the current economic recession, up to 100 thousand peasant youth from poor Andean highland communities were now drawn into making the trek to work as seasonal or even day laborers, often employed as coca stompers ("pisacocas") in the pits where coca-paste is first formed. (House 1990c: 59-60; and Healy 1991: 96) While this provided quick cash inputs into the pockets of impoverished peasant families, it also provided a ready source of labor for coca processing. (House 1990c: 59-60; and Healy 1991: 96) As it was, the Bolivian Government was not able to meet its US Congressionally mandated eradication quotas in either 1986 or 1987. Because of its decertification over this issue by the US Congress, Bolivia lost over $8 million in security assistance funding for its military for both years respectively. Nonetheless, the US Department of State's INM funding continued for specific anti-drug programs. (Abbott 1988: 107; and GAO 1987: 4)

Only after Operation Blast Furnace was initiated did the US government authorize the Country Team in La Paz to begin to examine ways in which the US could further assist narcotics control efforts inside Bolivia once the operation was concluded. Apart from helicopter support for airmobile operations by the UMOPAR, river interdiction was seen as a significant problem which needed to be addressed. The US Military Group (MILGP) in La Paz and the Country Team's Narcotics Assistance Unit (NAU) were operating under distinct concepts of what ought to be done, each with somewhat differing goals and objectives. For the MILGP, not only was narcotics interdiction deemed important but assisting the Bolivian government gain effective control of its borders was also of equal importance. The NAU had a more parochial focus, attempting to choke off the riverine entrance and egress from the coca growing regions to inhibit both precursors and paste from reaching the laboratories deep inside the Beni, La Paz and Pando Departments. (GAO 1988b: 3 and Hayes 1988)

At this time in Washington INM was writing and coordinating most of the NDPB's interagency anti-drug strategy and its implementation plans. For Latin America in general and specifically the Andean countries of Bolivia and Peru the policy goals were:

1. Reduce the amount of cocaine shipped from Latin America to the United States through an integrated program of narcotics control.
2. Eliminate major trafficking networks and cartels through increased seizures, arrests, prosecutions, convictions and forfeitures of assets.
3. Secure increased international cooperation in worldwide narcotics control matters through diplomatic program initiatives. (DOS INM 1988: passim)

Attorney General Meese identified the control of cocaine as the first priority for the US anti-drug policy. To further this end a significant portion of the entire INM budget was now to be devoted to controlling cocaine, along with heroin and marijuana in Latin America. The INM believed that eradication in the short term and institution-building over the long term were required to reduce the supply of cocaine and other related drugs at home. (Van Wert 1988: 8) A multi-agency intelligence effort to support anti-drug interdiction efforts in the Andes was coordinated. This enabled the government to bring together and analyze all information gathered on narcotrafficking activities and then pass this on to the the various country teams as well as US government agencies. (ONDCP 2)

During the mid-1980s the smuggling dimension of the anti-drug policy problem for the US in terms of stopping cocaine and heroin was significant. Faciltating smuggling was the fact that every year some 290 million people were crossing the US border. Another 30 million air passengers were arriving on roughly 500,000 commercial airline flights from all parts of the world. In addition 7.5 million cargo containers entered the US through its seaports, 100 million pieces of mail arrived from overseas and 89 million land vehicles crossed into the US and Canada. Additional thousands of pleasure boats and private aircraft came and went from the US mainland every year. The problem was so complex that US Customs was only able to seize some 27 of the 138 mt of cocaine estimated at that time to have been smuggled into the US during the period of a year. (Mabry 1988: 54)

In 1987 interdiction had been noted by the US General Accounting Office (GAO) as probably being ineffective since the transportation costs to the traffickers was only about 10 percent of their actual earnings from the cocaine being sold on the street. (GAO 1988a: 17-18; and GAO 1991c: 26) In this regard the GAO was supported by the 1986 RAND Corporation study which implied that even if one could triple the costs of production for coca farmers cocaine prices in the US would rise by only one percent. In short it would be extremely difficult to reduce cocaine consumption by as much as five percent through more stringent interdiction since the traffrickers could always absorb the additional costs of business (Figure 1). (Senate 1990c: 34 and 95)

Cocaine Prices' Distribution Chain
(Per pure kilogram equivalent in dollars)

At the Farm	$ 1,200
Export (Colombia)	7,000
Import (Miami)	20,000
Wholesale (1 kg. in Detroit)	40,000
Retail (1 gram units)	250,000

Source: Senate Hearing 101-712, 19 April 1989, p. 95.

Figure 1

Nonetheless, buoying up the anti-drug effort's current course was the knowledge that enough evidence had become available to US authorities so that a formal indictment of a number of key Colombian Medellin cartel members took place on 18 November 1986. (Miami Herald: 19 Nov 86)

Cocaine consumption patterns continued to show a steady increase between 1984 and 1987 with the Drug Abuse Warning Network

(DAWN) of the National Institute for Drug Abuse reporting an approximately five-fold increase in its annual metropolitan cocaine-related emergency room mentions, going from 8,831 in 1984 to 46,020 in 1988. Cocaine related deaths reflected a several-fold increase rising from 566 in 1984 to 1,793 in 1987. (DHHS 1987: 38; and 1991: 21) Three-quarters of all robberies in the US during this time were reported as drug related. (Seyler 1991: 1)

At the same time the wholesale price of cocaine had now dropped to a low of about $11,000 per kilogram or about half of the 1985 wholesale price. The purity of the drug was recorded by the DEA as having increased by some 30 percent, reaching a mean-high of about 70 percent. (House 1990: 6) The implication was that, despite efforts to the contrary, cocaine had continued to flow into the US in ever greater quantities and ever increasing quality. In FY 1987, after spending some $40 million on maritime interdiction operatins, the Navy and Coast Guard reported seizing 20 vessels, making some 110 arrests and capturing 550 pounds of cocaine. The Air Force spent $2.6 million, flying 591 hours which resulted in six aircraft seizures and ten perons arrested. (GAO 1988a: 28-29) This was not an especially significant return for the amount of time and money invested.

The US anti-drug policy was incorporated as part of the US national security strategy for 1987 which depicted narcotrafficking as breeding violence, fueling instability and threatenting governing institutions. (White House 1987: 5 and 34) Throughout 1987 the primary goal of the US anti-drug policy remained supply reduction or reducing not only the amount of illegal narcotics coming into the US but also reducing the amount of illegal drugs being cultivated and processed in the souce countries. To this end the country teams were expected to work with their respective host nations to reduce the production of narcotics crops as an immediate, short term goal and to influence the local laws of the host nation so as to better control and ultimately eliminate narcotrafficking altogether. (Hayes 1992 and Callahan 1993)

The Bureau of International Narcotics Matters (INM) had determined that there should be five main elements to the US anti-drug policy for the Andes: crop control, developmental assistance to coca farmrs to replace drug related income, enforcement of the source nations's anti-drug laws and policies, training for those involved in implementing the anti-drug laws and policies, and a general public education about illegal drugs and their usage. In conjuction with the INM efforts, the DEA initiated a law enforcement initiative called Operation Snowcap whereby the DEA would advise the law enforcement efforts of the various

Andean countries in order to better focus their operations in support of the US anti-drug policy. Snowcap was to last several years or until the end of 1989. (DOS INM 1987: 1)

Ironically, despite the reported devastating effects that drug usage was having on the American population, the Reagan administration in its war on drugs did not want to decertify or otherwise confront Panamanian Dictator-General Manuel Noriega's notorious, narcotrafficking-linked government which was both assisting in the trafficking of drugs through its territory and serving as a convenient money laundering site for narcotrafficker funds. The DEA, NSC and the CIA all considered Noriega to be an "asset" whose importance to US intelligence operations concerning Cuba reputedly outweighed any damage that his complicity and fostering of narcotrafficking operations inside Panama might have on the US population and the US national secuirity threat that narcotrafficking in cocaine allegedly represented. (Callahan 1993) This policy continued despite the fact that Noriega had been indicted for narcotrafficking by US legal authorities in Florida in 1987. Finally, on 5 February 1988 a twelve-count federal indictment was formally announced, charging Noriega with drug related crimes taking place as far back as 1982 and linking him to Colombia's Medellin cartel. (Miami Herald: 6 Feb 88) This action and its publicity over the extent of Noriega's activities tended to force the US government's here-to-fore protective hand.

Although in early 1987 Bolivia had agreed to provide three Bell 205 helicopters and pilots to support the UMOPAR's operations, the situation had proved to be unsatisfactory. It was felt by Ambassador Rowell that a permanent, dedicated airmobile force in support of UMOPAR would render more reliable and timely service. All too frequently the Bolivian Air Force's pilots had given various excuses for not flying missions against priority trafficker targets. This and the frequently poor maintenance condition of the helicopters further convinced Rowell and his staff that a change was necessary. Rowell took action. Beginning in 1988 a fleet of 12 UH-1H helicopters was loaned from the Department of Defense (DOD) to the DOS's NAU. Rowell then directed that his US Army-Navy Attache, Lieutenant-Colonel Edward Hayes, himself a rated helicopter pilot, take charge of the airmobile force personally as its commander. Renaming the force the Red Devils ("Diablos Rojos"), Hayes took command. As some Bolivian pilots proved to be incompetent or otherwise uncooperative, they were summarily relieved by their US commander and replaced with others retrained by a US Army helicopter instructor pilot who also served as an operations and maintenance advisor. (House 1990c: 49; and Hayes 1992) Over a period of a year's time the UMOPAR, assisted by the Red Devils, increased its operational tempo and located and destroyed a reported 4,237 coca paste maturation pits, 54 cocaine paste and 48 cocaine HCl laboratories. (House 1990c: 50) The airmobile force gained such notoriety for its successful support of the UMOPAR that the traffickers attempted to assassinate Hayes as he left the US Embassy's main entrance. The attempt failed. (Hayes 1992 and Montalvo 1993)

Despite the fact that there was no formal, operational riverine interdiction strategy in existence and that no formal evaluation had been made as to which types of boats and equipment would best address Bolivia's unique conditions (GAO 1988b: 12), in 1987 the DOS purchased eight Piranha swift boats to support a 35 man US-Bolivian riverine program. Due to doubts about the ability of the Bolivians to supply and maintain the Piranhas, only five were allowed to become operational. The others remained in storage, significantly reducing the potential riverine capability of the force. In reality, it was discovered by the NAU that the boats were too complicated and expensive for the Bolivians to maintain. It was also observed by Hayes that the Bolivian Navy disliked both the UMOPAR and the DEA and had from time to time attempted to disrupt their related US-Bolivian riverine operations. In addition to providing limited security and official government presence on Bolivia's rivers, the Navy often used some of its US purchased boats as river taxies to transport drugs, precursor chemicals and equipment to resupply the traffickers - all for the purpose of earning a few dollars when the overseeing DEA agents were not around. Although the US military training teams (MTTs) had completed their mission and the swift boats were in the water, the lackluster performance by the Navy in support of supposed Bolivian governmental anti-drug support operations was also undermining the very success of the Country Team's own anti-drug mission and became as a result very frustrating to Ambassador Rowell. (Gamarra, 1991: 33; DOS IG 1989: 20; and Hayes 1992)

To bring the Bolivian Navy's riverine force into line with the US anti-drug policy and, remembering the riverine portion of the Country Team's pre-Blast Furnace strategy concept, Ambassador Rowell now assigned Lieutenant-Colonel Hayes the new mission of taking command of the riverine force. Exploiting his previous experience with the Red Devil helicopter force, Hayes renamed the riverine force the Blue Devils ("Diablos Azules") and went to work. As part of his effort he conducted an investigation into the Navy's operations, finding that of the roughly 200 line officers assigned, about 30 percent were found to be actively involved in trafficking and another 40 percent were passively involved. This left a minority of relatively honest and apparently uncorrupted officers who either truly felt that it was morally and legally wrong to engage in trafficking or were not working in assignments which would bring them into direct contact with the traffickers. The investigation also indicated that the drug related corruption reached into the highest levels of the Navy's command structure. (Hayes 1992 and Moantalvo 1992)

With Hayes insisting that the key Navy narcotrafficking-linked ring leaders had to be replaced, President Paz Estenssoro, feeling considerable pressure from Ambassador Rowell, relieved the Navy's Commander-in-Chief (Admiral Douglas Estremadoiro) and its Vice-Chief of Staff. Their links to the narcotraffickers were undeniable and the evidence was overwhelming. In addition the DEA found that groups of naval officers were purchasing cocaine base and HCl as an investment and then selling these to narcotrafficker buyers or directly to the laboratories. Official Navy aircraft, as well as vehicles, swift boats and ships and Admiral Estremadoiro's own official sea-plane, were involved in facilitating the drug trade. With naval outposts situated along every major river throughout the region east of the Andes, the Navy was essentially operating a series of narco-transhipment cells which significantly facilitated the transportation of coca products and precursors to the drug-processing laboratories. In addition, Admiral Estremadoiro was controlling the Navy's officer assignments, placing corrupt officers at the key outposts which were most useful to facilitating the narcotraffickers' transportation system. Besides identifying and eliminating corrupt naval officials, Hayes also directed appointments of those officers deemed both honest and efficient. This included one Navy Captain Alberto Saenz Klinski, who was appointed as the new Commander-in-Chief of the Bolivian Navy, over the heads of far more senior officers. (Hayes 1992 and Montalvo 1993)

With Hayes at the "*helm*," the Blue Devils began operations to complement those of the Red Devils. Beginning in March of 1988, operations were begun south of Trinidad to choke off the riverine entrance and egress points along the northern outskirts of the Chapare and the eastern routes into the Yungas. The initial results seemed promising as over a full metric ton of cocaine base was intercepted and scores of narcotrafficker laboratories were attacked and destroyed. While not happy with the situation, the Navy's officers, under the scrutinizing eye of their new Commander-in-Chief and Hayes' dynamic and uncompromising leadership in the field, were forced to comply with the new turn in US-Bolivian anti-drug policy. (Montalvo 1993 and Hayes 1992)

In 1988 the US government still believed that by reducing the supply of drugs flowing into the US one could reduce drug abuse by US citizens. The idea was to discourage people from experimenting with or becoming chronic drug users by making drugs difficult to obtain and increasingly expensive to use. Supply reduction in this sense was to stop the traffickers from smuggling their illegal goods and services to the American people by seizing their products and production infrastructure, their profits and investments and otherwise prosecuting them for engaging in a criminal enterprise. It was also presumed that attacking the traffickerts at the source would defend countries friendly to the US whose own security and stability might be affected by the power and influence of the traffickers themselves. (Van Wert 1988: 1)

Nonetheless, there was no coherent policy and related strategy and only a series of operations and programs, sometimes operating in tandem and sometimes not. Highlighting this fact was General Fred Woerner's annual SOUTHCOM conference on Latin American issues in early 1988. When querried at the conference if the Department of State had an anti-drug strategy for the Andean region, Ann Wroblesky, The Department of State's Assistant Secretary of State for International Narcotics Matters stated openly to those in attendance that: "We have no strategy; we just operate!" (Author recollection 1988)

By early 1988 both the UMOPAR and the DEA were being accused by the Bolivian Congress of human rights abuses which only further assisted the drug traffickers in inciting the Chapare coca farmers to protest more strongly on their own behalf. The Permanent Assembly of Human Rights of Bolivia reported that the DEA directed UMOPAR routinely attacked coca farmers, stealing money, goods and other personal property. This is not to say that the narcotraffickers themselves did not coerce and use the threat of terrorism against those who refused to cooperate with the cocaine production industry. They did! But this was not reported upon as heavily as the DEA-UMOPAR activities. (DA 1991: 265) In one notable case, Bolivian Congressman, Edmundo Salazar, was shot dead in his home as he was intensifying his investigation of the drug traffickers involved in the Kempff-Huanchaca murders of 1986. During a visit to Bolivia in early August, 1988, US Secretary of State, George P. Shultz, became the target of an attempted bombing. Whether this attempt was conceived by narcotraffickers or minor insurgent movements such as the *Zarate Wilka* clan was never determined. Prior to that, during March of 1988, two members of the FELCN were murdered in Santa Cruz by narcotraffickers. The DEA itself became subject to a May 1987 bombing attack against the Cochabamba home of one of its members. (DA 1991: 255) But this was not all, as another factor - *corruption* - was still in play.

Corruption was perceived by both the Country Team and Washington as a major and perennial problem in Bolivia. The narcotraffickers not only successfully bribed the Bolivian military, police and UMOPAR but also routinely tried to bribe judicial and other governmental officials in exchange for releasing captured key traffickers and destroying incriminating evidence and narcotrafficker related files. Paz's government, at the urging of the US Country Team, suspended thirteen judges in La Paz, Cochabamba and Santa Cruz over drug related corruption. Nonetheless, relatively few prosecutions or forfeitures of narcotrafficker assets actually took place. (DA 1991: 270 and GAO 1987: 5) Confusion also took place as to how much coca was under cultivation. Estimates ranged from 35,000 ha and 60,000 ha by the DOS's INM and the Country Team's NAU respectively, to a high of over 100,000 ha by the Bolivian Ministry of Agriculture. A US government study questioned whether it was realistic to develop a narcotics control program for Bolivia if one could not accurately estimate the coca growing capacity of the country. (GAO 1987: 6)

If this was not bad enough, it was reported towards the end of 1987 to the Country Team that the Bolivian government's eradication assessment team officials, in league with certain coca farmers in the Chapare and the Yungas were exaggerating the amounts of hectares actually being eradicated. In specific cases the coca farmer was being given full credit for his eradication effort and a $2,000 payment for only eradicating as little as a quarter to a half of a hectare of coca. The money received was then divided between the farmer and the authenticating assessment team official. While not necessarily rampant, this defrauding of the Bolivian and US governments, did force the issue and the personnel involved were replaced. Given that eradication took place over an area involving hundreds of square miles, with limited road networks, verification of the accuracy of the eradication effort would remain a serious problem. Even the DEA's own eradication figures were thought to have been inflated to make the US effort appear more successful than it actually was. (Montalvo 1992 and Gamarra 1993)

That July 11th the Paz Estenssoro government, in accordance with the Principles of Narcotics Cooperation, approved a new coca control law (*Ley del Regimen de la Coca y Sustancias Controladas - Ley 1008*) which, for the first time in Bolivian history, officially declared coca cultivation illegal in most of the country. *Ley 1008*, which consisted of 149 distinct articles dealing with narcotrafficking in Bolivia, articulated what was legal and illegal in terms of coca growing inside Bolivia. In Article 3 legal coca was defined as growing in a *natural state* and producing no ill effects on one's health, and illegal coca was defined as that which was used in the process of economically transforming the leaves into cocaine alkaloids of any form. (Seamos 1991: 134) Ley 1008 also laid out a series of penalties of up to two years in prison for the mere planting and growing of illegal coca (Article 46), from five to fifteen years in prison for fabricating cocaine products (Article 47) and from ten to twenty years in prison for narcotrafficking in general (Article 48). A coca stomper working in a maceration pit was liable for a prescribed penalty of one to two years in prison (Article 47) and anyone who illegally provided controlled substances (called *precursors* by DEA), such as acetone, ether, and sulfuric acid, among a dozen others, to narcotraffickers was subject to a period of from eight to twenty years in prison (Articles 50-52). (Seamos 1991: 146-147) These were serious penalties and comparable with those meted out in the US and other countries.

No one was to be exempt from or immune to the provisions of Ley 1008 (Article 81). (Seamos 1991: 155) For this reason the law became the subject of intense debate among members of the Bolivian judiciary; some of whom had serious reservations as to its legality and its application to Bolivian society in terms of respecting individual civil rights. (Seamos 1991: passim) This debate produced some frictions and even divisions within the Bolivian judicial system and tended to undermine the impact of Ley 1008 with respect to how the judiciary would actually apply the penalties relevant to each narcotrafficking case.

There were now to be *traditional* or legal growing areas, *transitional* or areas where coca would be gradually eliminated over a period of five years, and *illegal* coca growing zones where cultivation was prohibited and eradication could take place immediately. Legal or traditional coca (Article 9) cultivation involved some 12,000 ha (Article 29) and was concentrated for the most part in the Yungas region of the La Paz Department as well as a block of land in the Cochabamba Department to the south-east. (Seamos 1991: 135; and Alcaraz 1989: 51-52) All the remaining coca crops in those regions were designated as essentially illegal. (USAID 1991a: 2) Ley 1008 also meant that officially the vast majority of the coca leaf farmers could now be technically categorized as criminals. (Healy 1991: 90) All zones were to be monitored by the government with a one year voluntary eradication program to be followed by a two-year forced eradication period in the illegal areas. Annual coca bush reduction bench marks of from 5,000 up to 8,000 ha were established (Article 10) for the transitional zones so that the Bolivian government could receive US economic aid and its farmers earn a US-Bolivian compensation of $2,000 per hectare eradicated. (CEDIB 1992: 116; and USE-BL 1992a: 24) Mandatory eradication, without compensation, was established for the illegal zones. The US-Bolivian goal was said to be the complete eradication over a ten year period of the 80,000 ha of illegal coca considered to be growing inside Bolivia. (House 1990c: 47-48 and GAO 1987: 4) Despite mass rallies, marches, hunger strikes, sporadic road blockages and intensive lobbying on the part of the coca grower federations, President Paz's government held firm in its policy.

The coca eradication project was to take place under the direction of the US-funded Bolivian Coca Reduction Agency (DIRECO). Any farmer desiring to voluntarily eradicate his coca crops could contact DIRECO which would then measure the farmer's field and determine the amount of compensation. Both the Country Team's NAU and DIRECO personnel would verify both the destruction of the coca and the fact that no further new coca crops had been planted. Yet it would not be until December of 1989 that DIRECO would ultimately conduct a forced eradication of some 105 ha; the first law enforcement action directed by the Bolivian government against the now mostly illegal coca farmers. (House 1990c: 50-51) Complementing DIRECO was the *Fuerzas Especiales para La Lucha Contra Narcotrafico* (FELCN - Special Force Against Narcotrafficking) which would control UMOPAR, as well as serve as an investigative element. It was commanded by a retired Bolivian Army general officer.

The Country Team reasoned that, using a $40 per *carga* ("hundred weight") cost factor and taking set up and operating costs into consideration, the first batch of 500 pounds of coca leaf would net the coca paste processors about $76 and about $200 per subsequent batches of 500 pounds. What could not be determined was how many days and nights the producer's team of stompers would be able to work, and what was a satisfactory profit margin. There were also concerns that the kerosene used in the maceration pits could be reused a second time, cutting costs of production. (USE-BL 1988: Cable 4962) Another Country Team report on the Chapare indicated that coca leaf prices tended to be lower for those producing areas in the vicinity of UMOPAR operating bases inside the Chapare than for those 45 minutes or more by road away from the bases. Despite the conclusion that "law enforcement presence has a downward effect on leaf prices," the prices had actually spiraled upward from lows of $21 per carga in the Ivirgarza area in early May of 1988 to well over $120 per carga in not only Ivirgarza but also the Eteramazama and Sinahota areas of the Chapare. (USE-BL 1988: Cable 12644) This indicated that, in spite of an eradication effort which destroyed 1,800 ha during 1988, coca cultivation expanded roughly 4,000 ha, reflecting a net gain for the narcotraffickers and a net loss for the US anti-drug policy (DOS IG 1989: 16)

There were, during this period, other incidents which plagued the US anti-drug policy efforts in Bolivia. Several Bolivian military officers, including a general, were dismissed and charged with being narcotrafficking accomplices. Also at this time two DEA agents were held incommunicado for some days at gun point by the Bolivian Navy's riverine command. A US DOS effort to involve other countries in a regional anti-narcotics police network fell apart when the latter refused to participate if the Bolivian police (perceived as notoriously corrupt) were involved. The Bolivian airline, Lloyd Aero Boliviano (LAB), was found to be transporting cocaine in its planes arriving in Miami, Florida. UMOPAR's Bolivian leadership was constantly being undermined by corruption in the form of narcotrafficker bribes in exchange for information pertaining to future operations or insuring that certain anti-drug operations were less than successful. This situation forced the DEA to change the UMOPAR's principal leaders every few months. (House 1989a: 15-16; and Hayes 1993) But this was not all.

The author noted in late 1988, during a visit to the Country Team in La Paz, that DEA's 29 permanent agents, analysts and supporting personnel were very often in disagreement with the NAU's 31 employees over what should be done, when and where in terms of executing the US anti-drug policy. This apparent working all too often at cross purposes, while not readily known outside the US Embassy in La Paz, did have a debilitating impact on the execution of operational aspects of the policy and tended to undermine the smooth functioning of the Country Team effort. In addition, Roberto Suarez Gomez, an infamous narcotrafficker kingpin for over a decade, released video film footage showing prominent members of General Hugo Banzer Suarez's ADN party fraternizing with the narcotraffickers. The scandal over this event tended to undermine the image of a supposedly resolute Bolivian government trying to fight the narcotraffickers. (MacDonald 1989: 80 - 81) Nonetheless, Roberto Suarez Gomez and several other major narcotraffickers were eventually arrested and imprisoned. (Westrate 1989) In addition the Bolivian government, on 23 December 1988, agreed to Annexes I and II of a US-Bolivian *Framework Agreement* which helped to implement the interdiction and eradication components of Ley 1008. (CEDIB 1992: 258)

Among the 1988 US election campaign issues, drugs had been at the forefront. There had been considerable frustration over the lack of visible progress in shutting down narcotrafficking. Consumption within the US was reported on the rise as was drug related violence and presidential candidate George Bush indicated that to resolve this situation he would assign a high profile to international narcotics efforts. (Bagley 1991: 13; and Washington Post: 27 Mazy 88)

The Congress wanted to centralize the management of the US anti-drug programs to bring about better control and continuity. As a result a drug-czar was created to provide for a more unified approach to anti-drug policy making and policy implementation. Also considered was a powerful anti-drug agency with budget certification authority mandated by law which could achieve enough influence to insure that Congressionally allocated anti-drug monies for the some twenty-five or more agencies in the federal government which had an interest in the anti-drug issue could not be diverted for other purposes. This was importatnt for prior to 1988 there was neither a single document which outlined the priorities and policies of the federal government in its war on drugs nor a single high-level official accountable for the success or failure of the anti-drug effort. (ONDCP 1: 1993)

With drug control being reflected in national polls during the first half of 1988 as the number one issue of concern to US citizens, the Congress responded with its Omnibus Anti-Drug Abuse Act of 21 October 1988 (Public Law 100-690) which built on earlier legislation promulgated in 1986. Monies were now not only allocated in quantity for interdiction but also for demand related programs, indicating that Congress was not satisfied with the supply sided approach. (Bagley 1991: 13)

Created at the mandate of Congress under the Omnibus Act was the Office for National Drug Control Policy (ONDCP). To demonstrate its importance, it was to be headed by an Executive Level 1, cabinet level official or Director (the drug czar). In this case William Bennet was initially appointed as the ONDCP's Director. Nonetheless, while Bennet was technically serving at the cabinet level, President Bush did not want him present at cabinet meetings unless drugs were being discussed. While the ONDCP did take some authority away from the Department of Justice, it was felt that under the circumstances it could better define the anti-drug problem and begin to understand what was needed to attain a solution to the war on drugs. (ONDCP 1: 1993) The ONDCP's primary function was to develop a comprehensive anti-drug strategy and to coordinate the anti-drug effort. (House 1990: 1)

The problems the ONDCP faced were considerable. While policy formulation could always be achieved in a relatively easy manner, the overseeing of its implementation was a significant problem which was never wholly resolved. That the ONDCP did not directly control the anti-drug budget process after it had been approved and therefore could not shift Congressionally earmarked anti-drug monies to better focus on priorities or influence the solutions to demanding and ever evolving problems meant that each government agency was essentially in control of its own affairs in terms of spending the monies allocated to it by the Congress. What the ONDCP could do to influence the general thrust of the US anti-drug policy among the various federal agencies was to use its stipulated authority to certify the budget requests of each agency in terms of the latter's role in the drug war. If an agency's budget was insufficient to meet its anti-drug obligations, it would be decertified and both the President and the Congress informed immediately. The idea was to ensure that the goals and objectives contained in the national anti-drug strategy were matched with sufficient resources to accomplish the agencies' respective goals. To this end the concept was considered generally successful. (Interview ONDCP 1: 1993)

Still, the coordination of the activities of several dozen federal agencies had to be carried out within a general plan. The drug Interdiction Committee (made up of the FBI, DEA, Customs and Coast Guard) was a case in point. No strategy existed and no one had bothered to sort out where some missions began and others ended. In short there was no team or fully integrated effort. To resolve some of the problems it was confronting over this issue, the ONDCP fomented the formation of a national drug intelligence authority which was to operate in the manner of the CIA but focus exclusively on drugs. As a result, El Paso, Texas became the site of the El Paso Intelligence Center (EPIC) which conducted drug intelligence collection and analysis operations in support of all federal agencies involved in the anti-drug effort. (Interview ONDCP 2: 1993) In addition, Congress passed in October 1988 the 1989 National Defense Authorization Act which directed that the Department of Defense (DOD) would serve as the lead agency of the US government in the detection and monitoring of aerial and maritime transits of illegal drugs into the US. This also applied to the Andean region. DOD's funding for this anti-drug activity accordingly rose to some $450 million. (Bagley 1991: 14; and ONDCP 2: 1993)

Here also the Congress asserted its authority whereby the cooperation of drug-producing and transit countries with US anti-drug policy was linked to determining the eligibility of those countries for US aid. The process, called certification, required the President to withhold at the beginning of each fiscal year (1 October) some 50 percent of the US foreign assistance to be dispensed to a given country until such time as a favorable determination and certification was granted on or after the beginning of March of the following year. In short it meant that each fiscal year some five or more months might pass before allocated monies could be brought into play on behalf of US interests in the Andean countries. To obtain certification, either support of a vital national interest to the US on the part of the receiving country had to be demonstrated or that full cooperation was forthcoming in terms of curbing illicit narcotrafficking and preventing drug production, processing, trafficking, drug-related money laundering, bribery and public corruption. (Perl 1988: 24-25)

To stem the flow of precursor chemicals flowing into the Andes, Congress was also instrumental in supporting ONDCP initiatives and in 1988 it enacted the Chemical Diversion and Trafficking Act which imposed stringent monitoring requirements on all US based chemical companies that produced the so-called precursor and essential chemicals which could be used in the manufacture of coca paste and cocaine products. Violations of these requirements could result in criminal prosecution. In addition, the United Nation's 1988 Convention to deal with the international trafficking problem world wide was sponsored by the US. The Financial Action and Chemical Action Task Forces were formed, involving up to some twenty-five of the more industrialized nations of the world. As a result, shipments of chemicals into the Andean region from US ports fell off dramatically. Nonetheless, there was a corresponding increase of chemicals flowing into the Andes from Brazil, Ecuador and Venezuela which offset the US effort. (GAO 1992a: passim) The DEA also began its efforts inconjunction with the Department of the Treasury's Financial Action Task Force to freeze or otherwise seize narcotrafficker financial assets throughout the world. (ONDCP 2 and DEA 1993)

As part of the Omnibus Anti-Drug Abuse Act's Title IV, the Secretary of State was responsible for coordinating all US assistance to be spent in international efforts to combat the production and trafficking of illegal drugs within each target country. Previously, certification had been based principally on the willingness of a country to reduce its production of illicit drugs. This aspect was now reduced in importance to just one of a number of criteria or issues involving the taking of law enforcement steps to curb corruption, the entering into a bilateral counter-narcotics agreement with the US and the general nature of its support for US anti-narcotics policies and programs. Nonetheless, eradication goals for Bolivia and Peru were to be adhered to as the primary US government means for measuring progress in those two countries. Here too, the US hoped to exploit its initiative in the UN Commission on Narcotics Drugs' resolution in February 1986 which sponsored a convention which included an article promoting the required extradition of drug traffickers to stand trial in those countries that desired to formally carry out a prosecution effort. (Perl 1988: 24-25; and INM 1993)

The US military with its own two million trained personnel, extensive resources in equipment, and its ability to project and sustain its power worldwide was looked upon as the only national institution which could project power from abroad to carry out an attack on the narcotraffickers inside the source countries. If otherwise idle in the Cold War, why not exercise its capabilites on behalf of the US counter-narcotics' efforts? If nothing else, the intelligence gathering capability of the various military services could be used to track and assist in the capture of the narcotrafficking enemy, or so the thinking at the ONDCP went. (Mabry 1988: 56; and ONDCP 1: 1993)

While the use of the US military in an international role, as well as in a domestic role to seal the US borders, was seriously entertained by some policy planners, Secretary of Defense, Frank Carlucci, as well as his predecessor, Caspar Weinberger, both argued against a combat role for the military in what they perceived was essentially a law enforcement problem. They contended that the mission of the armed forces of the US was to protect the nation against attack from foreign armies and not narcotraffickers. (Carlucci 1988: passim; and Washington Post: 22 May 88) Admiral A.H. Trost, then Chief of Naval Operations, spoke out publicly, declaring that the smuggling of drugs into the US could not be stopped through interdiction measures because "the economic incentives are so potent and the network of communications from farm to market via thousands of boats and small planes is so extensive." New York Times: 23 Jul 88) While the DOD was reluctant to enter into the anti-drug fray, it was persuaded and authorized by Congress to support the anti-drug effort as the lead agency responsible for detection and monitoring of aerial and maritime drug smuggling. As a result the Joint Chiefs of Staff (JCS) became more directly involved as the US Atlantic, Pacific and Southern Commands were incorporated into the Andean anti-drug effort. (House 1989: 4 and 13-14)

With the ONDCP's encouragement, the INM increased its operational role by developing an air wing within the Department of State which used both contract and State Department personnel. This was done over the objection of the DEA which wanted to control all helicopters in support of anti-drug operations as part of its Operation Snowcap activities. While this was a distraction from the INM's fundamental mission of policy development and coordination, it was thought that assets being brought into play in each Andean country could be better controlled and focused in the anti-drug role through the INM representatives on each Country Team. (NSC and ONDCP 2: 1993) In sum, the ONDCP had better defined the roles of its players and could promulgate anti-drug policies and strategy. Yet, it still lacked the clout necessary to ensure that all the various government offices and agencies responsible for anti-drug programs (Appendix B) were operating in an efficient and synchronized manner. The election of George Bush as the new President would give the US anti-drug policy some added clout and focus that it had not had before.

Towards the end of the 1980s the US anti-drug policy found itself at a point where both the Bolivian and US governments had been galvanized to action. Nonetheless, adverse factors, involving the generally chronic economic situation, coca farmer intransigence, corruption, adroit narcotrafficker maneuvering, and international market demand for cocaine, had all served to undermine the US anti-drug policy and keep it from realizing its objectives. That coca cultivation was generally always expanding in Bolivia during these years indicates that the policy was not achieving the results it was intended to produce and was, despite all efforts to the contrary, a failure. The administration of President George Bush intended to reverse this situation and place the US anti-drug policy on a winning curve.

Chapter 3

The Andean Initiative

In his 1988 presidential campaign George Bush had commented: "The cheapest and safest way to eradicate narcotics is to destroy them at their source.... We need to wipe out drugs wherever they are grown and take out labs wherever they exist." (Andreas and Sharpe 1991: 108) Bush's statements, once he formally became President in early 1989 became part and parcel of an enhanced US national security imperative to eliminate the threat of drugs to US society by addressing the issue inside the source countries involved. It had been recognized early on in 1989 that all was not going well with Operation Snowcap which, despite the spending of some $350 million in a supply-sided interdiction and eradication focus in the Andes, saw coca production increasing some 7,000 mt since 1987. In addition some 2,496 cocaine related deaths or about five times the number reported in 1985 had afflicted the US population. (Senate 1992b: 21-22; and DHHS 1991: 21) Bush intended to take action to alter this situation dramatically.

In 1989, under the administration of President George Bush, the US anti-drug interdiction strategy in play (Operation Snowcap) was once again modified. This time the focus was on isolating the coca growing areas of the Yungas and Chapare regions from the cocaine producing laboratories in the Beni, Pando and Santa Cruz Departments. Using Tactical Analysis Teams (called *TATs*) made up of DEA and DOD personnel, clandestine airstrips, laboratories, and narcotrafficker assets in the form of planes and vehicles were specifically addressed. In addition, key narcotraffickers involving the 94 known coca paste buyers and representing some thirty Colombian linked drug trafficking organizations operating up to ten laboratories at any given time were also targeted. This was done in the hopes that by arresting the buyers and capturing precursor chemicals it would be possible to once again collapse the narcotrafficker laboratory system and marketing operation. The UMOPAR was still left out of the intelligence targeting and planning operations and only participated in the process as the strike force. Operations were conducted in earnest and approximately a year later about one-third of the coca paste buyers had been captured or forced to cease operations. (House 1990c: 53; and USE-BL 1990: Cable 17386) This apparent success brought about an increase in coca eradication for 1989, involving some 5,800 ha. While this did reduce Bolivia's total coca crop by about 10 percent, it failed to keep pace with the ever expanding amount of coca being planted by still other farmers. (House 1990c: 65)

During the first two years of Operation Snowcap, the US government reported that some 26 aircraft, 39 vehicles and over 6,500 barrels of precursor chemicals were seized and 30 cocaine (HCl) laboratories were destroyed, indicating that narcotrafficker processing and trafficking capabilities had been reduced considerably. At the same time 6,957 maturation pits were also indicated as having been destroyed. (House 1990c: 50 and 53; and Westrate 1989) Nonetheless, to the detriment of the US policy, the 2.2 and 1.2 metric tons (mt) of cocaine base and cocaine HCl captured respectively, represented only about one-half of one percent (Westrate claimed 9.5 mt or about five percent) of the total product allegedly produced in Bolivia during this period. It was also found that, unless US Border Patrol agents, on loan to the Country Team, were at the key road inspection check points leading out of the Chapare, no real interdiction of precursor or paste products took place. (House 1990c: 53 and 58 and DOS IG 1989: 16) Since UMOPAR personnel received only $50 to $100 per month as a salary supplement to an equally meager pay from the Bolivian government, they were readily susceptible to being bribed.

Narcotrafficking bribes ran the gamut from about $5 at a vehicle check point to many thousands of dollars to allow an aircraft safe landing and take off. In some cases UMOPAR officers and town officials in the Chapare were reported by DEA and NAU sources as being offered amounts of money ranging from $15,000 to $25,000 in exchange for seventy-two hours of protection so that narco-aircraft could land, load and then take off from the normally clandestine airstrips. (DA 1991: 257) In addition, the selling of captured coca-cocaine products and precursors back to the narcotraffickers had been alleged by the Country Team. (House 1990c: 63-64; and DA 1991: 257) In 1988 the US and Bolivia fought this by exposing blatant corruption wherever it could be found. The Army's 7th Infantry Division commander and a number of his staff officers were given dishonorable discharges when they were found to be protecting clandestine airstrips in the Chapare. (DA 1991: 257)

Two major interdiction operations highlighted 1989 and depicted some of the problems of the US anti-drug effort in Bolivia. On 22 June DEA and UMOPAR personnel mounted a nighttime air mobile assault on the town of Santa Ana in an attempt to capture a major Bolivian narcotrafficker, Hugo Rivera Villavicencio. The town's people and the Bolivian naval detachment stationed at the site resisted, firing on the UMOPAR helicopters and personnel. During the operation four people were killed and others wounded. Rivera was not to be found. Another raid, this time on 8 November at San Ramon, found a SOUTHCOM planned operation, involving several hundred UMOPAR personnel and nine helicopters, compromised before it was initiated. The expected narcotrafficker kingpin (*"Yayo"* Rodriguez) had fled a half-day earlier, having received advanced warning of the operation. (House 1990c: 56-57; and Gamarra 1993) This was a classic example of the government's efforts meeting resistance from sectors of Bolivian civil society, all to the detriment of the US anti-drug policy in play.

US Army civic action activities, used to soften the potentially negative psychological impact of the presence of the US military through the winning of grass roots popular support, were frequently criticized by the Bolivian Congress. Some of the latter's members had inadvertently discovered US medical personnel passing out medicines in rural towns. That the US soldiers' presence inside Bolivia had not been formally approved by the Bolivian Congress or even publicly announced by the government and that the Ministry of Health did not know what medicines were being distributed, further exacerbated Bolivian congressional suspicions that the US was supporting some form of a *"hidden agenda."* (Gaillard 1991: 36) Why the Country Team did not solicit joint civic action activities involving both the US and Bolivian military remains unknown.

After going through a lengthy process of naming judges and prosecutors to handle the anti-drug judicial processes in support of its Law 1008, it was found that the Bolivian government, although it had budgeted the correct amounts, had not authorized payment of their respective salaries. For at least several months no salaries had been received and the judges were threatening to stop working and trying cases. It was only USAID funding as part of a US program to strengthen the judiciary with supplemental salaries that kept most of them working. (Diario: 4 Oct 89; and Gamarra 1993) This was despite the fact that in its *Decree 22337* the government had decided that confiscated narcotrafficker property such as furniture, automobiles and airplanes etc would be sold by the former to defray anti-narcotics operating expenses and support government operations. (Diario: 19 Oct 89) Meanwhile, the newly elected President Jaime Paz Zamora, stressing political reasons, decided to allow the extradition (this could also be called an *expulsion* since no extradition treaty existed between Bolivia and the US) to the US for trial of the nefarious narcotrafficker linked former Minister of the Interior, retired Army Colonel Luis Arce Gomez. In addition Paz Zamora stated publicly that the Bolivian justice system was deficient, immoral and weak. (Diario: 12 Dec 89) Nevertheless, by early January of 1990, the Bolivian executive branch found itself censored by the Supreme Court for violating the Constitution when the former ordered the expulsion to the US of Arce Gomez. (Presencia: 3 Jan 90)

On 15 February 1990 at the Cartagena presidential conference attended by both George Bush, Bolivia's Jaime Paz Zamora, Peru's Alan Garcia and Colombia's Virgilio Barco, a new anti-drug policy perspective was to be brought into play. It focused on the conclusion that the anti-drug effort could only be won by reducing demand and by helping drug trafficking countries find suitable economic alternatives to the coca-cocaine production process. It was this conclusion and candid expression of the situation in the Americas that heralded a phase in the US anti-drug policy that was to become known as the *Andean Initiative*.

The administration of President George Bush, anticipating the possible conclusions of the early 1990 Cartagena summit conference, involving the need for economic development, as well as repression and eradication at the source country, had actually decided in September of 1989 to dramatically enhance its anti-drug effort in the Andean Ridge region. This was, in part, in response to the fact that cocaine-related deaths in the US had witnessed a four-fold increase over a four year period from about 554 in 1985 to about 2,500 in 1989, indicating that the anti-drug effort was still less than successful. (Miami Herald: 9 Oct 90)

To expedite President Bush's agenda, the ONDCP and the NSC

conducted a series of joint liaison visits (Dennis Miller of NSC and John Walters of ONDCP) to the countries of Bolivia, Peru and Colombia during March of 1989. Data was collected and over the period of a few months some studies were made as to how the narcotraffickers were operating and where they were thought to be most vulnerable. By that Fall, Presidential National Security Advisor Brent Scowcroft, Bennet of ONDCP and Deputy Secretary of State Lawrence S. Eagleburger were meeting to formulate anti-drug policy and, as a calculated effort, to keep the drug issue on the NSC agenda as a national security issue to force a still reluctant DOD to draw down equipment and personnel in support of the drug war. Despite this, the NSC was afraid of asserting itself more in an operational role due to the adverse domestic political repercussions that had taken place over this type of a modus operandi, stemming from the Iran Contra scandal and the revelations concerning the activities of Lieutenant-Colonel Oliver North in Central America. After several meetings a three-country Andean strategy was formulated. Miller wrote the implementing National Security Directive (NSD) 18, based on Walter's concepts for implementing the new strategy. So as to reduce the possibility of immediate resistance on the part of elements within DOD, Secretary of Defense Richard Cheney was not immediately informed about the plan and only read into it in its later stages of development. (ONDCP 1 and 2: 1993)

The Andean strategy, also known as the Andean Initiative (AI) or the "Bennet Plan," was formulated by the NSC and the ONDCP and concentrated on interdiction and law enforcement, focusing in the main on Bolivia and Peru, as well as Colombia. The reasoning of Miller and Walters was that, if Colombia could involve its own military against the narcotraffickers, why shouldn't Bolivia and Peru do likewise. (ONDCP 1: 1993) The long-term goal of the strategy was to effect "a major reduction in the supply of cocaine from these countries to the United States" through working "with the host governments to disrupt and destroy the growing, processing and transportation of coca and coca products." Specifically, the amount of illegal drugs entering the US was to be reduced by 15 percent within two years from the initial execution of the strategy and by 60 percent within ten years. (ONDCP 1990: 49-52 and 120-121)

A primary departure from previous narcotics control efforts was the Andean Initiative's deliberate incorporation of host country military forces into the counter-narcotics effort and an expanded role for the US military throughout the region. A phased approach that included a coca eradication program, crop substitution, and effective local military and law enforcement measures was to be brought into play. Primary objectives included interdiction of air, road and riverine smuggling in drugs and the destruction of processing labs and infrastructure important to cocaine production and trafficking in general. (House 1990b: 10)

The several short-term goals of the Andean Initiative's strategy were:
1. To strengthen the political will and institutional capability of Colombia, Peru and Bolivia to disrupt and ultimately dismantle the trafficking organizations by:
    a. providing military assistance, security training and equipment;
    b. strengthening the ability of the Andean governments to prosecute, extradite and punish narcotics traffickers; and
    c. providing economic assistance, beginning in fiscal year 1991.
2. To increase the effectiveness of law enforcement and military activities of the three countries against the cocaine trade by:
    a. isolating key coca-growing areas;
    b. blocking shipments of cocaine-processing chemicals; and
    c. conducting eradication programs.
3. To inflict significant damage to the trafficking organizations which operate within the three countries by:
    a. targeting key traffickers for arrest and prosecution;
    b. impeding the transfer of drug-generated funds; and
    c. seizing the assets of traffickers. (ONDCP 1990: 49-51; and House 1990b: 10-11)

Through the implementation of a five year, $2.2 billion plan, called the Andean Initiative (AI), it sought to cut by 15 percent over a two year period and by 60 percent over a ten year period, the amount of cocaine entering the US. (Funk 1991: 2) While military aid was to be increased substantially to encourage and enhance the receiving country's ability to focus on the anti-drug problem, economic and law enforcement assistance and aid were to be raised even more. Bolivia's initially projected share of the $2.2 billion was about $837.7 million (Appendix C).

Bolivia's portion of the $2.2 billion was considerably higher than either Colombia or Peru and demonstrated the US interest there. Over the years it would generally remain as such. It was obvious that the US had concluded that any approach to the drug trafficking issue would have to deal with the economic issues, involving the employment of some 350 thousand individuals in the coca production process also and not just a repressive interdiction of the narcotrafficking system. The Andean Initiative also emphasized that counter-narcotics efforts should be primarily the responsibility of the host nation's law enforcement agencies, supported by the military as required. In addition, it also indicated that economic and military aid would only be forthcoming from the US if host country narcotics control measures met US congressional criteria for coca eradication and a respect for human rights. (Funk 1991: 3-4) President Jaime Paz Zamora formally signed the Cartagena agreement on 15 February of 1990. (CEDIB 1992: 363)

The most significant departure from the Blast Furnace and post-Blast Furnace strategies of the Reagan administration was the greatly increased role projected by the Bush administration for the Bolivian Army in the drug control effort. This was highlighted on 9 May 1990 when Jaime Paz Zamora also signed an unpublicized bi-lateral anti-narcotics agreement, *Annex III*, with the US. To this end, he agreed to not only increase the efforts and involvement of the Bolivian Air Force but also the Army and the Navy. Selected Army units were to be made available for anti-drug operations. The Air Force was to receive additional helicopters (UH-lHs) and form an aerial military police unit and provide up to ten T-33 armed jet aircraft for interception missions, working in conjunction with US provided mobile radar platforms and units. The Bolivian Navy was to make available one Marine infantry company, as well as focus most of its twelve river patrol boats on anti-drug missions. The Army was to provide two infantry and an engineer battalion for training, equipping and eventual operational employment in the anti-drug effort. Some 56 US Army trainers from SOUTHCOM would support this effort. After having kept the Annex III agreement a secret for well over half a year, Paz Zamora was eventually found out by the Bolivian media and received heavy criticism over the agreement from his own Congress; members of which accused him of being a *"cats paw"* of the US Embassy. (Presencia: 29 May 90; and Gamarra 1991: 19 and 22)

At this same time General Maxwell Thurman, now the CINC, SOUTHCOM, declared that anti-narcotics operations were now his command's number one priority in the region. (Gamarra 1992) This meant that, with the revolutionary war in El Salvador drawing to a close and a peace process there gradually coming into play, DOD was now reallocating and refocusing much of its previous efforts in Central America to the Andean Ridge. This included intelligence gathering assets which were to report to a National Joint Narcotics Intelligence Coordinating Center (JNICC) located in La Paz, operations and related logistical efforts, as well as training. (USE-BL 1990: Cable 15712)

The enhanced SOUTHCOM involvement may have been timely, as it was reported inside Bolivia that the *Nestor Paz Zamora Commission* (NPZC) terrorist group had begun operations by kidnapping a prominent businessman and staging a series of bombings.(Presencia: 6 Dec 90) While initially alarming and thought to have links to Peru's *Tupac Amaru Revolutionary Movement* or even the *Sendero Luminoso*, the NPZC was generally decimated and quashed by government security forces who captured seven members of the group while killing four others. (USE-BL 1992a: 39) As time went on however, power lines and gas transfer pipelines came under attack from another group, the *Tupak Katari* guerrilla movement (EGTK), which was said to have conducted some 48 terrorist type actions from July 1991 to April 1992. (USE-BL 1992a: 38) More alarming yet was the report that General Lucio Anez, then commander of the FELCN, provided to the Bolivian Congress, indicating that certain narcotrafficking interests intended to assassinate both Bolivian and US government officials, including President Paz Zamora, his Minister of Interior, and US Ambassador Robert Gelbard. (Presencia: 9 Oct 90; and Nuevo Herald: 21 Sep 91)

Mid-1990 Cost-Price Relationship Per Kilogram
(US dollars)

Product	Production Cost	Selling Price	Profit Margin
Coca leaf	$ 0.83	$ 1.57	$ 0.74
Coca paste	182.70	262.00	79.30
Cocaine base	644.00	1,500.00	856.00
Cocaine HCl	2,168.00	3,917.00	1,749.00

Source: Machicado, Flavio. 1992. "Cocaine Production in Bolivia" in *Drug Policy In The Andes*. Peter H. Smith ed. Boulder: Westview Press: 94-95.

Figure 2

The Bolivian reaction to the US SOUTHCOM initiative was intense. From July through November of 1990 in a storm of protest, coca farmer unions involving some 60,000 persons carried out a series of road blocks, strikes, and announced the establishment of armed defense committees. (Washington Post: 23 Aug 91; and Christian Science Monitor: 15 Apr 91) One can understand why the coca farmers and narcotrafficker-linked producers in the cocaine production process were up in arms. Their profits were considerable as the table below shows (Figure 2). The above table does not account for possible recycling of precursor chemicals which would reduce production costs by as much as 10 to 30 percent or more. In short, a hectare of coca producing leaves selling at $1.57 per kilogram (profit margin of $0.74) was providing an annual profit of about $4,340 per ha to the coca farmer. (Machicado 1992: 92) The profit spread gave the producers in the chain some flexibility in which they could absorb temporary setbacks due to UMOPAR operations and invest in unsold coca paste as the situation required.

The coca grower opposition to a fuller apparent militarization of the situation was promptly labelled by the Bolivian government as a concerted effort to cooperate with the traffickers. (Gamarra 1992) Ambassador Gelbard publicly reminded the Bolivian government that US economic aid would only be forthcoming if the Bolivian military formally entered the anti-drug effort. The Bolivian foreign minister, Carlos Iturralde, explained to his Senate that the US economic support, involving hundreds of millions of dollars in aid in the future, was important to the Bolivian economy and that the Army's non-involvement in the anti-drug effort would jeopardize that aid. (Presencia: 17 May 91; and Gamarra 1992) Despite this the Bolivian Congress initially delayed in approving the use of the Bolivian Army in the drug war. US military assistance was then temporarily withheld from the Army and refocused on the Air Force and Navy. (WOLA 1991:122)

The opposition on the part of the Bolivian Congress was rooted in the fear that a further militarization of the anti-drug effort would increase military intervention in politics, fuel corruption, spark militant confrontations and cause political unrest in the coca growing regions of the country, possibly undermining the economy, as well as the still very fragile democratic initiative in play. Despite reluctance among Paz Zamora's own ruling political party coalition (*Acuerdo Patriotico*), the Congress, feeling the combined US economic pressures and the agreement entered into by President Paz Zamora with George Bush, eventually approved the arrival of the US military trainers and advisors. (Presencia: 3 Apr 91; and Aqui: 3 May 91)

To this end the disruption of narcotrafficking activities and organizations as well as eradication would carry equal weight. The country teams would carry out the strategy through their respective US Embassy INM, DEA, DOD, AID and CIA offices, as well as a host of other supporting agencies' personnel which included the Departments of Justice and Treasury, US Customs, the Border Patrol etc. (Perl 1992: 15; and author observations 1992-93)

Since all the programs and activities were to be executed largely by each government agency under the control of their respective host nation US Country Team and, as there was no designated mechanism or office for actually directing a coordinated implementation of the strategy among the several countries, ONDCP concluded that it did not have sufficient operational control. To resolve this problem it attempted to influence the strategy's implementation through a series of study groups and the release in September 1989 of its own National Drug Control Strategy which represented the first integrated US national approach to narcotics control, consolidating the various separate agency and department policies to reduce both supply and demand. To accomplish this some $6.4 billion was requested from Congress to fight the drug war. Later budgets in the 1990s would double this amount. With inadequate staffing and lacking the trust of the other key US government agencies, the ONDCP found it difficult to enforce its mandates and edicts and, only through NSC support, was it able to keep the Andean anti-drug policy on track. (ONDCP 1989: passim; and NSC and ONDCP 1: 1993)

Ironically it was the impact of the Colombian government's crack down and seizure of large numbers of narcotrafficker aircraft in August of 1989, as well as other anti-drug cartel internal operations, which ultimately reduced the number of narcotrafficker planes flying between Colombia and Bolivia from about six per day to about six per week. (Ferrarone 1992) This indirect disruption of the Bolivian aerial link between the Bolivian laboratory system and Colombia produced another coca leaf glut on the internal Bolivian market and a sharp decline of about 90 percent in both demand and prices paid ensued. In this case, prices went from about $89 to less than $10 by April of 1990. (USE-BL 1990: Cable 17386; and USE-BL 1993: Cable 1096) It should be noted that this period also coincided with the advent of the rainy season (November to May) when DEA-UMOPAR operations were generally at a minimum due to the difficulty of detecting targets and flying in the poor weather. (House 1990c: 62-63; and Financial Times: 15 Feb 90) As it turned out, the on going operations in Colombia, in conjunction with the UMOPAR's Red and Blue Devil's own activities, caused the coca leaf prices to remain relatively low throughout most of 1990. This lead to an increased eradication and, over time, an overall drop for the first time in net coca leaf production in Bolivia from 239,650 tons in 1989 to 234,920 tons in 1990. Coca farmers, facing little or no profits, were again encouraged to seek cash compensation payments in exchange for voluntary eradication. (Espectador: 17 Mar 90; USAID 1991a: 1; and USE-BL 1991a: Cable 1278)

Despite glowing reports that *"hundreds"* of Bolivian coca farmers were uprooting their coca plants in return for the $2,000 per hectare and were substituting fruit and other crops for coca, eradication was slow at best because of factors other than mere price levels. (Christian Science Monitor: 24 May 90 and New York Times: 20 May 90) A more somber USAID study summed up the situation facing the US anti-drug policy in Bolivia at this critical juncture, concluding:

1. No crop could compete with coca's prices, markets, and added value, unless prices paid to the primary producers of coca leaf were driven down by effective law enforcement,
2. Successful technical assistance cannot be effectively provided, or received by target populations until such law enforcement takes place, and
3. It was critical that viable economic opportunities be available outside of the Chapare for labor presently employed in the coca sector, (particularly non-landowning labor), along with alternative agricultural inputs to coca growers remaining on the land. (USAID 1991a: 3)

As a result of this perception, the scope of the alternative development project was broadened to incorporate not only the Chapare region but also areas outside the region to include as a priority the high valleys of the Andes mountains. It was from the highland areas that much of the temporary labor (estimated to be as high as 60 percent of the Chapare labor force) for coca leaf processing was coming. (USAID 1991a: 9)

Since alternative development has among its purposes the progressive transformation of the Bolivian economy from one that relies on cocaine production to one that does not, the creation of jobs to attract people away from coca leaf processing and meeting the basic needs of Bolivia's poorest population sectors, was the priority US focus to assist in diversifying Bolivia's economic base. At the same time, the Bolivian government would have to depress the coca prices sufficiently to make economic alternatives attractive. Whether the Bolivian government would fully cooperate at this juncture was another question, as President

Paz Zamora reported that the cocaine trade and not just sound economic adjustment policies was significantly responsible for the reduction in the nation's previous hyperinflation of the mid-1980s to its about 1.9 percent by April of 1989. The parallel cocaine economy was allegedly earning about *$1.5 billion*, of which 600 million was remaining inside Bolivia. (Latin American Weekly: 1 Feb 90; and Economist 1989: passim) The strategy thus called for continuing the AID funded agricultural research, credit extension, marketing and infrastructural developmental activities in both the Chapare and the high valley regions, including rural road enhancement, electrification, and investment and export promotion of small enterprises or cottage industries. (USAID 1991a: 3-4)

During the above period, DEA-UMOPAR operations were on-going in one form or another. A September, 1990, operation in Santa Cruz netted not only one of Bolivia's 35 major narcotraffickers, Carmelo *"Meco"* Dominguez, but also almost all the senior members of his organization, including numerous pilots, chemists, money managers, and paste buyers of that entire cocaine production network, as well as records, safe houses, front businesses and nine aircraft. (USE-BL 1990: Cable 15712; and Miami Herald: 29 Sep 90) This effectively dismantled a complete narcotrafficking organization. Other operations in the northern Cochabamba and Santa Cruz towns of Isinuta and Ascension, while often resisted by the narcotraffickers and coca workers armed with automatic weapons and other firearms, resulted in the killing or capture of dozens of narcotrafficker personnel and an Air Force officer. Information captured in these operations enabled the US to arrest Jorge *"Techo de Paja"* Roca Suarez at his mansion in San Diego, California. The Roca Suarez capture was significant as he was known to have corrupted over the years virtually hundreds of government officials, including presidents, lawyers, pilots, customs officials, passport control officers, the police and the military. (Ferrarone 1992 and Gamarra 1993; and USE-BL 1991a: Cable 1278) The riverine force (Blue Devils), in an operation called *Pique Macho*, operated throughout November on the rivers exiting the northern Chapare in an attempt to further isolate the remnants of the Meco Dominguez group from its sources of coca paste supply. Besides arresting over 180 persons and occupying narcotrafficking centers at Isiboro, Isinuta and Eteramaza, the force captured weapons, explosives, and quantities of cocaine and money. (USE-BL 1990: Cable 17982)

In October 1990 an official of the Ministry of the Interior was claiming that the anti-drug operations were costing the narcotraffickers up to $1 billion in profits over the past year. (Presencia: 9 Oct 90) While this was undoubtedly true, clashes occurred between personnel of the Bolivian Army and UMOPAR stationed in the Chapare, indicating that the traditional police-Army rivalry involving resentment over US aid to the UMOPAR was ongoing. This raised concerns within the Country Team that an enlarged Army presence in the Chapare would further increase frictions and undermine the joint operational effort. (USE-BL 1990: Cable 17386; and Barrios Moron 1992) The effectiveness of the anti-drug effort was still being noted in terms of coca crop control where during 1990 some 8,092 ha of coca crops were eradicated - about a 200 percent increase over 1989. This reflected the lower prices then being paid for coca. (USE-BL 1990: Cable 1278; and Funk 1991: 10) President Paz Zamora maintained that his country had eradicated so much coca in 1990 that the economic growth rate of the country had fallen from about 3 percent to 2.7 percent. (Miami Herald: 28 Apr 91)

Yet it was only in early 1991 and only after much pressure from the US Country Team that the hesitant Bolivian Congress and government agreed to permit actual Army training and anti-drug operations under the auspices of US direction, if not control. The Bolivian government's position was that interdiction, prevention and alternate development were the goals of its anti-drug strategy and not merely eradication through the use of coercive military force. (Presencia: 1 Apr 91) The $33 million in promised US military aid was conditioned on the participation of all the Bolivian armed forces in the drug war. (Los Angeles Times: 26 May 91) These operations were to focus only on cocaine processing and trafficking routes outside the coca growing regions. Nonetheless, there was considerable fear among the coca farmers that the Army would be used to attack them directly. (Nuevo Herald: 21 Mar 9l; and WOLA 1991: 128)

By early 1991 training was going on across the board. UMOPAR forces were themselves now being trained by Bolivian trainers. US Special Forces began *Operation Stone Bridge* in which advice, and operations and training assistance were provided to both DEA and UMOPAR forces. The US Army's *Red Dragon* UMOPAR basic training mission was declared complete and returned home. (USE-BL 1990: Cable 1278) US Navy SEALs trained the Bolivian riverine force and Marine infantry company, and US Army aviators continued to train the Bolivian Air Force's 12 helicopter, anti-drug air wing. Finally, US Army trainers began instructing two Bolivian Army infantry-commando (Ranger) battalions in counter-narcotics operations and an engineer battalion in civic action construction missions. The Army counter-narcotics infantry battalions were intended to operate in tandem with the police (UMOPAR), since the former had no civil arrest authority. (USE-BL 1991e: Cable 7877; and WOLA 1991: 83-84) It was also publicly announced that an aviation radar detection system was being installed in the Santa Cruz and Beni regions. (Presencia: 23 Jul 91) Also indicating an increased effort by the US in Bolivia, the Central Intelligence Agency (CIA) announced that over a quarter of its resources were now being devoted to the drug war. (WOLA 1991: 24)

The US anti-drug strategy's Andean Initiative implementation focus was called *Operation Safe Haven* and had as its principal target the drug trafficking leadership. Called by some the *kingpin strategy*, the DEA, supported by the Country Team and its US government augmentations, attempted to identify and attack the vulnerabilities of the principal narcotrafficking organizations in Bolivia which had been estimated as being from 26 to 30 distinct groups purchasing paste and operating cocaine production laboratories at any given time. The main idea was to remove from operation the complete narcotrafficker organization or group, beginning with the coca paste buyers through the entire laboratory complex and its supporting personnel, leaders and aircraft. (House 1990c: 53; and House 1992: 49) It was ambitious and designed to render a series of knockout blows to the narcotraffickers; thus closing down their operations inside Bolivia for the long term and allowing the AID programs to work.

Paradoxically at this time in February 1991, the Bolivian government announced that retired Colonel Faustino Rico Toro, previously a narco-tainted intelligence officer in the infamous Garcia-Meza regime, was to command the Bolivian special narcotics force (FELCN). He was to replace General Anez, who himself had been implicated in a corruption scandal surfaced by the Country Team. (Interview 1992 USMTT:BL) Perceived as a slap in the face, the US government reacted bitterly, threatening to withdraw all support from Bolivia, including $100 million in economic assistance unless Rico Toro was removed. (Presencia: 27 Feb and 2 and 5 Mar 91) In this case the Bolivian government recanted and selected General Elias Gutierrez to replace Rico Toro. The Country Team, still not pleased, then pressed for the removal of the Bolivian officials generally associated with Rico Toro's appointment and suspected of complicity in narcotrafficking operations, including Interior Minister Guillermo Capobianco, National Police Chief, Felipe Carvajal and even General Elias Gutierrez. They were accordingly all dismissed by President Paz Zamora. (DOS INM 1993a: 94; and USE-BL 1991d:

Cable 5444) Nonetheless the Country Team would remain skeptical, reporting to the Department of State (DOS): "Corruption continues to impede enforcement programs...." (USE-BL 1991g: Cable 10375) Shortly thereafter, the government, claiming corruption as its reason for doing so, removed the Deputy Commander and a half dozen company commanders or most of the senior leadership of the UMOPAR. (Presencia: 7 and 17 Mar 91; and USE-BL 1991e: Cable 7877) Ironically, this tended to negate and undermine some of the training being provided by the US Army to that unit. (WOLA 1991: 10) Not helping matters was the generally accepted allegation from an opposition political party that President Paz Zamora's government did not have a coordinated anti-drug strategy and that each government ministry tended to operate according to its own agenda. (Presencia: 3 Feb 91) Paz Zamora contended that the $100 per month average salary of the UMOPAR force indicated that it was badly underpaid and therefore susceptible to being bribed. That his government had carried out a purge, "served to improve" the Bolivian-US relationship which he went on to describe as "excellent." (Miami Herald: 28 Apr 1991) Nonetheless there were some successes in the US-Bolivian effort.

In June, the largest and by far the most complex of any Bolivian anti-drug operations was targeted, as part of Operation Safe Haven, on the now infamous town of Santa Ana de Yacuma. This town was known to be controlled by three of Bolivia's principal narcotraffickers, supporting both the Cali and Medellin cartels in Colombia with shipments of cocaine. (USE-BL 1991g: Cable 10375; and Gamarra 1993) Most of the UMOPAR's roughly 600 men and the US's 33 DEA agents, as well as elements of the Red and Blue Devils respective airmobile (12 helicopters) and riverine forces (4 swift boats) participated. These forces, using a plan formulated by a SOUTHCOM TAT, itself consisting of DOD, NAU and DEA personnel, conducted the raid. Although some of the targeted narcotraffickers were not apprehended, the results appeared to be significant. Some 54 persons were arrested, 15 cocaine base and HCl laboratories were destroyed and 42 aircraft were seized, along with quantities of cocaine base. (DEA 1992: 17; USE-BL 1991g: Cable 10375; and Larmer 1992: 21) The seized aircraft were estimated to be about half of the narcotrafficker fleet then operating in Bolivia. In addition, some fifteen narcotrafficker properties, including ranches were seized. The raid effectively disrupted narcotrafficking operations in west-central Bolivia and eventually frightened six major Bolivian traffickers, including Erwin Guzman-Gonzalez, a key leader of a large narcotrafficking cartel group, into surrendering to Bolivian authorities. (House 1992: 48 and 56 - 57)

That September another carefully planned raid, based on satellite reconnaissance and radar sensor systems, enabled the UMOPAR to successfully target a major HCl cocaine laboratory complex inside the Chapare and capture the Carmelo *"Meco"* Dominguez narcotrafficking group along with another 17 cocaine producers and traffickers. In addition some 25 coca leaf purchasing organizations operating in the Chapare were driven out of business. These successes and the threat that these operations implied, prompted some narcotraffickers inside Bolivia to begin to negotiate with the government for a way out of their now more precarious and illegal situation. (House 1992: 255; and WOLA 1991: 79) To encourage this change in attitude on the part of the drug dealers, as a key strategic move in its anti-drug efforts, the Bolivian government announced in July an offer to grant amnesty from possible extradition (expulsion) to the US, if the narcotraffickers turned themselves in within a 120 day period. As an inducement, it was announced that the maximum sentence that could be applied under Bolivian law was five years in prison. (Christian Science Monitor: 22 Jul 91) Despite this success, not everything had gone well for the US.

It was eventually revealed that during the Santa Ana raid, the DEA directed UMOPAR did commit some excesses which were perceived as civil and human rights abuses by the Bolivian government. Some homes had been ransacked, private belongings damaged or destroyed and tear gas used against two hundred protesting local residents, some of whom were also roughed up. In addition, the commander of the Bolivian naval garrison at the town had been interned against his will by the DEA-directed UMOPAR during the operation to prevent another shooting incident as had happened before. These revelations, as well as Ambassador Gelbard's public comments and accusations of high-level Bolivian armed forces complicity in drug trafficking, sparked a nationalistic, anti-American backlash and a call from some Bolivian circles for the expulsion of the DEA agents and less US meddling in Bolivia's internal affairs. (Youngers 1991: 15-17) Despite this, the Bolivian Army and police were reported as having broken up militant coca farmer protest marches and road blocks, carried out by the Bolivian Peasant Workers Sole Confederation (CSUTCB). Clubs, tear gas and the threat of fire arms were used to end the marches and open the roads in the Chapare. (Presencia: 16 Jun 91; and Aqui: 5 Jul 91) Despite the heavy repressive measures, in August coca eradication cutting teams were attacked in the Chapare by unidentified gunmen. (USE-BL 1992a: 38)

During this period the US Country Team and the Bolivian government still sought to exploit the residue of the low prices of coca leaves during 1990 by continuing to offer $2,000 for each hectare of coca eradicated, as well as offering crop substitution loans ranging up to $20,000. The USAID goal was to use these incentives, along with the enhanced law enforcement effort in the illegal coca growing regions, to provide a secure environment to assist the government in changing the economy in those areas to a diversified one and away from one dependent on coca. (DOS IG 1991: 60-61; and USE-BL 1991e: Cable 7877) The funds available under the Andean Initiative were to serve as the support mechanism to induce farmers to grow a variety of crops including citrus, coffee, rice, soy beans, corn, coconuts and different nuts and spices. By the end of 1990 in response to the low coca prices paid by the narcotrafficker buyers and the glut on the market of coca leaves, some four thousand farmers out of roughly thirty thousand had actually participated in the program. (DOS IG 1991: 63; and Presencia: 1 Apr 91)

Nonetheless, coca prices per hundred weight for 1991 steadily increased from a January average of $23 to around $40 to $50 for the year. (USE-BL 1992: Cable 1494) The Bolivian government agreed to eradicate 7,000 ha during 1991 as part of the FY 1991 Economic Support Fund Agreement with the US. On 17 July the government of Bolivia began its uncompensated, forced eradication campaign in earnest with the UMOPAR police personnel protecting the machete wielding DIRECO coca cutters. The situation was tense and progress slow as the *campesino* (peasant or poor rural) coca farmers tried to organize, block or otherwise harass the highly mobile DIRECO cutting teams which relentlessly pursued their mid-year goal of eradicating 3,500 ha. (USE-BL 1991h and j: Cables 10517 and 13952) Ironically, in response to farmer appeals and fearing increased violence against the DIRECO eradication teams, the Bolivian government suddenly ordered forced eradication without compensation to be suspended. While the farmers were opposed to forced eradication, they were still generally in agreement to allow the voluntary eradication program to proceed. (USE-BL 1991k: Cable 15969) The dialogue that developed between the Bolivian government and the farmers was well received by the latter, many of whom who also felt that for the first time someone was interested in their welfare and not merely exploiting them. That the coca economy was vulnerable to price fluctuations was still an influencing factor that gave the government some leverage. (Ramirez 1992)

While this sounded promising, there were some problems recognized by the US government. USAID had not been using proper market analysis in support of its Bolivian program. Likewise it had stopped building roads in the Chapare as early as 1986 for fear that they would merely benefit coca-paste transhipment operations, involving local markets and production efforts which required the bringing in of precursor chemicals by road. The relatively straight roads were also found to have served as reasonably good landing strips for narcotrafficker aircraft. While US road construction had come to a halt, USAID had not coordinated its efforts with the United Nations (UN) Development Program which was in the process of upgrading or otherwise rehabilitating 208 kilometers of roads and now working at cross purposes with the USAID policy in this case. In fact, not until a 1991 audit report pointed out the discrepancy, did the USAID mission in Bolivia contact the UN program representatives to learn what they were doing in the Chapare and to try and coordinate the efforts of the two programs. USAID was unaware that, besides road construction, rural electrification projects were also being undertaken by the UN. (USAID 1991c: 13-14; and Funk 1991: 12) Nonetheless, despite the Alternative Development Strategy goals and the UN's own limited work, there was a generally inadequate road network to promote the marketing of alternate crops.

It was also found that only 16 percent of the farmers who had eradicated coca had received proper certification so they could apply for the crop substitution program and receive the prescribed benefits. (DOS IG 1991: 65-66) By the end of 1990 it was reported that, while the certification process had improved, of the ten thousand farmers certified as eligible for loans, only a little over a thousand had been approved and received actual loans from the Bolivian PL 480 Secretariat. No one could determine why 90 percent of the eligible farmers were not participating in the credit program. As it turned out, there were administrative policy qualification factors causing the delay in processing the loans. One example of this was the requirement for farmers to live within three kilometers of an all-weather access road as part of the qualifying process. Since most of them did not, this bureaucratic stipulation was bogging down the entire US program. (USAID 1991c: 16-17)

Possibly of more importance were the two US proposed initiatives involving the Andean Trade Preference Act and the Enterprise for the Americas Act. These acts were to allow duty-free access to the US for a broad range of Andean imports, including some crops. Former Ambassador Edwin Corr indicated that the fostering of these acts implied that the US was truly committed to the economic development of the region. Not to have enacted or implemented these initiatives would have tended to induce a backsliding in counter-narcotics control initiatives, undermining the entire anti-drug program of the US. (DOS IG 1991: 68) In accordance with the initiatives and the US International Narcotics Act of 1989 passed by Congress in 1991, the Bush administration wiped out $370 million in debts owed by Bolivia to the US under the foreign aid and Food for Peace programs. Nonetheless, there was no mandatory reciprocal commitment on the part of the Bolivian government to use these savings in support of the US anti-drug policy. (Senate 1992: 78)

Yet for these acts to succeed, productive exports would have to be developed. Citrus, coffee, cacao, coconut, macadamia nuts, pepper, pineapple, vanilla, rice, maize, peanuts, tumeric and ginger were among the crops deemed most suitable for agricultural exploitation. As time went on, during 1991 some 31 percent of the farmers who had eradicated and reduced their coca production received loans totalling $5.2 million (about $5,300 per farmer) to make the transition into crop substitution and, in a few cases, livestock activities. (USAID 1991a: 8, 10 and 12) While the AID strategy recommended that farmers raise annual crops (rice, yucca, ginger and tumeric) in conjunction with high value, long-term crops (pepper, pineapple, and tropical fruit) to ensure that they would receive a reasonable income at the outset or up to one year while waiting for two to five years for the longer term crops to come on line, it was not an easy process. One crop, coffee, demonstrates the problem. In the Yungas, the Agro-Yungas Coffee Development Project was rendered ineffective due to the low earnings realized by the farmers. Decreasing international coffee prices made it difficult for the small and medium size farmers to earn enough to sustain themselves and absorb short term losses compared to larger, already well established coffee exporters who could render a long term profit and not go bankrupt in the short term, if the international market was unfavorable. (Aqui: 30 Jun 90)

While theoretically promising on the one hand, the alternative development strategy in its execution was continually meeting obstacles. In the Chapare a USAID evaluation in early 1991 stated that "although the project's success will depend on the economic viability of alternative crops adopted by farmers, there had been no studies of the markets for the proposed alternative crops." (USAID 1991b: 5) Highlighting some of the contradictions involved, the report went on to state that new roads "essential for marketing Chapare alternative crops were not constructed for fear of aiding narcotics traffickers." Likewise, lime compounds which were essential to neutralizing the acidic soils found in the Chapare were banned from use by the farmers because they could also be used in cocaine processing. (USAID 1991b: 5) Obviously AID's economic development strategy was clashing with the DEA/NAU coca growing/production suppression strategy. On a positive note, the AID evaluation did find that AID's small-scale water infrastructure and service extension projects in the high valleys had reduced the number of adult males leaving for work in the Chapare from about 60 percent to about 10 percent. (USAID 1991b: 8) In sum, the report contended that alternate development would have to be economically focused in a logical manner and that some risks would have to be accepted by the DEA/NAU narcotics suppression programs or Bolivian farmers would not see a viable incentive to switch away from coca. (USAID 1991b: 7)

Despite the plethora of potential crops which could be exploited, it appeared to USAID that only soybeans really had, at that time, any long term promise of competing with coca as a crop substitute. While this was recognized early on in the late 1980s and was considered critical to the success of the US effort in Bolivia, nonetheless the US Department of Agriculture (DOA), fearing undue competition with the US soybean producers, forced AID, beginning in 1989, to exclude Bolivian soybeans from eligibility for both credit and technical assistance as an export product. (GAO 1991e: 28, 32 and 37) In 1990 and 1991 the US Ambassador to Bolivia argued against this and the US General Accounting Office (GAO) concurred, that one could not hope to take effective action to destroy Bolivian coca production, leaving 300 thousand or more producers jobless, unless some adequate substitutes in the form of employment, income and foreign exchange were generated on behalf of Bolivia. (GAO 1991e: 34-35 and 37) As it was explained, even if Bolivia realized its considerable soybean potential, its exports would only equal about 3 percent of the actual world market (the US accounts for 38 percent of the world soybean market today). (GAO 1991e: 57) Despite this analysis and the US government's own position that drug trafficking was a threat to national security, USAID found itself unable to convince the DOA that there was little or no threat to the US soybean economy from Bolivian soybean export competition. As it was, there already were some 3,000 soybean producing farmers in Bolivia's Santa Cruz Department, indicating that it was a feasible crop (GAO 1991e: 37) Soya production, at that time, was reported as being 225,000 tons, up from 125,000 tons in 1990. (Economist 1992: 12)

Wheat was another potentially lucrative alternative crop that, because of its linkage to soybeans competing with the US international export market, met the same dismal fate in terms of the US policy. USAID was involved in a program to increase Bolivia's wheat production to as high as 30 percent as a key food staple for the people in general. Nonetheless, because storage, seed treatment and production and research facilities were similar to those used to support soybeans, it was deemed inappropriate to continue the project due to the presumed hostility that could be generated by a US soybean community that might contend that wheat production was merely a cover for soybean production. (GAO 1991e: 38) In the meantime, in late 1991 the price of coca leaves resumed a profitable margin of about $55 per hundred weight. (Funk 1991: 11)

While progress was slow, overall the Bolivian economy was growing and expanding, demonstrating that alternative development was making some impact. When coca prices had stagnated, an export boom in sugar, independent soya production, cattle and wood caused non-traditional export products to go from a 1988 base of $108 million to $292 million in 1990. While some of this probably could be accounted for as narcotrafficker reinvestment inside Bolivia, most of the expansion was apparently based on non-coca products and their profits. (USIA 1992: 22) During 1991 the Bolivian economy grew by 4.1 percent or the highest rate in a decade. (Tanoca 1992) Reflected in this growth was renewed international interest in Bolivia by such economic powers as Japan which, along with the World Bank and the Interamerican Development Bank, was involved in a $600 million project fostering Bolivian natural gas and petroleum exports to Brazil. (USE-BL 1992c: passim; and Nuevo Herald: 21 Oct 91) This renewed growth provided jobs for some fifty thousand new entrants into the labor force and absorbed an estimated fifty thousand more who were previously unemployed for a total of one hundred thousand jobs. (USAID 1992: 12) Economic stimulation caused the Bolivian government to develop its own six-year alternative development plan which, while supported by the US, still relies heavily on foreign donor assistance. Assistance to farmers displaced due to eradication, promotion of exports and agricultural growth, as well as balance of payments support to assist a Bolivian transition away from a coca dependent economy were its objectives. (Funk 1991: 13; and Ramirez 1992)

In terms of coca eradication, about 8,100 ha were eradicated in 1990, a *300 percent increase* over 1989! (DOS INM 1993a: 96) Because this was not replicated again in 1991 (5,486 ha were reported as eradicated), the success of the US program in Bolivia was challenged since only about 17 percent of the total cocaine products (3.1 mt of coca paste, 4.7 mt of cocaine base and .4 mt of cocaine (HCl) coming out of Bolivia enroute to the US was said to have been intercepted. (House 1992: 255; and Miami Herald: 4 Oct 91) Yet, if the 8.2 mt of cocaine products seized are compared to an estimated cocaine product total annual yield for Bolivia of at least 250 mt., this is equivalent to about a 3 percent capture rate or significantly lower than some US government reports were indicating. (DEA 1992: 16-17) Another criticism of the US efforts in Bolivia was indirectly alluded to during mid-year 1991 by the media. It was reported at this time that a February DEA-UMOPAR drug bust in Bolivia triggered a panic and scandal which bankrupted or closed down six banks and caused 50 thousand families to lose their life savings. Many of the depositors, former miners, teachers and public employees, as well as former coca growers who had deposited their $2,000 in exchange for their eradication efforts, demonstrated in the streets. The six Cochabamba *savings and loan association* banks involved had taken in nearly $58 million by paying lucrative monthly interest rates (9 percent) on deposits which they then used to finance portions of the region's cocaine business. Profits were frequently laundered through local investments. (Miami Herald: 29 Jul 91; and Gamarra 1993)

In October of 1991, the newly trained Bolivian Army anti-drug commando battalions, based in part at the former narcotrafficker stronghold of Santa Ana de Yacuma, began their operations in accordance with the Annex III agreement into some of the more remote and unpopulated frontier regions of eastern and west-central Bolivia, bringing on a substantial, critical reaction from the peasant-labor, coca farmer organizations, coca federations and some politicians. (USE-BL 1991k: Cable 15969; and Presencia: 5-6 Oct 91) Coca farmers of the Cochabamba Tropic Peasant Workers Special Federation, in response to a government ordered eradication of illegal coca fields beginning in November, were reported as stating that they were prepared to *"fight until death"* to defend their coca plants. (Aqui: 4 Oct 91; and Presencia: 28 Oct 91) Some days later clandestine airstrips and narcotrafficker radio equipment and firearms were reported as being captured by Bolivian Army troops. (Presencia: 9 Oct 91). In addition, a further large laboratory complex, controlled by Colombian narcotraffickers, was discovered and raided in the remote north-eastern Pando region of Bolivia. (Nuevo Herald: 29 Nov 91) As the narcotraffickers shifted the location of their production operations to avoid capture, so did the DEA-UMOPAR forces which, using a record 18 helicopters and 2 C-

130 aircraft, targeted and successfully raided in December the northern Beni Department town of San Joaquin, arresting two more key narcotraffickers. At this time the UMOPAR was also purging itself, arresting six of its own officers for selling seized cocaine products back to the narcotrafficker buyers. (USE-BL 1992 Cable 1494)

During this time the legal process in Bolivia was actually beginning to try some narcotraffickers. One Erwin Guzman Gonzalez, who had turned himself in under the government's non-extradition incentive offer, went to trial. (Presencia: 14 Sep 91) As mentioned, Guzman Gonzalez, feeling the pressure from the DEA Operation Safe Haven's kingpin strategy, surrendered to Bolivian authorities on 11 July 1991 on the condition that he not face extradition to the US for further trial. About a week later on 17 July, President Paz Zamora proclaimed a new *Decreto Supremo 22881* (Repentance Decree) under which the threat of expulsion to the US would be suspended for all narcotraffickers who turned themselves in to Bolivian authorities within 120 days. Non-expulsion was also conditioned on the premiss that drug-traffickers would confess their guilt and be willing to submit to a trial. In doing so they would not only have to confess to narcotics related crimes and provide details about their wealth, but also identify cocaine laboratory sites and cooperate with Bolivian government authorities against other narcotraffickers. Besides Guzman, six other narcotraffickers turned themselves in as the year went by. (CEDIB 1992: 529-530; USE-BL 1991i Cable 12352; and House 1992: 57) One of these included Hugo Rivero Villavicencio, considered the principal narcotrafficker in Bolivia and the leader of the Santa Ana cartel. He joined Roberto Suarez who was then serving out a 15 year sentence. (USE-BL 1991k: Cable 15969; and Nuevo Herald: 17 Sep 91)

That August, President Paz Zamora stated that he would use the threat of expulsion and possible extradition to both coerce narcotraffickers to accept the Repentance Decree and to keep violence from breaking out, much as had occurred in Colombia. (Espectador: 4 Aug 91) On 2 October Carmelo *"Meco"* Dominguez was tried, found guilty, and received 21 years imprisonment. (USE-BL 19911 Cable 17171) It should be noted that the Repentance Decree angered Ambassador Gelbard who felt that Bolivia was going back on its promises indicating a sincere interest in promulgating a formal extradition treaty with the US. That Bolivia did not enter into an extradition treaty was perceived as a setback by the US. That the issue of national sovereignty was a factor in the *Bolivian solution* did not matter to the Country Team.

After weighing the pros and cons of its Bolivian program and reviewing the relevant successes and failures, President George Bush, on 28 February of 1992 in his Presidential Determination 92-18, formally certified Bolivia as having "cooperated fully with the United States, or taken adequate steps... to control narcotics production, trafficking and money laundering." This was done despite the fact that Bolivia had admittedly not met its 1991 Congressionally mandated eradication target of 7,000 ha. It remained 1,514 ha short! Apparently the overall net reduction trend of coca (down 2,400 ha for a second consecutive year), the Santa Ana de Yacuma operation, which disrupted the narcotrafficker operations for some months, and the arrest or surrender of some twenty major narcotraffickers had convinced the Bush administration that Bolivia merited certification and continued economic and military aid. Nonetheless, the corruption factor was noted as an inhibiting factor, hindering the success of the US anti-drug policy in Bolivia. (USE-BL 1992: Cable 1494; and House 1992: 34, 251 and 255)

As the US economy began to falter in mid to late 1991, the Bush administration began to look for alternatives and measures which could save money. Most US government agencies were cut back in one form or another. The USAID and security assistance programs were no exceptions. AID's own quarterly report for early 1992 indicated that FY 1992 budget reductions had forced the cancellation of the Alternate Development Roads project in the Chapare. Likewise it was predicted that other programs such as the regional development, electrification, and even drug awareness and prevention programs for Bolivia could be impaired. (USAID 1992: 12) Equipment and training for the Bolivian Army's engineer battalion, called for in the Annex III agreement, were not forthcoming when the FY 92 FMFP funding was reduced from $40 million to $25 million. This undercut the US plan to have the Army involve itself more in the civic action side of the anti-drug effort. While the engineer upgrade was not possible, the US loaned Bolivia three C-130 cargo transport aircraft and five PC-7 patrol and aerial interdiction aircraft - all for the support of counter-narcotics operations inside Bolivia. (USE-BL 1992a: 50-51)

Despite the financial problems, other AID projects continued apace in 1991 with some success. Banana production ensued in the San Luis area with six packing sheds in operation and a cooling center completed. In the Mariposa Paraiso area, the Pineapple Producers Association was assisted in the construction of a pineapple packing plant. Farmers planted pineapple and citrus fruits on a small scale as they had a good market potential. Soy bean crops were planted for the farmer's personal consumption due to their relatively high nutritional value. (Sturm and Smith 1992: 5) Bridge construction was also begun in earnest with eleven (average length of 48 meters) projected for completion in 1992. Not to be outmaneuvered by the narcotraffickers, AID technicians conceived of a series of *"bus stops"* or barriers made out of heavy steel and positioned them along strategic stretches of the Chapare road network which could serve as potential runways for narcotrafficking aircraft. One narco-pilot, after having a wing sheared off his plane in a surprise encounter with a bus stop, found himself being solicited by irate community leaders to pay for the damages caused to the "bus stop." (USAID 1992: A-2) Also at this time successful eradication of over 6,000 ha granted Bolivia a badly needed $15.8 million from the US. In conjunction with that, export production involving gold chain, boric acid, medicines and alcohol completed the million dollar investments in Bolivia of foreign internationals and assisted the now relatively stable Bolivian economy. (USAID 1992: A-9 and A-13)

The DEA had also attempted over the years to stop precursor chemicals from entering Bolivia for illegal diversion and sale to the narcotraffickers. Argentina, Brazil, and Chile were all principal precursor source countries for the narcotraffickers. (DOS INM 1993a: 87, 97 and 107) While Bolivia has, as part of its Ley 1008 (Article 92), several laws that address the control of precursors, a bilateral, precursor chemical control agreement with the US, and a team of some twenty investigators from its National Directorate of Chemical and Controlled Substances (NDCCS) trying to control the operations of some 800 private companies, it has been unable to stem the smuggling. Most chemicals are purchased legally outside Bolivia and then smuggled via front companies to their illegal destinations within the country. (DOS INM 1993a: 97-98; and USE-BL 1990: Cable 15712) This was found to be particularly true of Argentina which, as one of the primary industrialized nations in South America, uses large quantities of many of the same precursors which are also used in processing coca leaves and the resulting cocaine products. (DOS INM 1993a: 85) While the Bolivian government did implement its Ley 1008, designating some 20 categories of chemicals as drug precursors, the Country Team remained skeptical that the NDCCS could actually extend its authority sufficiently to have any real effect on the smuggling taking place. (USE-BL 1990: Cables 15712 and 17386)

By the end of 1991, the Bush administration was full blown into the implementation of the Andean Initiative and Bolivia had been certified as cooperating with the US anti-drug policy. The Andean Initiative and its related operations had made an impact on the narcotraffickers' production and marketing operations. Nonetheless, despite enhanced US and Bolivian military involvement in the form of training and operational support activities, Bolivian governmental support, and the expenditure of some hundreds of millions of dollars in support of narcotrafficker repression and alternate economic development activities in the coca growing regions - all of which produced some temporary successes - the US anti-drug policy was unable to make significant inroads on the overall coca cultivation. While not expanding further, coca cultivation was able to maintain its relatively high level of production, ensuring the flow of adequate cocaine products out of Bolivia to meet the international market demand. This was not a satisfactory situation for the US government and efforts were made to ensure that 1992 would be a banner year in which an all-out effort would be made to defeat the narcotraffickers.

Chapter 4

Bolivia in the 1990s

In February of 1992 the US hosted a seven-nation (Bolivia, Peru, Colombia, Ecuador, Venezuela, Mexico and the US) drug summit in San Antonio, Texas, only to find a number of Latin American leaders, including Bolivia's Jaime Paz Zamora, rejecting the US call for reducing the regional cocaine supply by the year 2000. The short-term inability of the weak Latin economies to offset the loss in national income from lowered coca production was the main worry and obstacle cited. Through a bargaining process, Zamora was able to emphasize his position that the economic dimension of Bolivia's situation was his first priority and that its favorable resolution would also tend to resolve the narcotrafficking problem. In addition, he opposed the participation of Mexico and Ecuador in the summit, fearing that the US would diminish its funding for Bolivia to assist the other countries in the anti-drug effort. (Miami Herald: 27 Feb 92) Nonetheless, Paz Zamora signed the document of 27 February, affirming his support for the eradication and alternate development strategies based on bi- and multi-lateral cooperation with the US and other countries. (House 1992: 282) A few months later the US announced that it would sell-off significant portions of its strategic tin reserves in the world market. This announcement hit the remaining Bolivian tin metals interests and workers like a thunderbolt. The workers and miners publicly threatened to join the coca growers in the Chapare, if the US decision was not rescinded, which it eventually was. (Nuevo Herald: 2 Apr 92)

In response to the White House's 1992 National Drug Control Strategy, while still promoting democratic institutions in 1992, the principal US anti-drug policy goals for Bolivia continued to be "to reduce and ultimately eliminate the production of coca paste and cocaine HCl for export or for domestic abuse." (ONDCP 1992b: 4-5; and DOS INM 1993a: 95) Other goals for 1992 were:
1. Interdict and seize cocaine and other illicit coca derivatives, precursor materials, and assets of the coca trade;
2. Eradicate coca beyond that authorized for legal use;
3. Arrest and prosecute drug traffickers;
4. Provide economic incentives to compensate for the loss of revenues resulting from drug control efforts;
5. Expand Bolivian Armed Forces participation in counter-narcotics activities; and
6. Heighten public awareness of drug abuse. (DOS 1992: 19)

The key operation to support and enhance the effectiveness of the US anti-drug policy and alternate development strategy in Bolivia was *Operation Ghost Zone*. Begun in March of 1992, Bolivia and the US conducted a series of major law enforcement operations throughout the Chapare, involving the Blue Devil's now five riverine support vessels, 20 light patrol boats and 10 Zodiac inflatable rubber boats, as well as the Red Devil's 22 UH-l helicopters and two C-130 Hercules aerial transports. Ghost Zone hoped to not only destroy laboratories but also to disband the drug-trafficking organizations operating throughout the Chapare. (Mendel 1992: 78) It also sought to interdict narcotrafficker flights into and out of the region, as well as cutting off trafficking via land and riverine routes, and generally stop cocaine products from leaving the Chapare for processing elsewhere. At the same time precursor chemicals flowing into the Chapare were to be cut off. (USE-BL 1992: Cable 8710; and Senate 1992: 64) The operation accounted for the arrest of a number of leading traffickers, including a top operative of the Colombian cartels.

As Ghost Zone began in earnest and, much like the preceding year's operations, placed pressure on the narcotrafficker production and marketing systems, it was found that Colombian traffickers and even Italian Mafia types, such as Adriano Maesano Sequilacci, had arrived in Bolivia to ensure that a steady flow of paste and refined HCl continued. (Interviews 1992: CT:BL and NAS:BL) At the same time a number of purchasing organizations in the Chapare disbanded or merged with other trafficking networks. The Colombians themselves, displacing

Bolivian functionaries, became more and more directly involved in both purchasing and processing the coca leaf inside Bolivia. There was a significant difference in the way the Colombian narcotraffickers operated. Whereas in the past the Bolivian buyers would often extend credit to the coca leaf producers and paste makers, the Colombians operated strictly on a cash basis. This made it difficult for the Bolivian farmers and others who were attempting to set up coca processing/farming businesses or were trying to recover from losses due to UMOPAR operations. While the Colombians could ensure the continued operation of their marketing systems, they were much like fish out of water and, being unable to blend into the Bolivian social fabric as well as a local national, were relatively easy to identify and target. (DOS INM 1993a: 91)

Besides an awareness of the Colombians now operating in the Chapare, it was also recognized by US officials that coca production and its commercialization activities in the Yungas had also increased. This reflected a natural gravitation of the coca growers and paste producers away from the harassment they were receiving in the Chapare from the UMOPAR forces. The Yungas, with its rugged mountain slopes of the lower Andes, was more intimidating geographically to the UMOPAR and its supporting helicopters. The uneven terrain was adoptable to coca bushes but caused problems for the Red Devil helicopters which often found it extremely hazardous to land at the oblique angles obligated by the terrain. Fear of accidents and blade strikes reduced the propensity of the UMOPAR to willingly work in this part of the coca growing areas. This point was not lost on the narcotraffickers who, despite their own problems in marketing and transportation, took full advantage of the relative security offered by the terrain. (Ferrarone 1992)

As UMOPAR successes mounted in the Chapare, technological change was brought into play by the narcotraffickers to offset their losses. While not new to the coca growers of the 1980s, a process was developed and refined by which coca leaf could be processed into a liquid mixture in which cocaine products or coca paste could be suspended in a liquid mixture called *agua rica* ("rich water"). This meant that, if the coca leaf or paste purchasing or transportation system broke down for whatever reason, the coca producers could virtually stockpile large quantities of cocaine product indefinitely for future shipment to laboratories for further processing into HCl. Cocaine could thus be stored in large quantities at an intermediate stage of production without spoiling, preserving the producer's investment until such time as a buyer thought it was safe to make the pickup and payment. This extended the shelf-life of the basic cocaine product and enabled the lower end of the production system to survive the vagaries of the UMOPAR anti-drug repression. By late 1991 and on into 1992, the traffickers began using a more efficient and newer technique for producing agua rica, eliminating some chemicals in the process and reducing the time involved. (DOS INM 1993a: 94)

The DEA strategy for operations in Bolivia, especially in the Chapare, had evolved over a two-year period and consisted of several mutually supporting parts. One was the law enforcement element involving the arrest and seizure of illegal coca and cocaine products on the part of the UMOPAR. Another was an all source intelligence gathering and planning effort involving the use of signal intelligence intercepts, aerial photographic and visual reconnaissance and human intelligence in the form of agent reports to identify the most lucrative targets which would do the greatest damage to the narcotrafficker and production systems. After verifying the presence of a functioning laboratory complex, aerial and communications intelligence then confirmed the presence of the narcotraffickers of interest. Once this process was completed, the SOUTHCOM TAT and DEA Joint Tactical Intelligence Center in Bolivia clearly defined the *target*. Once identified and defined, the Country Team's DEA office would prepare the plan for a coordinated attack (Appendix D). (USSOUTHCOM 1991: 9-17)

Finally there was the paramilitary operational element which executed the attack and pitted UMOPAR forces, the riverine Blue Devils and the helicopters of the Red Devils against the identified narcotrafficker strongholds. To this end the DEA was sending many of its agents through the US Army Ranger (commando) school to prepare them for the rigorous reconnaissance and strike operations that typically characterized the anti-drug operations. (Ferrarone and Rather 1992) The UMOPAR personnel were frequently staged out of forward operating bases and even La Paz to attack the narcotrafficker targets (Appendix D). (USSOUTHCOM 1991: 9-18) Despite this relatively smooth functioning system, DEA officials were not always pleased with the way in which their operations were conceived and executed in the context of the rest of the region.

There appeared to be no regional strategy in play and each of the country teams (Bolivia, Peru, Colombia and even Ecuador) were largely left to their own devices. According to DEA Bolivia, all too often an intelligence coup or success in an adjacent country was not properly exploited; the information pertaining to Bolivia often being held in the

gaining country and not passed on in a timely manner. (Ferrarone 1992) Nonetheless, SOUTHCOM attempted to fill the gap with its own regional planning and was a ready and willing actor, frequently offering and dispensing intelligence, logistical and operational support at will. While well intentioned, with some frequency, SOUTHCOM plans were presented to and approved by the US Ambassador without a full Country Team review taking place. For this reason the required interaction on the part of AID, DEA and the various elements of the Embassy's military mission and the Narcotics Affairs Section (formerly the NAU), as well as the Bolivian government's respective agencies was not always smooth, sometimes untimely, and often became disjointed. With time lines for operational employment of SOUTHCOM assets already established, there was little that the Country Team and the Bolivian government could do except react as best they could in support of the otherwise potentially worthwhile operations and plans. Thus, insufficient and untimely coordination among the agencies involved sometimes caused radar and communications support for the DEA-UMOPAR and Bolivian Army operations to be employed at the wrong time, place and even frequently in a disorganized manner.
(Interview CT:BL 1992; and Ferrarone 1992)

Called *Operation Support Justice* and conducted in a series of iterations, the implementation by SOUTHCOM proved uneven at best. Sometimes at critical junctures the sophisticated AWACs intelligence detection and monitoring (D & M) aircraft were seemingly arbitrarily withdrawn by SOUTHCOM and placed in support of other countries, undermining the continuous flow of accurate and timely intelligence on which virtually all of the DEA-UMOPAR operations depended for success. (Ferrarone 1992) Towards the end of 1992, after having sent out dozens of appeals for sustained support, the DEA office in Bolivia threatened to close down its operations unless the critical resources were once again provided. Only then did the Support Justice assets come back into play in support of the anti-drug effort in Bolivia. (Ferrarone 1992)

The Ghost Zone operations directed by the DEA Director in La Paz, Don Ferrarone, replicating to a large extent those techniques and tactics he had used throughout 1990 and 1991, resulted in significant seizures of cocaine products and continued to disrupt the narcotrafficking organizations and their related transportation networks into and out of the Chapare. One organization in particular, the Colombian Cali cartel's Celimo Andrade network was dismantled. (DOS INM 1993a: 92) In response to accurate and timely intelligence, the UMOPAR was able to project its assault teams into the attack against known transshipment and laboratory sites, often yielding large quantities of cocaine and enabling the arrest of both Bolivian and Colombian narcotraffickers. As the Colombian presence grew, so did the action and violent confrontations as the narcotraffickers attempted to resist the anti-drug effort. Based in part on a full debriefing of several captured narcotraffickers and other informants, it was found that, of the 22 purchasing organizations originally operating within the Chapare over a year earlier, there were now only four functioning. This and the fact that the 30 major trafficking organizations had been now reduced to about ten mostly Bolivian groups indicated that considerable success had been achieved. (Ferrarone 1992) That the US continued to plan, coordinate and direct the operations indicated that the UMOPAR leadership and its staff was not capable of taking full control of their own operations or not trusted by the Country Team. (Interview CT:BL 1992)

Indicative of the relative success of Ghost Zone was the capture of 188.9 mt of coca leaf compared to the little more that 5.5 mt for 1991 and the 62 mt and 42 mt respectively of leaf for the years 1990 and 1989. In addition agua rica was recorded as being captured at the record rate of 50,000 liters (ltrs) for 1992, over the roughly 23,000 ltrs captured for 1991. While cocaine laboratories destroyed only numbered 17, compared to the thirty to forty for the previous two years, this still indicated a general success trend, continuing from the previous years' operations which eliminated portions of or even entire narcotrafficking organizations, thereby theoretically reducing the number of targetable laboratories available. Agua rica production sites, numbering some 723, in conjunction with 670 base and paste laboratories destroyed sustained a similar trend from 1990 (DOS INM 1993a: 98) The high capture rate of cocaine products, combined with the ever present or potential harassment by the UMOPAR police had a corresponding affect on the number of people living in the Chapare. By the end of 1992 much of the population had evacuated the area and was now less than half of its former size or about 100,000 persons. (Ferrarone 1992) There are other aspects of Ghost Zone that are of interest.

By the summer of 1992, through the coordination of SOUTHCOM intelligence assets with the interdiction potential of the DEA-UMOPAR, a critical mass was reached in terms of meshing operational and intelligence related activities with the result that the Chapare was virtually closed down to narcotrafficker aircraft. Some 15 percent (41 aircraft) of the total number of all legitimate small to medium size commercial aircraft operating in Bolivia had stopped flying on account of the number of aircraft destroyed or captured (reportedly about 150 over a period of two years) by the DEA-UMOPAR forces. (Ferrarone 1992) Apparently these aircraft had been flying weekly missions for the narcotraffickers as well as their normally legitimate commercial runs. (Interview CT:BL 1992; and Jennings 1992) Nonetheless, because of a lack of continuity in the anti-drug operational strategy and the sometimes uneven intelligence support rendered by SOUTHCOM, by the end of the year narcotrafficker aircraft had once again resumed their familiar pattern of activity as the traffickers reconstituted their marketing systems. (Ferrarone 1992)

The narcotraffickers, reacting to the threat to themselves, changed their production and marketing strategies to adapt to the unfavorable change in circumstances forced on them by the more aggressive UMOPAR operations. Of note was the reported massive use of backpacking by farmers and paste peddlers who avoided road check points, as they infiltrated coca leaves, paste and agua rica out of the region along trails to clandestine pickup points. (Ferrarone 1992) Other narco-related tactics involved the purchasing of more than what was needed of leaf, paste and cocaine products such as agua rica from some farmers and producers so as to maintain the demand and keep the latter in business. While some of this surplus was eventually used, portions of it were often captured and destroyed by the UMOPAR. In addition, narcotrafficking laboratory technicians were found to be using modern, state of the art recycling methods, which enabled them to use the same amount of precursor chemicals to produce multiple batches of coca paste, cocaine base and refined cocaine (HCl). (Interview NAS:BL 1992; and Ferrarone 1992) The coca farmers federations and their subordinate union groups expressed their discontent and printed leaflets which circulated throughout the region exclaiming: "Coca or Death - We will win!" (Mendel 1992: 80)

The narcotraffickers also reacted to the intensified DEA-UMOPAR operations in Bolivia by conducting a considerable amount of their production and exporting operations to the US and Europe in such countries such as Brazil, Paraguay, Argentina and Chile - all bordering Bolivia. (GAO 1992: 3 and 19) It was reported that in the Brazilian states of Mato Grosso and Rondonia, immediately east of Trinidad and the Chapare respectively, some 5 mt of cocaine was passing through the area per month or about 60 mt per year. Since western Brazil is poorly patrolled by the local police forces, the traffickers' operations there have had a virtual free reign. In some areas it was reported that cocaine was being offered in exchange for stolen automobiles. (New York Times: 20

Aug 91; Folha de Sao Paulo: 24 Nov 91; and Istoe Senhor: 4 Sep 91) Indicative of the quantities of cocaine making its way from Bolivia through Brazil was the 2 mt shipment captured in Porto Alegre in July of 1993. (Miami Herald: 3 Jul 93) As cocaine was also captured in Argentina over the past year (1 mt), as well as in Paraguay and Chile, it has become obvious that all of these countries were being exploited by the narcotraffickers operating out of Bolivia. (DOS INM 1992: 88; DOS INM 1993a: 90; Las Ultimas Noticias 29 Oct 92; and La Epoca 27 Aug 92) Despite the *"balloon effect's"* flow outside Bolivia, some successes were achieved as a joint Bolivian, Brazilian and Argentine anti-drug operation in late October of 1992 decimated the Luis Bernardo Salomon Soria trafficking group. Salomon was a millionaire cattle rancher from the Beni who used both Bolivians and Brazilians in his organization. (Nuevo Herald 24 Oct and 1 Nov 92)

The relatively uneven tempo of the DEA-UMOPAR operations was significantly influenced by the myriad of diversely funded anti-drug support programs which would frequently run out of monies at an inappropriate time or could not respond in a timely manner to changes in the anti-drug policy's focus. Initially, UMOPAR found itself in need of 860 police personnel but was only able to adequately equip about 600 due to budgetary constraints. While funding did increase $2 million to a total of $17 million to support the force and increase its size, often a year or more would pass before required supporting radar, computers and field equipment arrived in country. The bureaucratic nature of the US logistical system and the fact that Bolivia was competing with other countries throughout Latin America, especially Colombia, for support meant that SOUTHCOM and other US national assets, involving intelligence and logistical support, were not always available on a sustained basis or in a timely manner. (Interviews CT:MIL; CT:NAS; and Ferrarone 1992) Reflecting on his own experience of several years in Bolivia unsuccessfully trying to coordinate in a logical manner the various funding programs and at the same time formulate a coherent anti-drug campaign, a frustrated DEA program director, Don Ferrarone, commented to the author: "The war on drugs is a disaster!" (Ferrarone 1992)

When the US government, based on its 1900 US-Bolivia Extradition Treaty and the 1988 UN Convention which also dealt with the extradition issue, requested in July of 1992 the expulsion (*extradition* from the US point of view) of Asunta Roca Suarez, the Bolivia government, after considerable debate, complied. Nonetheless, the Bolivian Supreme Court later denied a December US extradition request for one Ronald Iriarte, declaring that the latter's offenses took place prior to the 1988 UN Convention having been entered into force in Bolivia. It further claimed that the 1900 Treaty was invalid in this case because it did not include a provision on narcotics violations. It was also a way out of the controversy for the Supreme Court which did not want anything more to do with the extradition issue. (DOS INM 1993a: 94; and Gamarra: 1993) Here the US found itself once again in need of trying to redefine and remold a new extradition treaty.

Toward the end of the year, several special narcotics court judges were summarily relieved of their duties by the Bolivian government for accepting gifts, involving travel and hospitality benefits from narcotraffickers and now faced possible criminal charges. (DOS INM 1993a: 93) While the Bolivian judicial system was willing to prosecute its own personnel, this incident does demonstrate that the corruption factor was always prevalent. This reflects the difficulties the US judicial enhancement plan of September 1990 was having. The plan was conceived to exploit a UN sponsored program to enhance the Bolivian judiciary by developing, in conjunction with the Ministry of the Interior, a series of special narcotics courts called for in Ley 1008. The US provided $2 million to this end. Despite the effort, the results were modest, if not poor. (USE-BL 1990: Cable 15712; and Gamarra 1993)

Assisting in the pursuit of exposing corruption was the Bolivian press corps which found that the hunting up of drug scandals made for good stories. On the other hand, the press was playing an important role well-known in liberal societies where the power of the press did tend to keep corruption in check by lowering the local society's tolerance for drug related activities. (Smith 1992) That the Bolivian free press worked hard to expose corruption for an avid readership did help to keep some government officials in line and others from overtly blatant relationships with the narcotraffickers. (Ferrarone 1992) Of the eight narcotraffickers who surrendered under the terms of the Repentance Decree of 1991, all eight were convicted. While retaining protection from expulsion to the US, they were serving no more than six years each in prison terms. Accordingly, a La Paz narcotics court gave key narcotraffickers Hugo Rivero Villacencio, Edwin Guzman and Antonio Naciff sentences of six, five and four years respectively. (USE-BL 1992: Cable 10382; and DOS INM 1993a: 93) For some Bolivians, that the convicted traffickers did not receive sentences of from 20 to 30 years was indicative of the corruptness of the judicial system. That condemned narcotraffickers Rivero Villavicencio and Winston Rodriguez were able to leave prison at will and celebrate the 1992 Christmas holidays in Santa Ana de

Yacuma further indicated the leniency and perceived corruption of the Bolivian judicial system. (Baldivieso 1992; and Nuevo Herald 8 Jan 93)

The US tried to offset the corruption factor involving the UMOPAR by paying individual members salaries of up to $25,000 per year. This *purchased loyalty* by the NAS made some Country Team members skeptical that the US anti-drug effort could ever succeed over the long term. Corruption within the FELCN command structure and the UMOPAR was notorious. Virtually every UMOPAR commander, except one, had been exposed and relieved over probable complicity with the narcotraffickers. One Bolivian officer stationed in the Beni-Pando Departments was found to have up to half a million dollars in a personal bank account which he could not explain. (Interviews CT: BL; USMTT:BL; and Ferrarone 1992) It was recognized that, if the US anti-drug policy and its corresponding strategies were going to succeed in Bolivia, any level of corruption could not be tolerated. Since there were indicators that the narcotraffickers continued to have links into the highest levels of the Bolivian government, this made the problem that much more difficult. It was also noted that Bolivian politicians, over and above the objections of the DEA, would frequently try to influence and even select specific UMOPAR and FELCN officials, who might then be bribed by the narcotraffickers. (Ferrarone 1992)

In time honest officials were actually looked upon by the country team and SOUTHCOM as *force multipliers* who could enhance the success of even poorly executed operations by merely ensuring that proper security precautions had been taken to limit narcotrafficker knowledge of what was transpiring. Not to have operational security tends to jeopardize an operation which is illustrated by what happened at the town of San Borja. Acting on an informant's report that several high-level, key Colombian narcotraffickers were operating out of San Borja, the DEA spent several months gathering detailed intelligence, obtaining Bolivian government permission, and planning and coordinating an operation involving a major assault by the UMOPAR on the town. Some 48 hours prior to the execution of the operation, it was learned that the Colombians had disappeared, causing the operation to be canceled. Much time and effort had been wasted due to an unidentified security leak during the planning and coordination process. (Jennings and Ferrarone 1992)

The eradication goal for illegal coca set by the US for Bolivia for 1992 was 7,000 ha. The idea was to reduce the then estimated 47,900 ha down to at least 40,900 ha. Yet despite the on going UMOPAR operations DIRECO was only able to purge the coca growing areas of a net 2,400 ha or well short of the desired 7,000 ha. Yet figures can be deceiving as DIRECO actually physically eradicated a reported 5,149 ha. Its effort was offset to a considerable degree by the several thousand hectares of new coca which had matured and became available for production. Thus, by the end of 1992, there were an estimated 45,500 ha still under cultivation. Albeit a 14 percent drop from the 1989 high of about 52,900 ha, progress was indeed slower than expected. This meant that from 245 mt to possibly as much as 410 mt of coca leaves were still theoretically available on an annual basis for narcotrafficking purposes. (DOS INM 1993a: 5, 13, and 15)

DIRECO might have made more progress in eradication but was plagued by several undermining factors. Perhaps the most relevant one was the effective opposition by the coca farmers' federations and unions. Fearing a violent confrontation involving the loss of considerable lives, the DIRECO leadership deliberately avoided eradication attempts which were going to be physically resisted by the coca farmers. Only when UMOPAR elements were physically present in force on an infrequent basis, could DIRECO cutting teams proceed with their work. (Interview CT:BL 1992) Contributing to the slowdown of the eradication effort were the reported management problems within DIRECO and the unusually heavy rainfall which occurred in the Chapare area. (DOS INM 1993a: 94) Also undermining the eradication program was the fact that frequently, when coca crops were destroyed, those left to the farmers were more intensively worked, achieving about the same level of production as the formerly destroyed crops had produced. It was also found that the electrification, water and road development projects of both USAID and the UN were benefitting the coca farmers equally as well as the intended alternate development crop farmers. Disquieting to the Country Team was a report out of Cochabamba which indicated that an alleged 90 percent of the legal coca produced under Bolivian government auspices was actually being diverted to narcotrafficker use. (Interview CT:BL 1992)

Alternate development for 1992 was on going and reflected the US appreciation that it too, along with repression, was part and parcel of a synergistic effort to convince the coca farmers to cease coca leaf production. Extensive field contact between Country Team agency and staff members and the farmers in the Chapare revealed that, despite the coca federations' 65,000 members and the narcotrafficker buyers' coercive tactics, including threats of violence (the Colombian influence), most coca farmers basically desired a tranquil life devoid of the pressures of being involved in an increasingly perceived illegal activity.

As such it was found that many would not mind switching to an alternate crop situation provided that there was no disruption in their income and that the new income levels were relatively equal to that earned by coca. (Interview NAS:BL 1992; and Miami Herald 16 Apr 93)

It is this point, involving the basic economies of scale, that continues to influence the situation in favor of the narcotraffickers. The farmer knows that there is a demand and that the narco-buyers will come to him to make their respective purchases. In this manner his product is marketed at no cost in transportation and purchases take place several times a year. If there were no purchases, then the leaf and paste could be converted into agua rica and preserved in jugs and barrels until someone eventually did purchase them. (USE-BL 1993: Cable 1096) Nonetheless, the farmers were not content with this situation as it contravened Ley 1008 and made them vulnerable to forced eradication and a loss of property. This apparent quandary over what to do about their technically criminal status created by Ley 1008 and the threat of coercive violence from either the narcotraffickers, their own peers, or even the UMOPAR, and the fact that they were generally earning only about a third of the income that had been available to them in the 1980s, made for a less than wholesome lifestyle. (Arrieta 1992; Miami Herald 20 Feb 93) Because of this the Chapare population in general had decreased from a high of 300,000 in the 1980s to little more than 100,000 by the end of 1992. (Salinas 1992)

Due to a natural farmer skepticism that alternate development crops could produce an income equivalent to coca, the farmers tended to take a *wait and see* attitude. Thought to generate only a third of the income produced by coca, the farmers were for the most part keeping small plots of coca growing to insure that there was a reliable income available to them in the event their respective alternate crops did not work out. (Miami Herald 20 Feb and 16 Apr 93) A survey of Bolivian farmer interests reported that the initial investment for alternate crops appeared to be too big for many of the farmers. Some thought the crops would not grow well; for others there was the uncertainty of market availability; and still others thought that the time for the crops to reach maturity was too long. (Sturm and Smith 1992: 3)

When USAID provided potable water pump generators broke down or eradication claims inspectors and technicians were said to be illegally charging the coca farmers, such as those in the Senda #5 area, and then spending their illegal profits on prostitutes and liquor, skepticism towards the alternate development program increased accordingly.

(Interview NAS:BL 1992) In one instance the coca farmers complained that no one from either the UN or USAID projects had inquired as to what they thought would be a worthwhile project. *Trucante* ("peanut brittle") was seen a viable light industry alternative product to coca. Paying wages on a par with coca and involving local dairy products, it was viewed by the farmers as a viable and readily marketable product for the Cochabamba and Santa Cruz Departments. USAID was slow to appreciate this fact and had not included it as part of its alternate crop strategy. (Interview NAS:BL 1992) Another factor tending to impact negatively on alternate development was the desire on the part of the Bolivian political party in power to only provide support for a development project, if the beneficiaries had the appropriate party affiliation. (Interview NAS:BL 1992)

The US policy towards eradication did clash with Bolivian concepts. While the US insisted on complete eradication of a coca crop prior to compensating a farmer and providing alternate crop development support, the Bolivian government realized that the US policy could leave the farmer destitute if eradication was 100 percent. It therefore took a more lenient view involving a transitional approach, allowing the farmer to temporarily retain a portion of his coca crop as a hedge for survival while making the difficult and time consuming changeover of up to four years into the desired alternate crops. Since coca farmers were encouraged to try two or three alternate crops for diversification purposes over the long term, this policy permitted the maintenance of some coca crops to provide an income for survival until such time as an equivalent alternate crop income became available. Over time the Country Team would eventually accept this position, given the delicate relationship with the coca farmers, as the only realistic solution to the issue. (Salinas 1992; and Dlouhy 1993)

The USAID and Bolivian governments' alternate development strategy for 1992 and the remainder of the decade was to revolve around agricultural research, infrastructure development and marketing. This reflected optimism that the growth of the Bolivian economy in light manufacturing, construction and trade would assist in the improvement of communications, transportation and a natural resource product distribution capability. (Salinas 1992) While declining from the 1991 high of a 4.1 percent growth rate down to 3.8 percent, the economic growth rate was still substantial despite a falling off of natural gas sales. If the Bolivian GDP of the 1980s could have been said to be have been 30 percent based on narcotics related commerce, that of 1992 reflected only about 5 percent. This did not necessarily mean that the coca industry was declining, but that the overall Bolivian economy was growing at a relatively much faster rate. (Tanoca 1992; Ferrarone 1992; and Miami Herald 20 Feb 93) Part of this was due to the roughly $380 million already expended by 1992 under the Andean Initiative. This was to be reinforced by an additional $120 million, spent over a period of the next five to seven years to assist in the development of an agro-industry which it was hoped would positively influence the behavior of the generally intransigent campesino coca farmer in favor of alternate development. The US was to provide $80 million in grant aid and the Bolivian government $40 million for this five year effort. In addition Bolivia was expecting to also receive $35 million in funding from the UN, along with lesser amounts donated by Italy, France, Germany, Spain and Sweden. (Interviews Salinas 1992 and AID:BL 1992)

An agricultural research institute was accordingly established with two operating stations inside Bolivia. To support this project, agronomists and soils analysis experts were hired by USAID to come to Bolivia from other parts of the Americas in order to determine which agricultural products would be best suited for the Chapare and the high Andes regions. (Cueva 1992) Research results indicated that the only cash crops which could be validated as potentially viable in the Chapare were as depicted in the table below (Figure 3):

Alternate Development Program Crops (One Hectare Unit)

Crops	Time to Maturity	Profit margin	Market
Bananas	18 months	$ 2,622	local
Pineapple	15 months	10,022	local
Passion fruit	12 months	4,280	local
Macedonia nuts	4 years	5,436	S. America
Black pepper	3 years	5,162	S. America

Source: *USAID 1992 Report of Crop Potential* (shown to author) and GAO 1991b.

Figure 3

These crops should be compared to a sliding scale of values for coca as depicted in the table (Figure 4) below.

As long as the price per carga was no more than $40, the alternate development crop would have some chance of competing with coca. A US Congressional hearing indicated that new market analysis indicated that the break even point for profitable coca was about $26 per carga of coca, invalidating the previous $30 per carga that had been used for more than a decade by DEA. (House 1992: 321) In all cases fungus, pest control and environmental constraints would be inhibiting factors which would increase the cost of production and reduce the relative profit. It was estimated that a fully diversified program in place at the end of five years, or around 1997, would provide $23 million per year or about $2,300 per year for an estimated ten thousand former coca farmers. Pineapples were expected to bring in $20 million, bananas $1 million and the remainder about $2 million. While the citrus crops were destined for local consumption, the excess was expected to be sold in Chile and Argentina, provided transportation costs were low enough. Transportation costs in the export equation were critical factors, which, due to the poor roads and long distances (1,200 miles) over the Andes, made the prospect for large profits very suspect. (Tanoca 1992; and GAO 1991e: 23) These costs could run as high as $0.60 for every dollar's worth of product exported. This contrasts to the $0.10 in transportation costs for each dollar of coca derivatives and largely speaks for itself. (Machicado 1992: 92) For the high Andean valley regions garlic was expected to be produced and exported to Brazil and haba beans to Japan. These were thought to be sufficient to hold the migrant coca workers in place and keep them out of the Chapare and Yungas regions. Other complementary UN projects involved the production of tea, mint oil and a lemon flavored oil called *citral*. (Interview AID:BL 1992; and Miami Herald 20 Feb 93)

Net Annual Profit of One Hectare of Coca
(US dollars)

Coca price per carga	Profit per hectare of coca
$100	$17,714
75	11,387
60	7,589
50	5,059
40	2,530

Source: GAO 1991 Drug Policy and Agriculture: 18.

Figure 4

In terms of infrastructure support for alternate development, USAID was continuing with projects originally started in the late 1980s and early 1990s, but temporarily stopped when DEA objected that some aspects such as road construction were being exploited by the narcotraffickers (aircraft). Drainage, roads and bridges, schools, health clinics and potable water, electricity and plumbing were seen among the basic necessities required for a successful USAID program. With 13 bridges under construction and 187 kilometers of roads being opened, using *bus stop* tactics, the USAID projects gained momentum. AID attempted to mesh its operations with the UN supported potable water, plumbing, road repairs, milk production and agro-industrial development projects, as well as the Bolivian Ministry of Alternate Development's own program. (MACA 1992: passim; and Interviews AID:BL and Salinas 1992) Nonetheless, the investment problems involving the poor roads, no readily available export-port facility, no comprehensive energy grid and poor rural services in general tended to prejudice the success of this portion of the AID program. (Lupo Gamarra 1992)

Marketing of the alternative development products remained a significant problem for AID. Who would purchase the farmers' products, when, and where still remained to be resolved. Because of the specialized and dissimilar nature of the coca and cocaine product markets, there was no parallel commercial, agricultural support infrastructure in place. Stores selling fertilizers and pesticides did not exist in the Chapare. The AID solution was to try and subsidize and otherwise facilitate agricultural commerce through the development of an artificial, AID supported infrastructure, including transportation trucking systems and companies which would be encouraged to go into the Chapare to procure the new products under development. (Interviews AID:BL and Salinas 1992)

Despite the on going programs, there appeared to be confusion in the Bolivian government as to what to do about coca. Viewing cocaine use as a social threat to the family, the Congress had passed Ley 1008. Nonetheless the same Congress, within that very law, had laid the groundwork for the defense of coca. President Paz Zamora's proposed industrialization plan for the legalization of coca as an export crop, exploiting coca derivatives in the form of toothpaste etc., while logically exploiting a natural, locally grown plant as a limited national resource to further economic growth, was seen by some Bolivians as undermining the intent of Ley 1008 and the related alternate development projects. (Interviews CT:BL and Baldivieso 1992) That coca provides a relative economic security to the farmer, while the very idea of alternate development proposed crops produced a certain amount of uncertainty and insecurity, was well known to the members of the Bolivian Congress. This resulted in considerable confusion and diverse views on the subject of eradication. It also brought forth an ambivalent attitude on the part of some members of the Congress towards the enforcement of the provisions of Ley 1008. (Barrios 1992) This was very disconcerting to the Country Team which, in accordance with Washington perceptions, still perceived drug-trafficking as a threat to US national security and assumed that the Bolivian government would also take a similar view. (Interview CT:BL 1992; and White House 1991: 17)

In discussing drug-trafficking as a threat to the state and its institutions with key members of the Bolivian government, the question was posed as to whether narcotrafficking inside Bolivia was perceived as a threat to national security. Not one official in the over twenty interviews conducted acknowledged this point. It was uniformly stressed as a social problem and nothing more. Within the highest levels of the Bolivian military, which at the time had deployed forces to the field against the narcotraffickers, there was deemed no real threat from the traffickers to Bolivian national security. The prevailing view at the Ministry of Defense was that social problems did not merit a military solution. (Interview MD:BL 1992)

Another contributing factor to the ambivalent attitude on the part of the Bolivian Congress and its sometimes uncooperative attitude towards the US anti-drug policy was over the issue of US Army civic action projects inside Bolivia. The concept of national sovereignty is jealously guarded in Bolivia. Because the Bolivian Constitution (Article 59) prohibits the presence or the conduct of any operations by a foreign military force on Bolivian soil without prior Congressional approval, the frequently not fully coordinated or approved civic action projects undertaken by the US Army, in support of its training programs inside Bolivia, became the subject of considerable controversy. (Interview MD:BL 1992; Nuevo Herald 2 Aug 92; and Gamarra 1993) Unfortunately for the US, the intended saving of lives and construction projects, while conceived and executed with the idea of ameliorating the impacts of the US military presence, initially had just the opposite political and psychological affects. (Interview CT:BL 1992; and Miami Herald 20 Sep 92)

In the town of Santa Ana de Yacuma in mid-1992, the people watched while 122 US Army engineers constructed a school. They assumed that there was an ulterior motive to the cost free project on their behalf. This appeared to be confirmed when rumors began to circulate alleging that *"nuclear waste,"* involving an engineer construction garbage dump, was being deliberately deposited at the site of the village. Other press reports amplified the rumors, implying that the US was actually constructing a military base and trafficking in kidnapped Bolivian children. (Miami Herald 20 Sep 92; Barrios Moron 1992; and Ferrarone 1992) The sight of uniformed foreign military personnel, apparently roaming around Bolivia at will, brought out such a hostile reaction and debate among the Bolivian polity, and especially those in opposition to Paz Zamora, that the US Embassy in La Paz tentatively canceled all future civic action projects for the years 1993 and 1994. (Smith 1992; and Nuevo Herald 2 and 11 Sep and 22 Oct 92) Despite this, a Bolivian Ministry of Foreign Relations investigation found that the people of Santa Ana had decided after all that the US civic action was more positive in nature than negative. Other villages were now clamoring for their own projects. (Analysis: 6; and Miami Herald 20 Sep 92) Even as far away as Washington, D.C. there were diverse perspectives on civic action.

One ironic twist to the US civic action effort in Bolivia was realized in Washington during 1992. A member of Senator Jim Sasser's staff, becoming aware that the Country Team in La Paz was planning to refurbish an all weather runway at the town of Cobija, misinterpreted the civic action project as a formal *base development project* which required appropriate Congressional base rights legislation. The legislation was drafted and went into effect before anyone in the Country Team knew about it, hampering that particular US Army engineer civic action effort. (Interview CT:BL 1992) That an all weather runway on the northern frontier of Bolivia would potentially enhance the forward displacement of UMOPAR in its operations against the traffickers, was apparently not all that well understood by Sasser's staff.

The Country Team, through its US Information Service (USIS) Public Affairs Office, worked to offset any advance publicity concerning the US anti-drug policy inside Bolivia by developing a drug awareness program within Bolivia. Started in September of 1991 under an agreement with the Bolivian government, a strategy was designed to generally target all elements of the Bolivian society. A public opinion poll taken at the time indicated that, while 89 percent of the people viewed drug-trafficking as a problem, only 12 percent placed it ahead of economics as being the most serious problem in Bolivia. (Interview USIA 1991) The Country Team intended to reverse the perception and was greatly facilitated by the Bolivian private sector's own institutions, the Educational System for Social Mobilization and Anti-Drug Addiction (SEAMOS) and the Center for Education About Narcotics (CESE). While cocaine related drug abuse inside Bolivia is low, affecting some 3 percent of the population, its derivatives are said to affect a larger number of people. Because of this situation the Bolivian community was willing to work with USIS to help resolve the problem. (Smith 1992)

Financed to a considerable degree by the US and Bolivian governments, SEAMOS and CESE were able to carry out mass media campaigns against drug abuse, involving television, radio, flyers and advertisements in the press, as well as educational and training programs for the population at large and community organizations. (USE-BL 1992b: 38-39) Teachers and students in both the rural and urban areas were priority targets. (Baldivieso 1992) A drug abuse center was established in La Paz, servicing some several hundred customers per month. All this effort was followed in detail by the Country Team. The USIS also developed its own campaign using printed media in the form of pamphlets in Spanish to drum up support for Ley 1008 and the eradication programs. (USE-BL 1991: Cables 8905; and USE-BL 1990: 17386) Despite the considerable effort in attempting to educate the population as to the threat of international drug trafficking, by late 1992 only 29 percent of the population favored the anti-drug policy agreements with the US. (USIA 1993b) But USIS did not give up and sponsored a Chilean chemical engineer to conduct a study to *prove* that coca chewing was detrimental to one's health. The leaves' nutritional value was called into question, claiming that the alkaloids from the leaves produced a long term poisoning of the human body. (Figeroa 1992)

Another of the factors which complicated US and Bolivian relations over the US anti-drug policy was the latter's apparent lack of manpower and professional talent within the national government to address the various facets of the anti-drug programs which the US was striving to bring into play. The Ministry of Foreign Relations only had two knowledgeable officials who could deal with and coordinate the up to a dozen or more daily issues and requests which were forthcoming from the Country Team. The Country Team, on the other hand, had some dozens of officials who did nothing but that type of work. (Gamarra 1993) The net result was that, in order to attain a timely response to the issues at hand, the Country Team staff often ended up coordinating for and in the name of the various Bolivian governmental agencies involved in the anti-drug effort, often writing the latter's position papers. At times this included the actual drafting of legislation which the Country Team needed to have the Bolivian government vote on or decree into law to enable the US policy to proceed. At times the Bolivian Foreign Minister did not know what was transpiring until long after the coordinations had been made and projects were ongoing (fait accompli) or the Country Team eventually got around to informing him. (Interviews CT:BL 1992; and Gamarra 1993)

The *Consejo Nacional Contra El Uso Indebido y Trafico Ilicito de Drogas* (CONALID - National Commission Against the Improper Use and Illegal Trafficking of Drugs), the Bolivian government's own anti-drug organization (similar to the US Office of National Drug Control Policy), was well conceived and organized in theory but only minimally staffed. As it had little or no authority compared to the formal ministries of the government, it had to request support from the latter. In short it found itself competing with the Ministry of the Interior over interdiction matters, the Ministry of Health over social welfare and civic action concerns in the Chapare, and the Ministry of Agriculture over eradication and alternative development projects. Lacking ministerial authority, it was only able to complete one of its 75 projects considered critical in carrying out an anti-drug program in Bolivia. (CEDIB 1992: 578; and Lupo Gamarra 1992) The Country Team took a dim view of the whole issue involving CONALID and retained the perception that this reflected a lack of will upon the part of the Bolivian government to take seriously the anti-drug cause, Bolivian institutional weakness, and even possible corruption. (Interviews CT:BL; NAS:BL; and Lupo Gamarra 1992)

Bolivian political outlooks and ideologies also have played a part and impacted on the US policy as it was implemented. Some members of the Bolivian government and its Congress reflected traditional hostile attitudes going back into the 1950s when Dr Paz Estenssoro led the MNR which crushed the Army, but also had anti-US sentiments. That Paz Estenssoro in the mid-1980s had embraced the US anti-drug policy and that this tended to ameliorate somewhat the traditional attitudes, still did not lessen the ingrained nationalistic hostility that tended from time to time to stifle somewhat and slow down the Bolivian anti-drug implementation process that the US desired. Despite the frequent displays of Bolivian nationalism as part of an expression of its assertion of its national sovereignty to resist the US hegemonic pressures (the Country Team in La Paz), the Bolivian government generally supported most of the US anti-drug initiatives. Exceptions to this were the issues involving extradition, forced eradication without compensation and the use of herbicides. Nonetheless, the Bolivian government feared a direct personal confrontation with the US Ambassador and the power that he represented. As a case in point, when the Paz Zamora government wanted to obtain US support for its Repentance Decree as a new thrust for its own anti-drug policy, it pointedly waited until Ambassador Gelbard was out of the country (on vacation in Chile) to coordinate the new initiative in Washington, D.C., bypassing the Country Team in La Paz. (Miami Herald 20 Sep 92; and Gamarra 1993)

The Paz Zamora government sponsored the Tenth International Conference on Drug Control in April of 1992, displaying an interest in controlling precursor chemical infiltration into Bolivia. (El Comercio 26 Apr 92) That the democratic process was confirmed by an October 1992 poll which indicated that 77 percent of the Bolivian population preferred democracy as the most appropriate form of government for the nation, reflected the coincidence of Bolivian political values with those of the US. (USIA 1993c: passim) President Jaime Paz Zamora, himself, saw his priorities for Bolivia as avoiding civil war and resolving the narcotrafficker problem peacefully without confrontation. (Interview CT:BL 1992) For this reason he did not personally like the idea of forced eradication as a part of the solution to influence the coca growers into accepting the alternate crop development program. Because of economic necessity and using a *strategy of survival*, Paz Zamora, much like his predecessor Paz Estenssoro, found himself acceding to the imposition of the US mandated eradication policy so as to insure an influx of funding needed to stimulate the Bolivian economy. (Interviews: CT:BL; and Ramirez 1992) Fundamentally Paz Zamora viewed the problem of narcotrafficking and the growing of coca as related to a deeper root cause involving the basic poverty of the nation. For this reason his top priority for Bolivia involved improving the health, education and most importantly the economy. Deep inside he did not view the traffickers as a national security threat, although to placate the US from time to time he took this position. (Interview Pres/Adv: BL 1992)

As part of an attempt to assert greater Bolivian sovereignty over its own affairs and as a response to falling natural gas prices that were viewed as causing an estimated decline in annual export earnings of up to $150 million, President Paz Zamora began to promote the legal export of coca leaves. Hoping that the leaves negative international image could be erased, the government's Ministry of Planning hoped it could tap into the world's herbal tea market to enable coca farmers to exploit a national product and enter into a legitimate market. (New

York Times: 17 Jun 92) In addition, it was hoped that coca wine and tooth paste would become part of a coca industrialization plan. (El Comercio: 27 May 92; and USE-BL 1992a: 4) To this end Paz Zamora travelled to Europe to promote his "coca diplomacy." While not particularly successful in selling the "new" national export product, he did instruct his representatives to the World Health Organization to press the Bolivian government's contention that coca leaves contained positive medicinal and nutritional qualities. To this end a commission was formed locally to ensure that the legal coca market in Bolivia, including thousands of street vendors was protected. The Country Team saw all this as working at cross purposes with the coca eradication policy and indicative of a weak will on the part of the Bolivian government to confront narcotrafficking in general. (Interviews CT:BL 1992; and Gamarra 1993)

There was some merit in the Country Team perspective as eventually in April 1994 a major scandal broke in La Paz, implicating and linking Jaime Paz Zamora to key narcotrafficker personalities. In this case the President was to admit that he had established a personal friendship with narcotrafficker Isaac ("Oso") Chavarria Diez de Medina (the financial backer of Garcia Meza and member of his government) who had represented himself as an active supporter of the former's MIR party. According to a FELCN report to the Bolivian Congress based on testimony of captured narcotrafficker Carmelo "Meco" Dominguez, Chavarria provided $1.5 million to support the 1989 MIR election campaign. Chavarria was a former army captain and one of Bolivia's more important narcotraffickers financially linked to General Luis Garcia Meza's overthrow of democratically elected President Lydia Gueiler Tejada at the end of the 1970s. (El Nuevo Herald 26 Mar and 8-9 and 11 Apr 94)

Paz Zamora and his advisors saw that Bolivia must continue to accept US aid until such time as Bolivia's own economic growth and development would eventually liberate it from its dependency status vis a vis the US hegemonic power. This was emphasized in a Ministry of Foreign Relations and Culture (MFRC) report in 1993 which stated that US aid and cooperation were "*impresindible*" ("indispensable" for the development of Bolivia. (MFRC 1993: 6) Issues involving national sovereignty, including the presence of US troops and the quasi-paramilitary forces of the DEA which enjoyed a diplomatic status, were confronted on a daily basis. Perceived US insults and a general meddling and interference in Bolivian domestic affairs, to include the approving and disapproving of President Paz Zamora's own governmental appointments by the US ambassador often tended to make the relationship tense if not bitter from the Bolivian point of view. (Jennings 1992) This was also the case over US accusations involving Bolivian corruption, which were found to be irritable but also generally true despite the government's efforts to curb it. (Presencia 6 Sep 92) Because of the $372 million in debt forgiveness which was granted by the US President George Bush in 1991 to Bolivia as part of his Enterprise for The Americas Initiative, President Paz Zamora tolerated the perceived verbal abuse and insults from US ambassadors Robert Gelbard and Charles R. Bowers, both of whom might otherwise have found themselves declared persona non grata. (Interview Pres/Adv:BL 1992; and Miami Herald 7 Jun 93)

That the Bolivian economy was improving and narcotrafficker influence over the GNP was now only considered to be about 9 percent compared to 20 percent in 1980, reflecting about $0.4 billion of the $5.0 billion rated GNP for Bolivia for 1992, indicated a positive change had taken place. (Presencia: 1 Oct 92) With the creation of some 182,000 new jobs since 1989, unemployment had fallen to a manageable 6 percent. (Presencia: 7 Aug 92; and Tanoca 1992) Also indicative of an improved economy and standard of living was the infant mortality rate which fell from 120 per thousand (1987) to about 92 per thousand for 1992. With a growth rate of 3.8 percent, the 1993 future for Bolivia looked bright as foreign investment continued to increase. (USE-BL: 1992d)

Paz Zamora gave the democratic imperative in Bolivia much credit for the economic progress made to date and felt that too much militarization of the anti-drug process might threaten democracy in the country. (Expreso: 29 Apr 92; and Dlouhy 1993) His own concept for dealing with the drug and trafficking problems revolved around prevention at the local level, continued repression at the trafficking level, and alternate development at the production or growers level. In this general sense the Bolivian anti-drug policy perspective coincided with that of the US. (Interview Pres/Adv:BL 1992) By mid-year 1993, Paz Zamora was calling for the capture of the former tyrannical, narco-tainted dictator, Garcia Meza, who had been convicted in absentia earlier in the year by the Bolivian Supreme Court and sentenced to thirty years in prison. That Garcia Meza had indulged in political murders, human rights violations, and the misuse of government funds - all in violation of the Bolivian Constitution - had been brought to the attention of the Supreme Court which began trying him in absentia as early as 1986 (He was eventually apprehended in Sao Paulo, Brazil in

March 1994). (Miami Herald 22 Apr and El Nuevo Herald 6 May 93 and 12 Mar 94) While this was going on the democratic process was in full sway.

National elections took place in June 1993 and former financial planning minister and wealthy mining magnate, Gonzalo Sanchez de Lozada of the MNR won the presidential election by a wide margin. (Miami Herald: 11 Jun 93) Ironically the democratic process also caused Guillermo Capobianco, Paz Zamora's former interior minister, who was forced to resign due to drug-related corruption, to be elected to the Bolivian Congress as a deputy of the MIR party. (Miami Herald: 11 Jun 93) While Sanchez de Lozada was reported to be in favor of worldwide legalization of the use of drugs as a method to defuse the narcotrafficking issue, he still intended to follow the fundamental anti-drug policy approach of Jaime Paz Zamora. (Vision: 16-31 Oct 93)

Despite the fact that President Sanchez de Lozada made combatting corruption one of his goals, by 1994 the US Country Team was reporting that narcotrafficking corruption of both the courts and the police were impeding the effectiveness of the anti-drug law enforcement effort. Several judges of the Court of Controlled Substances were removed from office after they had been accused of accepting bribes and for failing to carry out the Bolivian laws regarding the detention of incarcerated drug traffickers. In addition, the National Director of Intelligence from the Ministry of Interior was found to have provided government documents to an incarcerated drug trafficker. Making matters worse during this period were the accusations of corruption (non-drug related) against the President of the Supreme Court and another Supreme Court justice who now faced impeachment. (DOS-INM 1994: 91-92)

US Ambassador Bowers was able to report in early 1993 that during 1992 DEA-UMOPAR interdiction operations and DIRECO eradication operations had combined to prevent an estimated 82.67 mt of cocaine HCl, with a street value of $1.8 billion from being exported. This represented about 30 percent of the US estimated total Bolivian cocaine production potential of 291.63 mt. In terms of promoting democracy, he felt that the narcotraffickers had been prevented from gaining "meaningful influence" in the political process and that narco-related violence had been minimal with the Bolivian government able and willing to assert its authority. (USE-BL 1993: Cable 639)

In concluding his report to the Department of State, Bowers stated: "It is hard to imagine that we could have done more in 1992 on the interdiction side." (USE-BL 1993: Cable 639) A strong and well financed anti-drug effort in the form of the Andean Initiative had been brought into play in Bolivia. The US had indeed given the anti-drug effort in Bolivia its best "shot." But, if this was a successful "shot," was it enough?

The issues of national sovereignty and the economy of Bolivia had become a primary concern for the administration of Bolivian President Paz Zamora. While these influenced the Bolivian government to follow a different approach to solving the narcotrafficking problem, the overall objectives for both Bolivia and the US remained essentially the same. Institutional weaknesses aside, the Bolivian government was doing all it could to deal with the drug problem and still resolve the omnipresent economic situation which was its most pressing priority. In short the US-Bolivian anti-drug policy and effort in 1992 had reached "high tide." Despite this effort, strong international market demand provided the incentive to enable the narcotraffickers to sustain their coca-cocaine production and transportation operations. The relative profitability of coca compared to all other crops continued to prejudice the success of the US anti-drug policy. The eradication of over 5,000 ha of coca for the year 1992 still did not make a significant inroad in the overall level of coca crops in production. (DOS INM 1993a: vi-vii; and USE-BL 1993 Cable 1096) The end result was that 70 percent of Bolivia's cocaine production was able to be successfully exported out of country by the narcotraffickers.

Despite the election of a new president dedicated to supporting US anti-drug policy objectives in Bolivia, the situation for 1993 and early 1994 remained much the same. The Bolivian government eradicated only 2,400 ha of coca, leaving an estimated 47,200 ha still under cultivation at the end of 1993. This meant that coca hectarage was again expanding by about 2,000 ha per year. Cultivation was reported on the rise in the Chapare and the Yungas, reversing the previous three-year downward trend in net cultivation. The eradication effort was far below the goal of 5,000 ha agreed to for 1993. This placed in jeopardy the overall eradication goal of eventually reducing the coca hectarage in accord with the 1988 bilateral agreement with the US whereby coca cultivation would ultimately be reduced by 1995 to its legally prescribed level of 12,000 ha. (El Nuevo Herald: 3 Mar 94) Even the small amount of coca eradication produced considerable opposition on the part of the five campesino coca farmer federations in the Chapare. These protested vehemently, confronting the UMOPAR supported eradication activities with up to 20,000 farmers armed with machetes and rocks. (Miami Herald and El Nuevo Herald: 5 Mar 94) The Bolivian government's poor eradication performance brought about the ire of Ambassador Charles Bowers who threatened to terminate the $44 million aid program for Bolivia (already reduced from $66 million in 1992 for insufficient eradication progress) unless the adverse eradication trend was somehow reversed. (El Nuevo Herald: 25 Nov 93)

The US ambassador's ire was directed against the Bolivian government despite the fact that the DEA advised UMOPAR, supported by a 16 man Snowcap Team and additional US Border Patrol Agents for planning and executing anti-drug operations, had registered some successes against the local narcotrafficking infrastructure during 1993. Four major narcotrafficking organizations were dismantled. These included the "Mariposa" network of the Limalobo-Durado brothers and 36 other traffickers, the "Christian" and Ferrufino-Fernandez organizations and some 650 persons who were arrested on drug related charges. Although 201 mt of coca leaf and 6 mt of cocaine HCl and base (solid and liquid) were seized, trafficking continued much as it always had in the past. This took place in part because of the Colombian traffickers who moved in to replace the Bolivian-run coca leaf and paste collection organizations which were in disarray. Over time the Chapare and Yungas networks became more efficient in their respective production processes for converting coca leaf into cocaine base and only then transshipping it further into the Beni or into western Brazil and Colombia for final processing into cocaine HCl. (DOS INM 1994: 71 and 90-91)

President Sanchez de Lozada was faced with the same fundamental problem that had plagued his predecessors - how to eradicate the coca and eliminate the narcotrafficking problem without having to militantly confront his own people or peasant-farmer citizens in the Chapare and Yungas regions. In his favor was the fact that the Bolivian economy was relatively strong, having registered a 4 percent growth for 1994. There was the full expectation that this would continue for 1995. If coca had been estimated as accounting for some 9 percent of the Bolivian nation's gross domestic product during the 1980s, it was now only 2 percent. (Miami Herald: 15 Jun 95) Apart from its linkage to the livelihood of the farmers in the Chapare and Yungas regions, coca no longer was an important element for the Bolivian economy.

Although he had acknowledged in late 1994 that the US sponsored alternate crop program was failing, in early April of 1995 Sanchez de Lozada initiated a new offensive to eradicate coca. The stated goal was to eradicate 600 ha per month until a total of 5,400 ha for the year was eventually reached. For each hectare eradicated, the farmers would recieve $2,500 in compensation. (Nuevo Herald: 2 Apr 95) To show good faith in and support of the US anti-drug policy, a new bi-lateral extradition treaty was entered into. By doing this the Bolivian president hoped to earn Bolivia some $300 million in useful loans, credits and donations in support of key social and economic development programs. Decertification by the US over the eradication issue could cause Bolivia to lose $87.5 million in US aid, as well as see the US government work to isolate the La Paz government from other potential international financial backing.

While the eradication policy now offered $2,500 per hectare of coca bushes destroyed, many of the some 30,000 coca farmers remained unconvinced that they could make a livelihood outside the coca itself. The farmers and their respective coca federations began mass protests over the government's aggressive policy, blocking main roads and thoroughfares. While in response the government declared a "state of siege," calling out the police and even army units in an attempt to coerce the peasant farmers to return to their family plots and begin the process of eradication, it would not be that easy. As time went on over the next few days, the campesinos armed themselves with axes, spears, rocks and dynamite sticks to confront the UMOPAR, police and heavily armed army troops. Rather than face the people directly in a feared militant confrontation with the possibility of mass casualties leading to a major civil upheaval, Sanchez de Lozada ordered that the police withdraw. (Nuevo Herald: 20 and 21 Aug and Miami Herald: 20 Sep 95)

Despite this apparent setback, some eradication actually did take place as planned over the course of the year. Some 5,493 ha of coca was eradicated, exceeding the US stipulated goal of 5,400 ha. (DOS INM 1996: 70) This did keep Bolivia from being decertified and jeopardizing its financial support in 1996. The Bolivian and US governments could also point to some progress in the Chapare as, with over $300 million having been spent on economic development since the onset of the decade, electricity, pure water, improved roads and the establishment of food processing plants and a transportation system were now functioning. Legal alternative crops now occupied twice as much land as coca. Nonetheless, the legal crops (bananas, pine apples, tea and yuca) were expensive to ship and finding markets outside that region was proving difficult. (Miami Herald: 5 Jun and 20 Sep 95) In terms of the eradication effort, this "success" was offset by the stark reality of the related statistics which indicated otherwise. In 1994 an estimated 89,800 mt of coca leaf were produced, the highest figure ever recorded in Bolivian history and about 6.4 percent more than 1993. (DOS INM 1996: 72) This represented a potential of about 298 mt of cocaine that could be produced (based on a figure of 40,300 ha of mature coca estimated to be actually producing leaf, with each mature hectare of coca producing about 7.4 kilos of cocaine in a season). (DOS INM 1996: 69-70)

A new phenomena was also taking place in an apparent response to pressures generated by the Colombian and Peruvian anti-drug efforts. In this case the Bolivian trafficking organizations were becoming increasingly independent of their Colombian counterparts and were noted as being heavily engaged in both the processing and smuggling of cocaine (HCl) into Brazil, Paraguay, Argentina and Chile for eventual rerouting to US and European markets. To this end coca farmers, lured by the prospects of higher profits, had begun to process their own coca leaves into cocaine base. By early 1996 Peruvian suppliers, faced with depressed coca leaf prices, now began marketing their products to the Bolivians. (DOS INM 1996: 65)

The UMOPAR anti-narcotics forces, taking advantage of US developed intelligence, dismantled five major cocaine and chemical precursor trafficking organizations. The anti-narcotics police's successes in these operations were offset to some degree by the still blatant corruption pervading the Bolivian government. The FELCN anti-drug police became so mired in a corruption scandal, unleashed in mid-September 1995 over the seizure of a Bolivian cargo aircraft and 4 mt of cocaine (worth on the US market about $120 million) destined for Mexico, that it was necessary to reorganize the force. (Nuevo Herald: 1 Oct 95 and DOS INM 1996: 67) Also relieved over this incident was a senior Bolivian police colonel from Santa Cruz. (Nuevo Herald: 4 and 8 Oct 95) While the offices of the Bolivian Minister of Government were implicated in facilitating the aircraft's departure for Peru, other officials, including members of the ruling political party were discovered to have been attending parties given by convicted narcotraffickers in Santa Cruz. Even the Bolivian Navy was again implicated in trafficking as one of its ranking captains was apprehended for using navy vehicles for smuggling purposes. (DOS INM 1996: 68) Taking into consideration the factors of corruption, in conjunction with an increasing net production of coca leaves and the natural resistance of the coca farmers to turn over their highly profitable coca farms for more risky alternatives, the future of the US anti-drug policy in Bolivia appeared to be very bleak in the main.

Chapter 5

Observations and Conclusions - Bolivia

As Bolivia entered the 1980s, the distressing social-economic condition of the general population influenced heavily the involvement of the up to half a million people working in the coca-cocaine production process. Alleviating the dire economic situation to a significant degree was the demand for labor and coca production from the various narcotrafficking organizations which sought to meet a serious, and ever increasing, albeit illegal, consumer demand in the United States and Europe. The immense profits accruing to those who participated in the higher levels of the narcotrafficker marketing system provided the incentives to the traffickers to make the effort and take the risks to generate and maintain the cocaine business. People in Bolivia became involved because of the critical need for survival which the relatively lucrative profits of the coca-cocaine production business virtually guaranteed. It was against this economy of coca that the US anti-drug policy butted.

This eminently strong, social-economic factor was then, and still is, steadily confronting and thwarting to a considerable degree the forward progress of the anti-drug effort. This has been going on for well over a decade. Despite spending some $10 million to move the US anti-drug effort forward in the late 1970s, the coup d'etat of Garcia Meza, at the end of the 1970s, and his ensuing dictatorial regime with both its corruption and support of the narcotraffickers brought all anti-drug activities in Bolivia to an abrupt halt. The symbiosis of the narcotrafficker and the state, in addition to the socio-economic exploitation of the traditional and mythic coca, proved to be an overwhelming element working for the moment against the US anti-drug policy and in favor of the narcotraffickers. US INM program spending dropped off accordingly, reflecting an acknowledgement that all was not well.

With the advent of the Torrelio government and the reopening of the democratic process, the US anti-drug policy was resuscitated, as the Bolivians sought to break out of their international isolation and rejuvenate their economy. That the US government had significant and powerful international influence corresponding to its hegemonic position in Latin America helped significantly to sustain its interests in Bolivia which included democracy and the anti-drug policy. In this case helping actors for the US were the ambassadors who spurred the democratic process on in Bolivia, laying the groundwork and smoothing the way for new US anti-drug initiatives. As these factors helped to start to buoy the policy up, Bolivian coca growers and farmers asserted their eminently strong position with the Siles Zuazo administration which in 1982 did not want to confront the coca growers directly.

The Bolivian government's real fear of creating a civil war and its respect for the rights of those involved in growing the traditional coca were key elements in the process which would continuously pull or push against the US policy. That the USAID programs at this time were unable to meet the needs of the coca growers was ignored by the US as it sought to reengage the Bolivian government in supporting the US anti-drug initiative based, in the main, on repression. The US Congress attempted to assert itself by establishing mandatory eradication levels and threatening the Bolivian government with a loss of aid. The Bolivian government, reacting to this threat, attempted to comply by sending military forces into the Chapare; only to find that the narcotraffickers generally bought off the military leadership, both corrupting it and neutralizing the intended repression. The factor of corruption was now also cascading against the US policy with the end result that the anti-drug effort once again had bogged down.

With the election of the Paz Estenssoro government in 1985, there appeared the distinct possibility of rejuvenating the anti-drug policy. But this also floundered in the face of the need of the economically destitute Bolivian government to maintain the coca economy at least until such time as the overall economy could grow to such a degree to serve as a balancing factor, reducing the importance of coca. Paz Estenssoro's

New Economic Policy and its austerity process initially led to an increase in unemployment of scores of thousands of former miners, many of whom now headed into the coca fields in the Chapare and Yungas regions in search of a new livelihood. At this point in time one could have concluded that the US anti-drug policy did not have any real chance of success; there were just too many negative factors working against it and otherwise undermining its forward progress. Yet an unforseen event took place which produced a dynamic which was to drive the anti-drug policy forward and give it a new impetus unlike ever before - the national security imperative!

Beginning in the Fall of 1985 for the Country Team and for the US government officially in the Spring of 1986, the announcement that international drug-trafficking constituted a threat to the US national security (President Reagan's NSDD 221) was probably the most important, pro-policy effect to come into play over the next decade. This energized the anti-drug policy effort to the degree that it became a virtual, single-issue foreign policy, eclipsing from time to time the US interest in sustaining the democratic process in Bolivia. For all the diverse interests that might have existed within the Country Team in La Paz, there now was a crusading cause in play. Economics, cultural and political affairs, institution building, development, representational activities and security assistance, as well as all the rest of the many activities which traditionally involve a US Embassy, now had the underlying purpose of fostering a successful anti-drug program in Bolivia. It was an all-encompassing focus.

This focus and its momentum naturally led to a desire within the Country Team to militantly confront the narcotraffickers, over and above what the DEA was already attempting to do with little or no success (coca crops had expanded from 6,000 ha in the early 1980s to 35,000 by April of 1986). This came to fruition when Paz Estenssoro, for economic as well as his own professed moral reasons, agreed to allow the US to implement a militarized approach to resolving the drug issue inside Bolivia. Having the full cooperative support of a national president of Paz Estenssoro's stature, a virtual carte blanche in favor of the US interest, should have put the anti-drug policy in good stead. Unfortunately, what should have been an overwhelming factor to place the policy on a decisive, winning track did not turn out that way at all.

The unprofessional and experimental manner in which the initial militarization of the anti-drug policy was undertaken in 1986, ignoring the complicated situation and the series of resources and activities that needed to be brought into play and synchronized in the Bolivian context to see a strategy through to success, merely disrupted the narcotrafficking system and set back for only a few months the narcotraffickers' marketing efforts. The unintended legacy of Operation Blast Furnace was that it created a great deal of controversy and distrust within the Bolivian government concerning Paz Estenssoro, placing in jeopardy the sensitive democratic initiative on which the entire edifice of US anti-drug policy and effort were based. It now created the situation which found the Bolivian Congress, for legitimate reasons involving the assertion of its Constitutional prerogatives over the approval of foreign military personnel operating in Bolivia, now pitted against the US in an adversarial manner. The Bolivian Congress would tend to maintain its often critical and adversarial relationship with the US for the remainder of the 1980s and on into the 1990s, although in the end it would generally accede to the basic thrust of the US anti-drug policy.

Another point worth mentioning is that it was not that the Country Team's general strategy concept in early 1986 was flawed, but that the execution directed from Washington, D.C. was so constrained in both time, resources and coordination, failing to address the social-economic complexities of the Bolivian situation as well as the modus operandi of the narcotraffickers. That USAID was totally unprepared and not alerted in terms of having appropriate alternate crop and economic development plans ready to support the Washington initiated operation is indicative of the vacuum in which the initial militarization of the anti-drug policy was carried out with its sole emphasis on repression. Blast Furnace, while useful to the US and Bolivia as a learning experience for future counter-drug operations, did give the narcotraffickers a clear idea of what they would have to face in the future. The Reagan administration's own militant effort had the effect of merely alerting them as to what was coming in the future and they prepared accordingly. The phenomena known as the *balloon effect* immediately came into play whereby the traffickers extended their production and trafficking operations over international borders into the more benign and relatively secure areas of Brazil, Argentina and Paraguay.

Despite the fact that the anti-drug policy was once again bogged down and considerable wrangling was taking place within the Country Team, there was a renewed and very sincere effort, based on the national security imperative in play, to rebuild momentum. Between the leadership of Ambassador Edward Rowell and his Army-Navy Attache, Lieutenant-Colonel Edward Hayes, and the interests of President Paz Estenssoro, as well as a handful of other members of the Bolivian government and its security forces as key actors, there was a sufficiently large effect generated to ensure that the US anti-drug policy was once again reengaged. Both repression and eradication, now involving a theoretically logical and viable crop substitution program, were the activities that were expected to propel the anti-drug policy forward in the mid- to late-1980s. The US and Bolivian leadership went a long way to clear away the obstacles involving the corruption of the Bolivian Air Force and Navy as undermining factors in the success of the anti-drug effort. That US military personnel were now commanding Bolivian military personnel and units in action against the traffickers was an all time first in the US-Bolivian relationship. Yet, albeit successful on the one hand, the all-pervasive nature of the narco-corruption was so strong that the narcotraffickers were still able to reach out, contact and eventually bribe the UMOPAR's leadership, as well as selected members of the Bolivian government on their behalf. This and the ever present international demand for cocaine continued the effects which played havoc with the anti-drug policy's efforts to achieve success.

There was a dramatic turn down in the price of coca leaves during the time of Blast Furnace (mid-1986), followed by the obvious reconstitution of the drug-production process. The advent of renewed Country Team efforts (Red and Blue Devils) and the Colombian government's backlash against the narcotraffickers did much to bring coca prices down again in early 1988 and in 1989-90. Nonetheless, while the overall trend in coca leaf prices was lower, the factors of continued market demand, corruption, and the balloon effect were enough to enable the narcotraffickers to reconstitute whatever systems had been temporarily closed down and once again continue their illicit operations. These factors more than offset the efforts of the Country Team to keep a successful anti-drug policy in play.

An undoubted element in favor of the anti-drug effort in Bolivia was the 1987 agreement (Principles of Narcotics Cooperation) between the US and Bolivia whereby the latter's government set in place a three-year coca control program and a $300 million, US funded, eradication-reimbursement program ($2,000 for each hectare of coca eradicated). This built on previous agreements and created an incentive to work in tandem with the repressive efforts of the UMOPAR and DIRECO. Nonetheless, the DEA-UMOPAR refocus on the Chapare created much resentment and militancy among the now generally well organized and led coca farmers and their communities. Their lobbying successfully caused the Bolivian government and its presidents to prohibit the use of herbicides which would have given the US government a cheap and effective means of destroying virtually completely the coca crops growing in the Chapare. That the collateral effects of the use of herbicides would probably conflict with and place in jeopardy the livelihood of innocent farmers involved in other types of agricultural production was not lost on the Bolivian Congress which supported the coca growers over this issue and thwarted the implementation of this aspect of the US policy. On the other hand, since coca was still considered to account for about 30 percent of the Bolivian economy, it was not likely that the Bolivian Congress or government was going to allow the coca growers to become disenfranchised without some suitable, compensating economic alternative.

While coca prices, reacting to the international market demand process, had once again risen by mid-1988 and there had been a number of anti-drug scandals involving the Bolivian Supreme Court, the Paz Estenssoro government promulgated its Ley 1008 which effectively laid the legal basis by which coca farming was clearly defined in terms of what was legal and illegal. This gave both a moral and legal boost to the US anti-drug policy and both governments' policies now appeared to coincide to a considerable degree. Eradication goals were clearly established and DEA-UMOPAR operations continued apace. US Army, Navy and Coast Guard MTTs were all operating to enhance the capabilities of the UMOPAR and its supporting elements. Yet this operational momentum was, much like a proverbial chess game, offset by narcotrafficking activities which, as they became under pressure or suffered losses, attempted to become more efficient. In this case the recycling of precursors was now in play and, while not apparently noticed by the Country Team, was still making cocaine product production sufficiently cost effective so that the production system continued even in the face of the AID offers of compensation ($2,000 per hectare) for coca destroyed.

Despite the setbacks, there were some successes achieved by the US-Bolivian effort. Through SOUTHCOM influence and the provision of operational and intelligence assistance, the UMOPAR efforts did have an impact and some coca farmers, feeling the pressure as well as seeing the opportunity to escape from their now government declared illegal status, opted to eradicate and try other crops. This continued on into 1989 with the capture of dozens of narcotrafficker aircraft and vehicles, thousands of barrels of precursors, and the destruction of thousands of coca leaf maturation pits as part of Operation Snowcap. Yet when one compares the eradication effort to the ever expanding production of coca that actually took place, one begins to realize that the harder and further the anti-drug effort was driven, the harder and further the narcotraffickers correspondingly pushed and expanded their own production systems in order to meet the sustaining market demand.

Despite the fact that the US had spent several hundred million dollars on behalf of the anti-drug effort during the 1980s, there was little effect on the growing of coca in general. Market demand had been relatively steady and the coca crops in Bolivia had helped to meet that demand. This also meant that, despite a Department of State claim that five percent or 9.5 mt of cocaine products were being intercepted at the end of the 1980s, some 95 percent or the vast bulk of the cocaine base and cocaine HCl was being successfully produced and transshipped to its export destinations in Colombia, Brazil and other countries throughout the Americas. Spurred on by the high profits that the cocaine market provided, the narcotraffickers were consistently able to work their way around the US anti-drug policy. During the 1980s the positive anti-drug policy was more than often offset or had a reduced impact due to the agility, resilience and adaptability of the narcotrafficking systems in play. The 1990s would not see a very significant difference.

George Bush and his Andean Initiative (AI) attempted to come to the rescue of the US anti-drug policy in Bolivia. Now, after some five years of experience with a militant, repressive approach towards resolving the narcotrafficking problem in Bolivia, the US was to lay out a five-year policy involving billions dollars in the attempt to stem the narcotrafficker tide through a combination of both economic alternative development and repression. This was a monumental effort in support of the US anti-drug policy and all previous funding in Bolivia paled to relative insignificance in comparison. That Bolivia was the recipient of more AI monies than any other country in the Andean Ridge indicates the priority it held in terms of the US policy interest. Bush, of course, had reiterated the Reagan position that international drug trafficking was a threat to US national security. The US national security threat perspective on narcotrafficking in Bolivia continued to provide the basis on which the policy was implemented. The election of Jaime Paz Zamora merely confirmed the conviction within the Country team and the Washington, D.C. community that the democratic initiative was safely in play and that the US could continue to play all its cards towards winning the coca control, national security stakes.

That President Paz Zamora had signed the Cartagena agreement and declaration (1990) that he, too, was behind the anti-drug effort in Bolivia was a good omen for the US anti-drug policy as it entered into the 1990s. Paz Zamora had even gone so far as to agree to implement the "secret" Annex III agreement which, in support of Ley 1008 objectives, would now formally involve the Bolivian Army in support of the UMOPAR. This was a long sought US objective which was said to be indicative of the *will* of the Bolivian government to deal with the narcotraffickers in a serious manner. It would also be, from a Country Team standpoint, indicative of the government's leadership accepting the narcotrafficking situation in Bolivia as a national security problem, much as the US leaders did.

What was sometimes forgotten was that Paz Zamora agreed to the US sponsored initiative, not because he saw a threat to national security interests at play, but because he needed financial assistance to keep his economy moving. He also wanted to avoid a serious domestic confrontation involving the use of violence among his own people over the coca eradication issue. This conflict in interests tended to serve as a constraint and work against the potentially positive national security imperative upon which much of the dynamics of the US anti-drug policy was based. For both him and Sanchez de Lozada in the mid-1990s, the Bolivian economy and the reduction of poverty were the keys to ultimately dealing with the acknowledged social problems involving drug abuse and the illegal coca-cocaine production process. While his intransigence on this issue remained throughout his administration, as a policy it coincided to a considerable degree with the US Andean Initiative's own economic emphasis. To this end the US and Bolivian leaders were mutually supportive. The Bolivian Congress' opposition parties balked at the idea of committing its Army in a situation which could evolve into a bloody civil war, with Bolivian killing Bolivian. Remembered too was the chronic corruption which had ensued when the Army had entered the Chapare in the early 1980s and the corrosive situation which the Navy had fallen into in the mid-1980s.

Another effect which is significant to note was the ever greater involvement of SOUTHCOM as a spearhead for US military involvement on behalf of the anti-drug policy in Bolivia. Beginning in 1990 under the able leadership of General Thurman and his staff, enhanced organizational and intelligence elements and equipment were brought into play to improve the information gathering and targeting efficiency of the DEA. Other actors such as the CIA, Defense Intelligence Agency (DIA), US Customs and the FBI lent their capabilities and talents on behalf of the DEA effort to better engage to the maximum the UMOPAR against the traffickers, the narco-organizations, and their respective production and transportation systems. As US government agency and actor support increased on behalf of the Andean Initiative and its increased militarization of the drug war, the Bolivian reaction to this effort buffeted against and caused the policy to produce uneven results. Nonetheless, while the US achieved what it wanted in terms of more military involvement, the Army was employed on the fringe areas of the potential coca-cocaine zones of conflict and the UMOPAR remained the primary actor in the execution of the principal anti-drug operations.

Towards the end of 1989 and entering into 1990, another event took place which gave the anti-drug policy and unexpected boost. This was the noted anti-drug activity in Colombia against the cartels there and their aerial transportation systems. This brought about another precipitous lowering of the price of coca leaves and a correspondingly more intensive eradication effort inside Bolivia in response on the part of some farmers who felt that coca was no longer a viable business enterprise. The ideal situation had once again come about, with the price of coca leaves reduced to about $10 or roughly 25 bolivianos (Bs) per carga. This was most opportune as a USAID study, discussed in the previous chapter, had, just at that time, indicated that no crop could compete with coca unless the price was forced down. This had now taken place. But what happened is indicative of the unintended consequences impacting on a policy.

While the DEA-UMOPAR forces, exploiting their enhanced targeting capabilities and operational efficiencies, captured hundreds of narcotraffickers and dismantled entire organizations, leading to the eradication of the record 8,092 ha, the AID program was not able to meet the challenge. Ironically, it had stopped its road construction programs to placate DEA interests, creating a shortfall in the infrastructure to support an alternate crop program. A USAID audit reported that "this action delayed progress in establishing alternate cropping by as much as three years, agro-industries have not been developed, and farmers do no have ready access to markets." (USAID 1991c: 6) This and the fact that an unexpected actor, the USDA, had involved itself in the policy action to quash the bringing into play of the one best crop (soybeans) thought likely to compete with coca, was a coup de grace for AID. This fact and the often poor administration of its coca eradication-crop substitution credit program contributed to neutralizing a relatively successful repression campaign carried out by the UMOPAR in the context of what had happened in Colombia. One might be prone to ask at this point: "Of what importance was the national security imperative if a small segment of US agriculture could distort the US effort to thwart the alleged threat to the nation's security?"

As time went on and 1991 came on, under the leadership of the DEA Director, Don Ferrarone, the DEA-UMOPAR operations continued apace. Operation Ghost Zone, conceived and directed in large part by Ferrarone himself, was considered the epitome of US anti-drug policy success in terms of interdiction and the dismantling of narcotrafficker organizations. SOUTHCOM radar was brought into country and installed, complementing the aerial platforms already in play to assist in intercepting and targeting the narcotraffickers. The *kingpin strategy* of the DEA came to fruition and decimated many of the narcotrafficker organizations. The pressure became too much for some of the key narcotraffickers and, fearing Bolivian governmental reprisals, acceded to Paz Zamora's quasi-amnesty program (Repentance Decree) with reduced sentences for those who voluntarily gave themselves up. This carrot and stick strategy was carrying the repressive side of the anti-drug policy to its greatest heights of achievement. This, and the 4.1 percent growth achieved by the Bolivian economy in 1992 gave the Country Team the confident feeling that the policy was achieving considerable success. And it was, but only to a degree.

Throughout 1992 the US anti-drug policy was at high tide in Bolivia. It had attained the maximum support that could be expected to be forthcoming from a US government which still considered the narcotraffickers in Bolivia to be a threat to US national security. The Bolivian government had, itself, signed up to the better part of a dozen significant anti-drug agreements and their related amendments in support of the US anti-drug policy. The San Antonio summit of early 1992 had reinforced these initiatives and there was a significant US emphasis on economic development. Economic support increased dramatically, but, while albeit extensive, had only reduced the overall coca cultivation in Bolivia by a relatively small amount. This is to say that the "record" eradication effort was in fact offset by the always steady growth of new coca bushes which reached maturity and came on line to support the commercial demand requirements of the narcotraffickers and their international market. While coca seed beds were also destroyed in fairly large quantities, they were by their nature also very easy to replace, sustaining coca production. A country Team cable of mid-1993 was to state: "Despite years of interdiction and alternative development, coca remains the most lucrative crop a Chapare Valley campesino can grow." (USE-BL 1993: Cable 9641)

Despite the Ghost Zone operations, the balloon effect came into play as traffickers scattered and concealed their production and transportation operations across relatively open international borders in Brazil, Paraguay and Peru. Due to the sensitivity of the national sovereignty issue, it is more often than not very difficult and time consuming to coordinate multi-national, cross border operations. For this reason the narcotraffickers continue to have the upper hand in this sphere also.

An aspect undermining or otherwise offsetting Ghost Zone's indubitable successes was the Bolivian judicial system. Key narcotraffickers who, by US standards should have been receiving sentences of over twenty years in prison, have in fact received considerably less than that. This, in addition to other factors of corruption which have continuously raised their heads in various aspects of the US anti-drug policy, has contributed to a mitigating effect on the success of the policy in Bolivia.

One last aspect concerns the situation involving the indomitable coca farmers who, by asserting their democratic prerogatives on their own behalf to not only ensure their survival but also their livelihood, have endured remarkably well considering all the activity that has taken place to uproot them or otherwise wean them away from coca. Only when they were overwhelmed by events beyond their control, which rendered coca production relatively unprofitable, did they grudgingly, in the best entreprenurial manner, begin to accept the USAID and Bolivian government's alternate development projects. Nonetheless, the suspicion that the alternate crops might not compete with coca, leaving the farmers in dire economic straights, has tended to ameliorate the farmers' enthusiasm for switching to alternate crops and, in turn, produced an effect which has consistently served to impede the US anti-drug policy's progress. The end result is that AID has been unable to wean more than 15 percent at most of some 100,000 farmers away from growing coca.

Bolivia was perceived by the ONDCP as the best-run overseas anti-drug program. Nonetheless, because of its almost single issue interest in the Bolivian eradication goal (6,000 ha per year), Congress had been threatening to cut back its allocation of monies for the US economic and military aid programs, since Bolivia's coca eradication goals for 1991 and 1992 had not been met. Despite presidential certification to the contrary, the Bolivian government was not seen as fully complying with the US anti-drug policy. With Colombian traffickers entering Bolivia clandestinely to keep their operations running in the face of the US king-pin strategy, ONDCP felt that only the US presence was keeping the Bolivian government interested in anti-drug activities. This opinion had also been echoed by the Department of State's own Office of the Inspector General. The need for continuous US presence was unsettling as this implied that the anti-drug program would unravel and become neutralized if the US allowed the Bolivians a free hand to deal with the traffickers alone. (ONDCP 2 and Deering 1993; and SOUTHCOM J3 1993)

One of the first and primary lessons to come out of this case study of the US anti-drug policy experience in Bolivia is the danger that ensues when a country embarks on what is essentially a *single issue foreign policy*, ignoring for the most part or deemphasizing all other issues. In this case the US anti-drug policy became exactly that, as it evolved in 1985 and 1986 into an all-encompassing national security imperative. Other issues involving the political-economy of Bolivia were arbitrarily brushed aside or obscured by the intensity of the demands emanating from the imperative itself. The imperative tended to require the immediate implementation of a repression strategy at the source at the expense of other options as a solution to the narcotrafficking problem. In reality an economic approach or a combination of the two might have better served the US anti-drug policy in Bolivia. It took the US five years before it finally began to realize that the economics of the drug problem were as important as the law enforcement or repression elements. The other danger from this situation is the possibility of opening one's policy to an unanticipated vulnerability due to the single focus intensity of pursuing one's objective at all costs. This essentially happened to the US when the democratic government of Paz Estenssoro was challenged over the violation of the Bolivian constitutional process for permitting foreign troops (Operation Blast Furnace) to enter the country without the approval of its Congress. This possibility had only been slightly entertained, if at all.

Another or second lesson learned from the case study in terms of the application of foreign policy is the need for a Country Team and the US government to *study all sides of an issue* before implementing its policy. In the case of Bolivia, the White House made a significant change in policy in late 1985 and early 1986, implementing it in the form of Operation Blast Furnace without having evaluated the situation in depth or coordinated the operation with sufficient time to properly weigh its advantages and disadvantages in terms of either the Bolivian or Andean region context as a whole. As it was, the solution in Bolivia required at least an assessment from a regional perspective as to whether it stood a chance of successfully effecting the overall outcome of the narcotrafficking operations in the Andean Ridge. Here too, had the messianic nature of a national security imperative not come into play as it did in the mid-1980s, cooler heads might have prevailed in

Washington, D.C., realizing that, in a supply and demand business-economics situation, it is the demand which creates the incentive for the source to provide the required goods and services to make the business equation both functional and profitable. In this sense the demand is the key center of gravity which must be addressed to resolve the problem in the long run. In this case the national security imperative set Bolivia up as a source target or false center of gravity, causing it to become a windmill of countervailing factors against which the US anti-drug policy has tilted without generating a decisive result. Had the Bolivian situation been studied and evaluated properly, the US might have begun to address the demand side of the problem in such a way so as to reduce its intensity in animating the supply side, giving the source oriented strategy a chance to produce genuine, long lasting results in defeating the narcotraffickers in Bolivia.

As a third lesson, the Bolivian government has expressed frustration, fear, distrust and bitterness over the US involvement in its internal affairs. At issue is *national sovereignty*. The US can not afford to run roughshod over the leadership of a foreign nation with which it expects to deal on even terms in the future or obtain its willing support as an equal partner in dealing with complex social-economic and political questions. To do this in Bolivia was to place in jeopardy both the US relationship and its goals involving the reinforcement of the democratic process which is the moral foundation and legitimacy on which much of the US foreign policy is currently based. In addition, the US role in dealing directly with and often in secret with the Bolivian Executive to gain approval for intended US operations actually had the unintended affect of undermining Bolivian constitutionality. In short, US Country Team coordinating efforts did not promote the democratic process and tended to encourage the Bolivian presidents to violate their own constitutional process. While the US was often able to coerce to a considerable degree the Bolivian government into supporting the US anti-drug policy or risk losing economic and financial aid, it did not garner in the end an overwhelmingly positive attitude in support of the policy which the complex situation demanded.

While domestic corruption is a major factor and obstacle to dealing with narcotraffickers inside Bolivia, a fourth lesson learned suggests that it is ultimately the *element of trust and cooperation* which will make or break any international joint anti-drug program or venture of this nature. In Bolivia the lack of mutual trust undermined considerably the US anti-drug effort. This, in turn, has affected the political will of the Bolivian government which is very aware of its precarious social-economic situation. The US Country Team has often lamented the lack of will on the part of the Bolivian government, but will not share information or include the latter in critical planning or direction of the anti-drug operations which take place within the latter's national territory. This is both humiliating and insulting to the host government's leadership. That a foreign nation and embassy, in this case the US and its Country Team, have the coercive power and influence to enter into the host nation's domestic law enforcement environment and can act with apparent impunity, only highlights the perceived national embarrassment and disgrace.

A fifth lesson learned involves the *cost-benefit approach* to calculating host-nation national interest. It may very well be that whatever support the US is receiving for its programs in Bolivia is really predicated on how much aid is forthcoming in benefit of the Bolivian government's own interests. In this case one could suppose that Bolivia, because of its generally chronic economic condition, is going with whatever source gives it the largest national largess. In this case it balances the US government's grants in aid, as well as other foreign investment and bank loans, against the benefits and returns it accrues from its own socio-economic situation. It is doubtful that Bolivia will change its current policy and risk committing national economic suicide and civil war by jeopardizing the still remunerative coca and the welfare of scores of thousands of farmers in pursuit of US objectives, unless a suitable income substitute is in place and functioning.

While there have been increasing DEA-UMOPAR successes over the last several years in interdicting cocaine and breaking up the cocaine production systems and organizations, a sixth lesson shows that the narcotraffickers are involved in a *self-generating business* which means that, as long as there is a strong demand and high profits to be made, they can and will sustain themselves indefinitely. When some narcotraffickers are arrested or otherwise neutralized, others immediately take their place. US supply oriented anti-drug operations have produced at best an accordion-like effect with the narcotraffickers having to suspend operations temporarily; only to reconstitute their efforts at a later date. The demand pull of the supply and demand marketing system, in the truest sense of competitive capitalism, means that for the US anti-drug policy the *narcotrafficking market process can only be dealt with successfully if the demand side is reduced* in either its intensity or influence. This is a lesson that the US government has only grudgingly began to appreciate and accept at this point in time.

A seventh lesson learned deals with the problem of a *coherent policy*.

Because there is no real coordination between what transpires inside Bolivia in terms of the US policy in play and what is going on in other, adjacent countries, there has been no coherence to the anti-drug policy to insure that successful results produced within Bolivia are meshed with equal results in neighboring Andean regions of equal or greater importance to produce a decisive effect. It must be kept in mind that Bolivia produces but 30 percent of the total amount of cocaine exported to the illegal world market. Success in Bolivia must be weighed against what is going on elsewhere in the Andes. This means that, when repression does place pressure on the narcotraffickers inside Bolivia, they can and will shift to other adjacent countries (the *balloon effect*) in an effort to continue operations. For this reason an anti-drug policy or any policy with multi-national implications must be tied into the US policy effort for those countries concerned with the issue and its ramifications.

A final lesson learned which is relevant to Bolivia concerns the RAND Corporation study of *narcotrafficker profit margins* which showed that coca leaf farmers received something less than one percent and the producers, and exporters and smugglers only up to about ten percent of the profits from the sales of cocaine HCl in the world market. This means that roughly 90 percent of the profits are made outside of Bolivia, giving the narcotraffickers a windfall which they can then use to bribe or otherwise facilitate marketing operations within Bolivia. The RAND study concluded that even if half of the total cocaine market could be closed down, the retail price of cocaine would rise by less than about three percent inside the US. Since the profits are so high, supply side interdiction in itself does not appear to be a cost deterrent for the narcotraffickers. (Reuter 1990: 95; and GAO 1991a: 26-27)

Even if the total anti-drug program in Bolivia could be successful in its interdiction-eradication-crop substitution process, closing down most if not all of the illegal coca-cocaine production, there would be a time when the US will stop providing its economic and financial incentives. At this point, provided there is still an international market demand for cocaine, the lure of potentially astronomically high profits to be made will undoubtedly cause a new group of narcotraffickers to reintroduce this lucrative type of business in Bolivia. In turn a new group of farmers will then come into play to meet the demand and enhance their livelihoods. The process will have begun again. In the end it is the demand side of the supply equation which is the key center of gravity which will have to be addressed if the US expects to make any lasting progress in terms of its anti-drug policy in Bolivia.

If Bolivia is considered to produce 30 percent of the cocaine appearing on market, but intercepts or keeps from export 30 percent of that cocaine inside its borders (as the Country Team maintains), it can then be said to be stopping only ten percent of the world's total annual production! Is that enough? The final judgement of this case study will have to await the evaluation of Peru as an actor in the war on drugs. Nonetheless, one can conclude that, after spending well over a billion dollars in an effort involving a cast of thousands, including iterations of Washington, D.C. and La Paz administrations, their respective bureaucracies and militaries, US Country Teams and a host of paramilitary police forces (UMOPAR) and their associated US field advisors and trainers, the US anti-drug policy and supply side strategy in Bolivia has been unable to stem the tide of international drug production and trafficking at the source. To this end, despite some successes which this case study has noted, it has been a failure.

This happened despite the fact that the US leadership was generally successful in getting the Bolivian government's commitment and cooperation to at least attempt to do virtually everything the US government demanded. In addition, the availability of adequate resources to support the anti-drug policy in Bolivia in the 1990s went well beyond the fondest dreams of the Country Team of the mid-1980s which desired a more militant implementation of the anti-drug policy then in play to resolve the perceived threat to US national security. On this point and the evidence reviewed one must question the soundness of the entire US policy approach to drug trafficking in Bolivia and its generally all-encompassing, single issue foreign policy agenda. The US national security imperative and the intensity with which the related anti-drug policy was pursued appear to have blinded its executors to the many factors or obstacles, involving economic, political, social and even societal values in play which tended to buffet the policy much like a block of wood in rough water in such a manner to render a less than desired effect. This begs the question of whether the US anti-drug policy in Bolivia has been worth the effort expended and whether any lasting results could ever be achieved as long as there is a strong market demand for cocaine remaining in play. This suggests that chances for future success are already too badly prejudiced for the US anti-drug policy in Bolivia to achieve the aims for which it was conceived. As the case study of Peru will demonstrate, the factors and obstacles that the US anti-drug policy confronted in Bolivia were relatively mild compared to those it would encounter to points north.

That Peru is contingent to Bolivia's northwestern frontier is of some importance. The close proximity of two of the most important coca growing regions in the world provides mutual support for narcotrafficking operations and facilitates the movement of coca derived products in and around the Andes. In addition, traffickers can move with relative ease back and forth across the international border to escape pursuing counter-drug forces. If aerial interdiction poses a problem in one country, coca products in the form of paste or refined cocaine can be back packed at will into the adjacent country and then transshipped to points north. Nonetheless, Peru in itself is capable of producing sufficient coca leaves to sustain the worldwide demand for coca's end product. For this reason it is critically important to this study.

Chapter 6

U.S. Anti-Drug Efforts in Peru - The 1980s

Peru is the world's largest single source of coca leaves, providing about two-thirds of the total cocaine produced in the world. For this reason it has been important to the US pursuit of a supply oriented anti-drug policy in the Andean Ridge. (House 1991b: 2; and ONDCP 1989: 62-63) Peru is also one of the most daunting challenges to the US anti-drug policy in the Andean Ridge due to its unique social, economic and political problems which at once have placed it in a state of virtual civil war and on the brink of economic collapse. Here too, countervailing influences have been in play involving various actors, events, and environments which together have affected the outcome of the US anti-drug effort.

As a country of a little over 21 million people (UN 1990: 429), for almost a decade Peru underwent severe economic recession, hyper-inflation, and faced a huge ($24 billion) foreign debt. (Miami Herald: 11 Feb 91) While the Peruvian national flag displays a cornucopia as part of the nation's coat of arms, in reality the benefits are not known to the great majority of the population as a whole. Approximately 75 percent of the population is underemployed or not employed at all. Half of the remaining 25 percent traditionally earn about $56 per month (The official minimum wage is $42 per month). In addition, over half the population lives at a level one could call "nutritional risk." At a level of near starvation, mere survival is for many the only hope or aspiration in life. (Taft-Morales 1990: 1 and 13; and Werlich 1987: 31) Life expectancy in the early 1980s was said to be 62 years compared to 76 years in the US, (UN 1990a: 178). The infant mortality rate was about 86 per thousand births compared to 10 per thousand in the US and 5 per thousand in Japan. (UN 1990a: 232) Enrollment at the secondary (high school) education level was about 50 percent. For half the population it was more important for their children to be working to support their family rather than spend time in high school. (UNICEF 1990: 234)

About the size of Alaska, Peru is characterized by high Andes mountains running through the middle of the country from north to south. Its western Pacific Ocean coast consists of arid, desert-like coastal plains forming the region known as the Atacama Desert. To the east on the other side of the Andes, lie the tropical zones and jungles of the headwaters of the Amazon River complex. It is this Amazonian tropical section, bordering on Brazil further to the east and Colombia and Ecuador to the north, that is of paramount interest to this case study. It is here in the San Martin, Huanuco and La Libertad Departments that the major share of the Peruvian coca leaves, so important to the illegal cocaine trade entering the US, is produced. The remainder of the coca produced in Peru, or about 40 percent, generally comes out of the high Andean valleys to the south, such as those formed by the Urubamba and Ene Rivers, in the Departments of Ayacucho and Cuzco (also spelled "Cusco") which, over time, have also demonstrated their importance to the international narcotics trade. (Barsallo 1988: 24; and Taft-Morales 1990: 1) In short, coca was growing in 14 of Peru's 24 departments.

Complicating the drug issue in Peru is a serious social-economic problem, involving distinct but very important dimensions. Beginning in the late 1960s, agrarian reform measures were brought into play as the result of a military *golpe de estado* (coup d'etat). These measures were introduced by the Peruvian military led by General Juan Velasco Alverado in 1968 to resolve the issue of previously broken promises of land reform on the part of the Fernando Belaunde Terry government of the mid-1960s. This raised the level of expectation of virtually all the *campesinos* ("peasant farmers and laborers") who found it frustrating to have to eke out a survival level of existence within a governing system which centuries ago was perceived as a cornucopia of abundance and social welfare but was now perceived as generally unresponsive to their needs. Yet, even though the *campesino* farmer under the Velasco regime could now own his own private plot of land or work it as part of a cooperative effort under the government sponsored agrarian reform movement which began in 1969, life was at best still very hard. (Craig 1990: 322)

Ironically it was the permanent workers and squatters who received the main benefits of land ownership from the agrarian reform. About ten million hectares out of a total of some 30 million hectares of farm property were actually distributed by the Velasco regime. (Alvarez 1992: 73) The transient or seasonal workers (over half the labor force), apart from their wages, generally received no land and were therefore inclined to go to either the urban areas or to the tropical zones where coca farming was reported as a flourishing business. (Vassilaqui Interview 1992; and Sheahan 1987: 258) In the end the Velasco regime ignored the plight of the impoverished rural workers and merely contributed to the overall dissatisfaction and frustration felt by many people in the high-Andes which set the stage for a violent alternative that was not long in coming. (Sheahan 1987: 264-265)

To offset some of the difficulties of life, the high Andean Indians centering around the Cuzco region and numbering over four million or about a quarter of the Peruvian population have traditionally chewed coca leaves. (Deustua 1987: 44; and Cabezas Interview 1992) To relieve the monotony of life, dull the pains or twitchings of a half-empty stomach, and otherwise feel the stimulus that the coca leaf juices generally gave to their sense of physical well-being, the Peruvian Indians indulged in a traditional past time which has been passed down over the generations - the chewing of coca. This and the rituals that go with it out of respect for *Pacha Mama* ("God of Earth"), as well as other gods, have become part of the cultural and socio-psychological makeup of the Peruvian Incan Indian traditions and peoples going back well over a thousand years. (Gagliano 1963: passim; Cabezas Interview 1992; and Craig 1990: 324) Up to 70 distinct folk medicines are based on one use or another of coca leaves and over 80 percent of the rural high-Andean population use the coca leaf for some form of health-care purposes. (Lee 1989: 24)

Erythroxylum, the species of coca which is the most commonly found in Peru generally grows in a narrow geographical band or high tropical altitude between 1,500 and 3,600 feet above sea level. Adapted to this environment over thousands of years, the coca generally needs and receives 80 inches of rain each year. The US Drug Enforcement Administration (DEA) Special Testing Research Laboratory rates the quality or alkaloid content of the Peruvian species at .75 of a baseline of one, while that of Bolivia is rated at .68 and that of Colombia .32

respectively. (Stickney 1993) Traditionally cultivated in terraces during Incan times, coca can be planted and cultivated successfully on steep slopes of up to about 45 degrees which are frequently encountered in the Upper Huallaga Valley (UHV) of north-central Peru and the high Andes valleys in southern Peru. (Senate 1990a : 5 and 65) That it grows in soils that are high in acids and low in nutrients, essentially means that coca grows well under conditions that most other crops find inhospitable. Some bushes in the UHV are said to have grown as tall as 12 to 15 feet. (Lee III 1989: 27) Another species is the *Ipadu* variety which is found in the lowland rain forest of Peru's Loreto Department. In addition, a highland variety known as the *Novogranatense* or *Truxillense* ("Trujillo") coca can also be found in some areas of the Andes Mountains of northern Peru.

Narcotraffickers, operating mainly out of Colombia to exploit a lucrative, high demand market in the US and Europe involving billions of dollars in profits, saw great potential in not only the highland regions of Peru where coca had been grown for a millennium, but most importantly in the lush tropical zones at the base of the eastern slopes of the Andes. One area in particular, the Upper Huallaga Valley covering an area of about a 8,000 square miles of which 3,000 square miles was considered eminently suitable for growing coca, was deemed particularly valuable due to its high quality coca leaf which could be produced in large quantities through several or more growing seasons each year. (House 1990c: 19; and Taft-Morales 1990: 19) It was into this region that 90,000 migrants, responding to the 1968 Agrarian Reform Laws of the Velasco era (1968-75), came looking for both land and work. By 1981 the population was roughly 134,000 or several times over what it had been just twenty years earlier. (Aramburu 1989: 234, 237 and 245) In addition, some of the landed elites who were forced to turn over much of their properties to the campesino workers also found the lure of the coca business as a means to offset their losses. (Cabezas 1992)

Informal contracting enabled the narcotraffickers and their buyers to purchase coca leaves for conversion into first paste and then ultimately into the high quality cocaine demanded by the consumer markets of North America and Europe. During this time coca production had risen from an estimated 18,000 hectares (ha) in 1976 to about 40,000 ha in 1980. (Gorriti 1990: 188) While raw coca converted into paste was generally produced by the local campesinos and then sold to Colombian cartel-linked buyers, the cocaine products actually produced inside Peru included cocaine base and even some refined cocaine HCl (about ten percent of the total HCl produced) were processed at Peruvian and Colombian run laboratories. (McClintock 1988: 128-129) By the mid-1980s's the region was producing roughly half of the world's known supply of cocaine on some 18,555 of registered plots of five hectares (one hectare is equal to 2.2 acres) or less. (Craig 1990: 323; and Aramburu 1989: 254) In 1986 it was estimated that the 105,000 metric tons (mts) of coca leaves picked from this valley alone produced some 54,000 mts of paste and base which was then exported to processing laboratories located in Colombia. Business boomed and the poor Indian *campesinos*, numbering up to a million in the various coca growing regions of Peru, for the first time in their lives began to subsist reasonably well with their now readily exportable coca leaf crops. (Deustua 1987: 45; and Vassilaqui Interview 1992) While a peasant farm family typically grew up to two hectares of coca and from five to seven hectares of food crops, the farmer could earn an annual income of from $1,500 up to $10,000 per one or two hectare plot of coca bushes alone. Wage laborers picking leaves or making paste could earn as much as $5 per day or about double the official minimum wage. (Clawson and Lee 1992: 32-33) Even so the coca farmers received less than one percent of the coca product's final street value (Figure 5).

Production Price Chain For One Kilogram of Cocaine
(in 1986 dollars)

Production/Transhipment Process	Price Charged
Coca leaves at the farm	$ 1,200
Export of coca paste to Colombia	7,000
Import of cocaine into Miami	20,000
Wholesale cocaine in Detroit	40,000
Retail cocaine (in 1 gram units) on street	250,000

Source: 1986 RAND Corporation study by Peter Reuter in House Report 101-991. 30 November 1990. p. 34.

Figure 5

But all this activity was not lost on the US government which, since the late 1970s had begun its fledgling, yet ever intensifying anti-drug effort in Peru which was trying to stem what was becoming an ever increasing crescendo of illegal cocaine leaving Peru to eventually enter the US. Through the US Embassy (Country Team) in Lima, the Department of State and other affiliated organizations such as the Department of Justice's Drug Enforcement Administration (DEA) began to take a considerable interest in reducing and controlling the coca and cocaine product trade and attempted to place pressure on the Peruvian government to do likewise. DEA officials known to the author in 1980 felt that, if Peru could not or would not do its part in quashing the drug trade, then it should allow the US a free hand to intervene and stop narcotrafficking through eradication of the coca crop. Yet it was not that Peru was not trying to do its part.

Coca growing in Peru was known to be contributing to the then relatively small international cocaine market in the mid-1970s. Despite US efforts to focus the Peruvian government's attention on this point and promote an eradication effort, little was done. Nonetheless, efforts on the part of the DEA so impressed Peruvian authorities that they made an attempt to assert the government's authority over the coca industry. Beginning in 1978, through its Ministry of Economics and Finances' *Empresa Nacional de Coca* (ENACO - National Coca Enterprise), Peru tried to gain control of the coca growing areas by declaring them to be national enterprises whose leaves would have to be sold to the government. Under the government's Decree Law 22095, legal coca growing areas of some 18,000 ha were established by ENACO and acknowledged to be under the control of about 25,000 legally licensed and registered coca growers. (USAID 1986: D-1; and House 1990c: 18)

ENACO was to purchase the coca leaves from the registered growers and then sell the leaves to retailers for further distribution and sale to the traditional coca chewing and herbal medicine consumers throughout Peru. It also produced a limited amount of cocaine (HCl) for legal export to the international pharmaceutical community. Nonetheless, the *campesino* farmers largely ignored ENACO and the Peruvian law, selling their leaves to other *campesino* paste producers or narcotrafficker buyers who paid far higher prices than what the Peruvian government could afford to offer. Throughout the 1980s ENACO would never be able to purchase in any given year more than from five to about 40 percent of the legal coca trade which was spread over an area running from Tingo Maria to Cuzco. (Barsallo 1988: 144)

To assist the Country Team's DEA office to reduce what was known to be illegal or non-registered coca growing in Peru, the Peruvian government of the now reelected President Fernando Belaunde Terry agreed in mid-September of 1981 to establish an agency called CORAH or *Control y Reduccion del Cultivo de la Coca en el Alto Huallaga* (Control and Reduction of Coca Cultivation in the Upper Huallaga) to complement ENACO. This was part of a five year, $26.5 million USAID economic assistance program for Peru. The US State Department's Bureau of International Narcotics Matters (INM) agreed to provide $1.25 million towards the formation of an anti-drug police field force. (Walker 1989: 208; and Reid 1989: 156) CORAH, with a budget of some $4.3 million, was supposed to begin a forced eradication process targeting all unregistered or illegal coca that could be found. (Barsallo 1988: 197)

With the UHV becoming more and more a focal point for the illegally grown coca, the Peruvian government with USAID financial support began the *Proyecto Especial Alto Huallaga* (PEAH - Special Project for the Upper Huallaga) in December of 1981. It had the objective of introducing the *campesino* farmers growing illegal coca to legitimate, alternate crop substitutes. The Peruvian narcotraffickers, initially viewing the government's initiatives as serious threats, responded by attempting to infiltrate and gain control of the principal political parties, hoping in this manner they could influence if not dominate or otherwise neutralize the anti-drug policies in their favor. Their overtures and attempts to gain control of the various political parties failed, (Vassilaqui 1992) and by 1986 US funding for the CORAH and PEAH efforts would reach $23.4 million. (Barsallo 1988: 193) Thus, by 1982 the US policy in Peru had changed from its original late 1970s' concept which envisioned intimidation and the threat of eradication as sufficient enough incentives to cause the campesino farmers to desist from producing illegal coca to one which involved a carrot (PEAH) and stick (CORAH) approach. Now economic or positive incentives were also deemed necessary for the policy to succeed. (NACLA 1989: 16)

Yet almost from the very beginning of the serious US and Peruvian efforts to stem the drug trade in Peru in the late 1970s and early 1980s, there was an important complication looming. This took the form of a deadly, rural based insurgency, called the *Sendero Luminoso* (SL - "Shining Path") which had begun a campaign (initiated in the late 1960s) to ultimately overthrow the national government in Lima. While this insurgency began with a relatively narrow minority base in the 1970s, it rapidly expanded, attracting the discontented from all levels of Peruvian society. Beginning in May 1981 after a decade of preparation, it unleashed a reign of terror throughout most of Peru, increasing in such strength and ferocity that the insurgency became a destabilizing force far beyond the ability of the local police forces to cope. The SL operated on two principal fronts, one that was revolutionary and focused on the high Andean regions around Ayacucho and another that was very much a commercial enterprise, as well as a revolutionary effort in its methods and relationships with the people, which was centered on the coca growing regions of Peru. (Zapata Interview 1992) As such, the SL became a salient enigma which seriously challenged the US anti-drug policy in Peru.

The roots of the SL phenomenon have been traced to a synthesis which took place during the 1960s and 1970s in the Ayacucho Department between a dissident high-Andean intellectual elite and a group of young, energetic and impressionable men and women of Indian and mestizo origin. Taught by professors such as Abimael Guzman at the Huamanga University, this group eventually formed the core cadres or central vertebrae of the SL revolutionary movement. Exposed to Marxist analytical concepts of human exploitation as an explanation of the Peruvian reality, they were told that they were the "children of the deceived." In addition the group learned that the Spanish language and culture had been deceitfully imposed upon their Indian ancestors by the Iberian conquest as part of a strategy of domination and monopoly control by an oligarchy centered on Lima. (Degregori 1989: 7-8; and Palmer 1992: 3-4)

An ideal or utopian society, which they were told they had been denied, was depicted as a people living in absolute peace and harmony, without exploitation, greed, graft, or corruption without the dominating structure of the state, political parties, classes or even democracy. (Degregori 1989: 14) Guzman taught this as a dogma and said that anything that smacked of the trappings of the "old state" or "semi-feudal order" was contaminated since it was not legitimate in its protection of the people's interests. Contamination included among other things the national governing structure, elected mayors, unions, cooperatives (symbols of exploitation and corruption), other parties of the left, and all non-governmental entities such as churches and businesses. Modern Peru's concepts of liberty and equality were scorned as falsehoods and myths when confronted with the reality of the human misery and degradation which was the visible lot of the poor in Peru. All this was said to have to be extirpated through revolution in order to make way for the "new" and "just" society in Peru. (Degrigori 1989: 25; and Strong 1992: 8-9)

It was very easy for the Huamanga University generation of the 1970s to relate to Guzman's perspectives and dogma about the reality of Peruvian society at large and to themselves in particular. The failure of the reform military government of General Velasco to allow the natural thrust of the agrarian reform movement to take place and permit the high-Andean peasants access to and real influence at the national level of government was one part of this reality. Corruption, combined with an unresponsive and uncaring government and its administrators was a fact of life in Ayacucho and contributed to a loss of considerable legitimacy on the part of the government not only in the eyes of the university students but also the *campesinos* in general. (Zapata 1992)

Finally there was the young, idealistic and now relatively highly educated minority in the Peruvian Andes that found itself as neither part of the world of their parents with its myths, traditions and state of abject poverty and bare subsistence agriculture (agricultural wage labor earned 50 cents per day), nor part of the western-oriented, urbanized criollo classes who both rejected and looked down upon them as Indian-mestizo and Quechua speaking outcasts. (Palmer 1992: 4; and Degregori 1989: 14) The frustration over knowing what ought to be theirs in terms of a new and better economic and social status and the relative indifference of the national government in Lima to the plight of its citizens in the Andes only added more fuel to the smoldering revolutionary fire that would eventually break out. Thus, the expanding educational opportunities and stagnant employment prospects on the periphery of Peruvian society combined with a callous disinterest and rejection by the Lima based center to produce a catalytic situation waiting to be exploited. (Zapata Interview 1992)

Offering a "solution" to the Andean society's problems and the psychological vacuum in which a number of its young people found themselves was an organization offering an identity to this new generation, an ideology in which it could believe, and a captivating *caudillo-maestro* (leader cum teacher) who could guide them in their own "long march" to a utopian destiny. This was Abimael Guzman and his *Partido Comunisto del Peru* (PCP - Peruvian Communist Party. The "way" or movement was called the "shining path" from whence the name *Sendero Luminoso* sprang. (Degregori 1989: 19) To escape from their perceived conditions of virtual feudal slavery, Guzman told his followers it was now necessary to engage in a revolutionary war which would both educate and cleanse the society and eliminate the dominating illegitimate state structure and government. This was to be the "popular war" or revolution as advocated by Mao Tsetung and Jose Carlos Mariategui (Peruvian Communist Party leader of the 1920s) to overthrow the government. (Degregori 1989: 27 and 42; and Strong

1992: 15, 17 and 23)

Seeking to exploit the Andean campesino's tradition of independence and distrust of the government, Doctor *Puka Inti* or the "Red Sun" as Guzman was known to his followers, opened his revolutionary campaign against the Peruvian government, beginning in the Ayacucho region. (New York Times: 14 Sep 92) Attempts were made to win over entire communities of *campesino* farmers and their families. By discrediting the government and Peruvian societal values, the SL hoped to be able to substitute its own standards of law and morality. Cattle thieves, disloyal husbands, dishonest merchants, corrupt government officials, and those who drank alcohol and caroused were subject to stern SL justice and retribution. A number were killed outright. While there was a guarded positive response on the part of the peasant communities to these actions and the stern prescriptions of revolutionary morality, the SL demanded in return an autarkic society based on economic self-sufficiency with little or no political and administrative links to the national government. (Smith, M.L. 1992: 25; Degregori 1989: 43 and 45; and Palmer 1992: 5 and 8) In some cases where a major land lord was killed or forced to flee his land, the SL then redistributed the property among the villagers and canceled any outstanding debts that remained. Likewise some paramedical and literary services were provided in lieu of those sometimes offered by the government. (McClintock 1984: 81)

Not fully cognizant of all the complexities of traditional agrarian communities, the farm to market system, and the deep hatred of any domination felt by the campesinos, the SL all too often tried to forcibly reorganize the communities into unrealistic economic and social arrangements which included shutting off access to local markets and imposing improper planting techniques for the local food crops. (Palmer 1992: 5) Through its use of selective political violence or terror against uncooperative individuals, wealthy peasants, and hostile cooperatives and its imposition of its own new regime and standards of morality, over time the SL made as many enemies as friends. Nonetheless, the low wages and lack of free and simple access to land, as well as the indiscriminate and heavy handed tactics of the Peruvian national security forces involving the police and military kept considerable peasant sympathy on the side of the SL. Those who opposed the SL were rejected, humiliated or killed outright in retribution. (Palmer 1992: 6, 8 and 9) As the SL gathered more popular support and expanded, Guzman organized the revolution into six regional commands, supported by networks of cells and guerrilla units which provided the intelligence, logistics and operational support for the SL's revolutionary strategy. (Palmer 1992: 9)

The *Tupac Amaru* Revolutionary Movement (MRTA) competed with the SL as a second revolutionary movement and attempted to appeal to those disaffected people throughout Peru who believed in the more standard revolutionary ideologies and processes for overthrowing the government. In this case, the traditions of the Cuban Castro revolution and that of the Sandinistas in Nicaragua were more the preference of the MRTA's leadership and followers. Its operations, while employing car bombings, kidnappings, extortion and murder, were usually conducted on a vastly smaller scale than the SL and had a more intensive urban focus. Targets typically included symbols of "imperialism" or foreign enterprises such as the US Embassy in Lima, Kentucky Fried Chicken and Pizza Hut restaurants, Mormon churches, radio and television stations and some government offices. While the SL could be considered a real threat to Peruvian society, the MRTA was looked upon more as a nuisance. Nonetheless, the MRTA did compete with the SL for the Huallaga Valley as a source of funding for its revolutionary efforts. (Strong 1992: 214-215; House 1991b: 118-119; and Zapata 1992)

With the need for a reliable source of funding to finance its efforts, the SL began in 1983 to extend its operations into the coca growing regions of all parts of Peru, contesting and frequently ousting from most areas the competing MRTA insurgency. (Taft-Morales 1990: 11) In the Upper Huallaga Valley (UHV) the SL guerrillas effected a type of protectorate relationship in support of the coca growers in exchange for a type of "tax". By this means the SL was able to gain control of up to 90 percent of the UHV. (McClintock 1988: 127-128; and Palmer 1992: 7) In so doing it ruled by the law of the gun, protecting the coca growers from being swindled or underpaid by the narcotrafficker buyers and the purchasing and shipping organizations which formed the traffickers' infrastructure for the drug trade. Here too the buyers and traffickers also paid their share of "taxes" or fees charged as a price for not being molested by the SL and allowed to ply their trade. (Strong 1992: 102-103 and 109-110) In exchange for exacting taxes, the SL also provided the "service" of protecting both coca growers and traffickers from the distrusted and bothersome government officials, coca eradicators, police and military forces. (Soberon 1992; and Smith 1992: 102-103) The SL used coercion in the form of terrorist acts and related threats against the government, the traffickers and campesino farmers alike who refused to pay their taxes or otherwise did not cooperate sufficiently to the former's liking. (McClintock 1988: 138) Nonetheless, as the only organization in the UHV that openly defended the coca growers' rights to production, the SL guerrillas gained a certain amount of legitimacy in the eyes of the campesino farmers. (Senate 1990a: 8-9)

The US government wanted to go directly to what it perceived was the source of the coca production problem in Peru: the coca bush which generated several or more coca-leaf crops per year. This supply side strategy could best be carried out, or so it seemed in the early 1980s, through a process of complete eradication of the coca bushes. To protect the coca-growing *campesino* who was both the mainstay of the insurgency against the government in the UHV and a principal source of revenue, the SL opposed and openly contested the US sponsored eradication program. This put the US policy in Peru on a collision course with both the SL guerrillas and the coca farmers. The situation was complicated and did not set well within the Peruvian government. (Vassilaqui 1992) In addition, the coca farmers, prodded in part by their Colombian cartel refiners and buyers and the SL guerrillas, formed loose coalitions and interest groups consisting of both legal and illegal local coca growers. Called *Frentes Para la Defensa de Intereses Populares* (FEDIPs - Fronts for the Defense of the People's Interest), these groups had a political connotation relating to the SL as well as an economic interest relating to the traffickers. Militant support for the FEDIPs came from the SL and MRTA guerrillas who were attempting to build a base of political support among the coca growers and not just merely exploit them for financial gain. All attempts, however, on the part of the growers and the FEDIPs to legalize coca production and terminate the efforts at eradication and crop substitution were to no avail in the face of an intransigent Peruvian government supported by the US anti-drug policy. (Lee 1989: 59, and 79-82)

At this time in the early 1980s, the accompanying increase in brutal assassinations of government officials, drug addictions, prostitution, infamous boom towns such as Tingo Maria and Tocache and the fact that the local coca farmers were squandering their newly begotten wealth on luxury items such as dish antennas atop their peasant shacks, new cars and discotheques, often at the expense of their families and agricultural development on behalf of society, made for a bad public image. (Craig 1990: 325-326; and Lee 1989: 79) With some prodding on the part of the US Country Team and other socially concerned elements within Peruvian society, the government began to react to this situation. In August of 1984 a state of emergency was declared and the Army was ordered into the UHV to destroy the SL guerrillas operating there and to protect the DEA and its Peruvian manned eradication teams. (Interview CT:PE)

By mid-1984 President Fernando Belaunde Terry was concerned about both the drug trafficking and the insurgencies taking place in Peru. He believed that narcotrafficking operations had replaced the traditional international assistance from communist countries and organizations as a source of earnings for the revolutionary movements in Peru. (Lee 1989: 157) Unfortunately for both the Peruvian and US anti-drug policy in the UHV, the Belaunde administration had not taken the early SL activity seriously, and it was only after several years that the government finally declared in 1983 an emergency zone in the Ayacucho area in recognition of the insurgency problem. Besides this there were economic problems too.

Belaunde, as a part of his Popular Action (AP) party administration, had tried to stimulate the Peruvian economy through an export-led economic growth policy supported by international loans. The policy had the misfortune of being implemented during a period of volatile world commodity prices which undermined its effort. As time went on inflation increased and real wages were eroded by some 30 percent. World market prices for Peru's exports (copper, oil, sugar, fish meal and minerals) remained low or declined further. Not helping the situation were natural disasters in the form of rains and flooding in northern Peru and a severe drought in the south. By late 1983 this economic reality saw Peru's GDP falling 12 percent and manufacturing declining 17 percent. In 1984 about 60 percent of Peru's total labor force was underemployed and public external debt had risen 21 percent ($13 billion total by the end of 1984). The 1980s world recession had a devastating impact on Peru, placing it in a situation where it could not assist its people economically or meet its international debt payments. (Wise 1989: 169; and Palmer 1990: 268) All this prejudiced Peru's efforts to deal with the insurgencies and narcotraffickers.

The two Peruvian Army missions of confronting the guerrillas and the narcotraffickers, albeit important to both US and Peruvian interests, were actually working at cross purposes. The Army, under the command of General Julio Carbajal D'Angelo, maintained that its number one priority in the UHV was the elimination of the SL insurgency and not the destruction of coca bushes. It therefore made a deliberate effort to befriend the coca growers whose support was seen as critical to defeat the SL guerrilla movement. *Campesino* support was perceived as conducive to isolating the SL from its sources of funding, logistical support and valuable information on the government's counter-insurgency operations. If isolation was not always possible, at least information could be obtained from the coca farmers to assist reconnaissance units to better target SL guerrilla elements. (Craig 1990: 325-326; and Gonzales 1992: 107) General Alberto Arciniega Hubi, one of a number of the Peruvian Army commanders ultimately sent to the UHV to run counterinsurgency operations against the guerrillas, summed up the situation saying: "There are 150,000 *peasant coca farmers* in the zone. Each of them is a potential *guerrilla*. Eradicate his field and the next day he'll be one." (Andreas and Sharpe 1991: 116)

To offset and work around the Army's top priority in the UHV, the DEA, with permission from the Belaunde government, created its own rural, mobile strike force called the DIPOD or *Directorio de la Policia de Drogas* (Directorate of Anti-Drug Police). This was made up of Peruvian National Police (PNP) and was similar to the Bolivian UMOPAR and often referred to by that name. Unfortunately, this force was often ignored, left undefended and sometimes even actually prevented from carrying out some of its own operations by the Army. The conditions under which it worked were not easy. In November 1984, 23 coca eradicators and government inspectors from CORAH were murdered by the SL. In addition, in January 1985 fifteen farm laborers including women and children were killed by the SL, bringing the total of murdered innocents in the UHV to over fifty campesino farmers and their family members. These events were suspected as having been carried out on the part of the SL guerrillas as retribution against those farmers who had become involved in the PEAH alternate crop projects. They also had the aim of coercing and otherwise discouraging other local coca farmers from cooperating with PEAH in the future. By mid-1985 USAID became concerned over the fact that some Peruvian civilian officials were losing their enthusiasm and initiative for their work as they became more concerned about their personal safety. The violence was also having a negative affect on outside commercial investment in the UHV as well. (USAID 1986: D-9 and D-10) At the same time, the longer Army and police personnel were involved in operations in the UHV, the more they became susceptible to corruption in the form of narcotrafficker bribes. The campesinos themselves did not particularly like or trust the soldiers and became more and more irate as the latter roamed around their plantations, disrupting an otherwise relatively tranquil accommodation and business relationship that had been developed with both the SL and the traffickers. (Craig 1990: 325 and 326) At this time it was estimated that coca farmers were earning a level of income per hectare of coca approximately at least twice that of a hectare of coffee and up to twenty times that of a hectare of rice. (USAID 1986: D-8; and Andreas and Sharpe 1992: 79)

Corruption among the Peruvian military had been reported to the Peruvian government by the Country Team. As a result, General Carbajal and 32 of his officers were placed under court-marshall arrest by the Ministry of Defense for allegedly taking bribes and having links to the narcotraffickers. (Gonzales 1992: 123) Observing that the Army was vulnerable to being corrupted and was not making any progress in fighting the SL, the Peruvian government eventually ordered its military forces out of the UHV in December of 1985. The Army mission had failed and narcotrafficking as well as the SL guerrillas could carry on very much as they had before. Despite this a series of DEA instigated operations (*Condor*) were underway. One of these, Condor III, was reported as having destroyed 44 cocaine laboratories, disabled 40 airstrips and seized 725 metric tons (mt) of coca leaf as well as one-third of a metric ton of cocaine itself. While statistically impressive, the impact of the Condor operations on the flow of cocaine base and cocaine HCl of the UHV was minimal. (McClintock 1988: 131)

In 1985, Alan Garcia, the newly elected President of Peru on a nationalist economic-reactivation ticket of the American Popular Revolutionary Alliance (APRA) party, inherited an economy in chaos, an ever growing and violent insurgency threat, and an ever expanding and influential and powerful narcotrafficker network plying its trade. In his acceptance speech before the Peruvian Congress he stated: "*Una lacra historica amenaza a nuestro pais: es el narcotrafico*" ("A historical scum threatens our country: it is narcotrafficking."). (Barsallo 1988: 11) He also noted that Peru's institutions and people were being corrupted and degraded by the narco-dollars circulating throughout the land. Garcia's own strategy concept for dealing with the narcotraffickers and resolving the illegal coca production problem revolved around the idea of taking away the economic incentive to grow coca through a more militantly coercive and harassing interdiction effort which was supposed to bring about the collapse of the coca market. (Craig 1990: 323-324)

To deal with Peru's worsening insurgency situation, Garcia hoped to direct resources to the rural sector to raise productivity and reduce poverty. This was the most difficult end to achieve since it required profound structural changes in the conditions of production. The government had neither the resources nor the time to allow it to overcome its rural economic problems. In addition, influential economic elites lobbied the Garcia administration to concentrate on stimulating the urban industrialization process. They advocated a national industrial strategy which involved forging a pact between the state and the domestic business and financial groups. (Sheahan 1987: 268)

To resolve poverty in general, productive employment had to occur at rates faster than the growth of the labor force (and unemployed). Labor intensive methods of production in industry were what Peru needed most, but proved unable to achieve. Due to fear of the SL and its activities, both foreign and domestic investment was not taking place in sufficient quantity to provide the stimulating current necessary to enable the economic development process to take place. (Sheahan 1987: 268-269) As a result, President Garcia took other measures in an effort to improve Peru's economic situation and resolve its acute debt crisis.

A deliberate decision was made on the part of Garcia to embark on a debt service strategy whereby Peru would only pay off only 10 percent or what he thought was reasonable for the contracted international debt service. It was perceived by Garcia that to do any more would necessitate the use of the nation's several billion dollar budget and leave the government completely bankrupt and unable to conduct its internal governing operations. (House 1990c: 27) Based on this perception, he called for a unilateral debt moratorium since debt payments now surpassed the total of the country's export earnings. Further international financing was out of the question as Garcia announced his "10 percent solution." The international banking community was put on notice that Peru would limit its international debt ($14 billion in 1986) service to 10 percent of its export earnings. At the same time the Central Bank began to purchase dollars from regional banks which were flush with the proceeds from the cocaine trade. (Wise 1989: 173)

Garcia's strategy did have a short term positive effect on the economy. Real wages in the countryside increased 30 percent and the GDP rose 8.5 percent. By late 1986 the economic boom made him one of the most popular presidents in Peruvian history. Nonetheless, the SL insurgents were targeting local industry and new private sector investment fell off. While Garcia's debt-service formula was undoubtedly appropriate from a Peruvian perspective, other international lending institutions did not agree. Peru was isolated from further international loans and by 1988, lacking international credit, its economy saw an 8.5 percent decline in its GNP. (Wise 1989: 174) Peru was again in an economic crisis.

At this time there were operating in Peru some seven or eight narcotrafficking groups which were dominated for the most part by Colombian cartels. (Interview DEA-PE: 1992) The majority of these were operating in the UHV where the Peruvian *campesinos* continued to sell their coca paste to buyers or gangs who in turn sold it to their cartel contacts. These contacts either shipped the paste to a laboratory complex in the UHV or had it flown to a processing site in Colombia. (McClintock 1988: 128)

The DEA's Condor operations continued throughout 1986, attacking coca paste and cocaine processing facilities and airstrips with the expectancy that the coca market would collapse if these vulnerable points in the trafficker's production system were shut down. The Condor operations were conducted independently of what was then going on in Bolivia and the Country Teams in neither La Paz nor Lima particularly cared what the other was doing at the time. In Lima, the Country Team felt that, in conjunction with interdiction and crop eradication as two pillars of the anti-drug strategy for Peru, an AID supported crop substitution program would serve as the third pillar which could be successfully pitted against the narcotraffickers. While all this sounded good to US government officials, President Garcia could not escape the fact that, much like the preceding administration, his government was also dependent to a large degree on the flow of coca dollars into the depressed Peruvian economy. (Craig 1990: 323-324)

By the mid-1980s the Peruvian government estimated the foreign exchange input into its economy from the coca trade as being upwards of a billion dollars annually or from 25 to 50 percent of its total exports of about $2.5 billion. (McClintock 1988: 129; and IADB 1987: 136; and IADB 1988: 488) This was a badly needed source of income, even if it was extralegal and formed an underground economy. Up to that time the previous Belaunde government had financed its operations through multi-billion dollar loans totalling some $10 billion. (UN 1990: 265) Funding of this nature was no longer available to the Garcia administration due to its reduced debt-service policy. While the mining of metals such as copper, iron ore, silver, zinc, and lead, as well as coffee and petroleum, served as the base of the export economy, after 1985 it was not enough. With export earnings reported as averaging $4 billion and imports running at $6 billion, the parallel coca economy was helping to buoy up the economy and take up a significant portion of the export earnings' shortfall. (World Bank 1991: 466-477; and IMF 1990: 424) Despite the economic and insurgency problems, CORAH was able to follow its mandate and eradicate a reported 5,000 ha during 1985.

This was offset by some 12,000 ha of new coca that had been brought under cultivation. (McClintock 1988: 130)

Another factor working to undermine the Condor strategy lay in the economic solvency of the coca farmer who for the first time in his life was enjoying more than a survival wage. The attraction of earning more than reasonable wages was causing most *campesino* farmers to ignore ENACO's offers of legal licensing to grow coca for the government as well as to encourage further large numbers of destitute peasants to migrate into the UHV to seek their fortunes growing coca. (NACLA 1990: 6) In exchange for eradicating his coca crop forevermore, the DEA offered to pay the farmer $300 per one hectare of destroyed coca bushes. (McClintock 1988: 130) Unfortunately for the DEA and the US anti-drug policy, the average farmer was now receiving from $4,000 to even as high as $20,000 for a year's worth of coca leaves from his generally one to three hectare plots year in and year out. (McClintock 1988: 133; and Craig 1990: 325) With this high level of earnings, one can understand why the coca farmer's allegiance continued to lie with his coca crops.

By 1986 there were twelve narcotrafficker purchasing groups or organizations in the UHV who, along with the SL and MRTA guerrillas, were constantly urging the coca farmers to resist, reject or otherwise militantly stand up against the efforts of the US and Peruvian governments to eliminate illegal coca and substitute other, less profitable crops. (Interview DEA-PE: 1992) During April and May of 1986 militant coca grower groups in the form of FEDIPs and other loose coca growing organizations staged a strike in the UHV against the US-Peruvian effort. Roads were cut, transportation was paralyzed and for several days the *campesino* farmers even laid siege to one of the USAID missions located at the town of Aucayacu about twenty miles north of Tingo Maria. (Lee 1989: 62 and 109) The following June up to 3,000 farmers and other persons surrounded and proceeded to stone a detachment of DIPOD troopers and burn two of the CORAH eradication trucks.

As a lobbying effort, this did get the attention of the Peruvian government in Lima which hurriedly sent a representative from the Ministry of the Interior on a low key visit to the UHV to negotiate with the growers. While not greatly publicized, the farmers did make 54 demands which, besides the legalization of a plot of two hectares of coca per family and a complete withdrawal of the CORAH, PEAH and DIPOD personnel from the UHV, included a rural development package. This package sought the construction of four rice mills, six agricultural processing plants, seven agronomic institutes and colleges (including a National Coca Institute), a weather station, irrigation canals, hospitals, clinics and even a hydroelectric power station. (Lee 1989: 83 and 86). The demands were acknowledged by the government's representatives, but little or nothing was done to implement them.

As the Spring of 1986 wore on and President Reagan announced his National Security Decision Directive (NSDD) 221 with its attendant "declaration of war" on drugs and the involvement of the US armed forces in the effort, the US anti-drug aid program for Peru began to see an increase in funding. In this case aid in support of interdiction efforts went from $3.2 million in FY 1986 to $5 million in FY 1987. While USAID programmed some $23 million for crop substitution, the coca farmers still found more profits were to be had by remaining in the coca growing business than opting out.

Nonetheless, by 1987 while the SL still provided its protection, the coca farmers found they were losing as much as 20 percent of their coca profits as taxes paid to the SL guerrillas for this service. The alternative was somber; the *campesinos* could either pay the SL taxes or probably lose their lives. It was estimated that in this situation the SL was earning some $30 million per year from its activities in the UHV alone. (NACLA 1990: 15; and Craig 1990: 331). The SL did not like competition and in March of 1987 fought a pitched battle with the MRTA over who would control the UHV. After some 60 persons had been killed between the two guerrilla forces, the MRTA was forced to withdraw in the face of the superior SL into the Central Huallaga and the Tarapoto area. (Lee 1989: 87) The SL now controlled the UHV and had successfully protected its primary source of finances for its ongoing revolutionary war to the south.

In the airports of Tocache and Uchiza between two and five narcotrafficker aircraft per day were reported as landing and picking up between 800 and 2,500 pounds of coca paste for shipment to laboratories in Colombia. These aircraft, after spending only about ten minutes on the ground to conduct their transactions, then took off for the return flight back to a laboratory site in Colombia. Paying from $600 to $750 per pound of paste and some $8,000 per landing and takeoff may appear prohibitively expensive to the reader, but, when measured against the profits earned outside Peru, one can appreciate why this was such a lucrative business and very much worth the relatively "small" transaction costs (Figure 5). The SL guerrillas received some $3,000 of the $8,000 paid by the narco-pilots or shippers as a "tax" for each landing and takeoff, while the corrupted police constables received the remainder in return for their "cooperation" in not impeding the transshipment operation. (Barsallo 1988: 91) When the police did get in the way, the SL asserted its authority in no uncertain terms. In one case in late May 1987 dissatisfied SL guerrillas overran and wiped out the Uchiza police detachment. (Gonzalez 1992: 123)

The significance of this price chain (Figure 5) is important for understanding the impact that drug prices can have in undercutting an anti-drug policy and supply-side effort in a country such as Peru. Note that the prices doubled between Colombia and Miami and, between Miami and the street, they increased some six times over. This meant that no matter how costly the US and Peruvian efforts appeared to make the narcotrafficking operations inside Peru, the losses could either be absorbed by the traffickers or passed on to the consumer. In the meantime the SL was cementing its alliances with the coca growing campesinos and making a modus vivendi with the local narcotrafficking barons. In addition it continued its guerrilla operations, blowing up two key bridges in an effort to inhibit government control of the UHV. (Gonzalez 1992: 109)

Things were clearly out of hand and the Peruvian government was visibly seen to be losing control over much of its territory in the UHV, which now appeared to be governed under a joint accord involving the collusion of the SL guerrillas and local police. While President Garcia and his government would have preferred to have ignored the situation in the distant UHV, it could not. International pressure, mainly from the US as well as local media highlighted the happenings in the UHV and constantly prodded Garcia and his ministers to address aspects of the situation. Since the taxes collected from the coca growers by the SL was acknowledged as a source of funding for the guerrillas, President Garcia was forced to conclude that the situation was indeed out of hand. (Zapata and Pedraglio 1992)

The Country Team in Lima consulted with President Garcia about the issue and was able to get some results. As part of a government declared state of emergency in the UHV, roughly 1,200 police using helicopters and staging out of Tingo Maria made a series of airmobile assaults called *Operacion Relampago* (Operation Lightning) to retake the towns of Tocache and Uchiza. There was little or no resistance from the SL to these operations which lasted from 15 July until 25 August 1987. Nine laboratories were located and destroyed in the process. (Barsallo 1988: 93) The DEA and its DIPOD forces persisted in their own efforts which, while destroying some 40 additional laboratories, disabling 140 airstrips, and capturing 14 aircraft along with thousands of pounds of coca paste and cocaine base, still did not appear to make any real progress in stemming the overall flow of coca products out of Peru. (Werlich 1987: 32; and McClintock 1988: 131)

In late-1987 the Country Team again approached the Peruvian government with a new strategy which envisioned the establishment of a formal forward operating base at a central location deep in the interior of the UHV. From this base, called "Santa Lucia", anti-drug operations were to be staged to attack the cocaine traffickers at their remote laboratory sites. Because the site selected was on the west bank of the Huallaga River in a relatively remote area without a road network connecting it to any of the major towns, it would not be until September of 1988 or a year later that construction would actually begin. (NAS 1991: 3) The Country Team in Lima, observing the less than successful results of Condor and the initial positive impact that Blast Furnace had had in Bolivia in terms of disrupting narcotrafficker operations, now modified its strategy.

As part of Operation Snowcap in Peru and initiated in the latter part of 1987, the US approach aimed to target the traffickers' advanced level cocaine processing laboratories. In this case it was hoped that further confrontations with the coca farmers could be avoided. With no advanced laboratories available to process the coca paste, it was theorized by the DEA that the coca market would become over saturated with an abundance of leaves, forcing the prices paid for the leaves to be reduced to where no reasonable profit margin could be achieved. At this point in time, the coca farmer, seeing no profits to be made, would be susceptible to being induced to take up an honest livelihood producing the USAID sponsored alternate crops. (Interview NAU-PE: 1988)

The Peruvian government had also adopted this strategy concept, calling it the *Plan Integral a Largo Plazo de Lucha Contra el Narcotrafico* (Long Range Integrated Plan Against Narcotrafficking). The Peruvian plan included public education and precursor control components as well as a program for drug user rehabilitation (Barsallo 1988: 73 and 211; and Interview NAU:PE 1988) The public education effort revolved around CEDRO or the *Centro de Informacion y Educacion para La Prevencion del Abuso de Droga* (Information and Education Center for the Prevention of Drug Abuse) which was to promote drug abuse prevention and mobilize public opinion in favor of the anti-drug effort. USAID supported CEDRO's effort with a $4 million grant which took effect in mid-1986. Via information bulletins, journal articles and advertisements, including radio and TV spots,

CEDRO waged an unrelenting campaign against drug usage and the narcotraffickers in Peru. The US Information Service from the US Embassy in Lima assisted in the coordination of meetings and seminars which eventually involved some 1,400 Peruvian institutions as participants. (USIS 1991: 17-20)

The precursor control aspect of the Peruvian plan, involving the interception of kerosene, sulfuric acid, potassium permanganate and ammonia as key chemicals in the paste, base and cocaine production processes, was not practical from the start. All these chemicals were common user items for a wide variety of commercial purposes inside Peru and were shipped in large quantities throughout the nation practically every week if not every day. As such there was no way to determine at the border entry points which chemicals were destined for legitimate or illegitimate end uses. (House 1990c: 20)

While there were some successes during Operation Snowcap, due to the inability of the government and the DEA to sustain its operations and the narcotraffickers' flexibility in rebounding from their losses and then shifting their activities in and around the UHV ahead of the DEA-DIPOD forces, the overall results were less than satisfactory. By using river craft, pack animals, vehicles, sea going vessels and human backpacking as alternate means of transportation, the traffickers were more often than not able to avoid the DIPOD's helicopter supported operations and move their products to their respective market destinations. (House 1990c: 20; and McClintock 1988: 131-132) The eradication effort suffered accordingly.

Despite the Peruvian government's Public Law 22095 which allowed the *campesinos* to own no more than five hectares of land legally, coca plots proliferated throughout the region. Of the from 107,000 ha to 180,000 ha of coca estimated to be under cultivation in the mid-1980s, only 3,200 ha in 1984, 4,800 ha in 1985 and some 2,600 ha in 1986 had been eradicated. (Senate 1990a: 126; Lee 1989: 23; and NACLA 1990: 16) This was despite a CORAH agreement with the US to eradicate 15,000 ha over a three year period. (Barsallo 1988: 148) Of the remaining total hectares of coca, 90 percent was still available for narcotrafficker use. This no doubt reflected to some degree the influence that market profits were having on the *campesino* farmers who compared their coca crop profits to what other crops were earning (Figure 6). The years 1987 and 1988 would see a similar trend and, as time went on, it was found that coca paste production had virtually doubled between 1985 and 1986, going from 320 metric tons (mts) to about 540 mts respectively. (McClintock 1988: 132) This took place despite 1,913 persons being prosecuted for narcotrafficking by the Peruvian legal system and another 243 having been fired for narco-related corruption. (Soberon Garrido 1992) At the end of 1987 in terms of repatriated dollars into the Peruvian economy, cocaine exports were estimated as being equal to about 25 to 30 percent of Peru's total legal exports for that year. (House 1990c: 20; Senate 1990a: 129; and Lee 1988: 89) The expansion in narcotrafficking had taken place despite the 78 distinct legislative acts on the part of the Peruvian government which had been promulgated since 1920 to control or otherwise suppress drug usage and drug production throughout Peru. (CEDRO 1988: passim)

Peruvian Agricultural Crop Profits Per Hectare
(in dollars)

Crop	Profit
Platano	$ 323
Corn	271
Rice	323
Cocao	969
Coffee	271
Achiote	1,085
Coca	5,000

Source: *Drogas Responsabilidad Compartida* by Jose Barsallo, p. 63.

Figure 6

In 1988 the Department of State's Bureau of International Narcotics Matters (INM) perceived one of its anti-drug policy goals in Peru to be the persuading the Peruvian government to establish a permanent police or security presence in all coca growing areas so that eradication could proceed smoothly. In addition, INM hoped to fund alternative development projects to the degree that campesino farmers would be more willing to abandon their coca crops for suitable alternates. Here USAID and other multilateral organizations were expected to help defray the costs of the effort. To these goals were added the traditional objectives of dismantling the narcotrafficker networks, reducing corruption, and enhancing public awareness so as to better engage the Peruvian government and the population in the anti-drug effort. (Van

Wert 1988: 13)

The backbone of the US sponsored effort during this period was the 500 man strong DIPOD Peruvian counter drug police force trained, equipped and paid for by the Department of State's Bureau of International Narcotics Matters (INM) which was represented in the Country Team as the Narcotics Assistance Unit (NAU). The field operating DIPOD was actually controlled by DEA and backed by an anti-drug operations planning and intelligence targeting cell in the form of a SOUTHCOM provided Tactical Analysis Team (TAT) which was on duty at the US Embassy in Lima. The TAT would guide the DEA-DIPOD effort and was intended to ensure that the DEA's effort was as efficient and effective as possible, targeting the narcotraffickers wherever they could be found inside Peru. In addition some five Bell helicopters and a C-123 aircraft with contract pilots were placed on loan by the Department of State to the DEA and constituted the latter's air wing, giving it considerably more capabilities in terms of reaching out to attack the narcotraffickers in their here-to-fore relatively immune laboratory sanctuaries.(House 1992b: 38; and NACLA 1990: 20)

The helicopter supported DEA-DIPOD forces frequently staged out of the forward operating base then under construction at Santa Lucia. The base would ultimately contain a 1,500 meter long earthen runway capable of handling up to C-130 medium size transport aircraft. In addition, living quarters for up to 500 persons, cooking and dining facilities, bunkers, lookout towers, barricades, wire fencing, a command-and-control center, power generators and a medical support center were ultimately constructed in a configuration which looked much like a "Vietnam style Special Forces camp." (NAS 1991: 3) To manage and sustain the overall US anti-drug effort some one hundred personnel, representing all the US armed services, DEA, NAU, US Customs, Coast Guard and a contracted, commercial aviation maintenance company called National Air Transport Inc. (NATI) worked with the Country Team. (House 1990c: 21; and GAO 1991a: 12-13) This US effort was costing some $10 million or several times the investment of just several years earlier. (McClintock 1988: 132)

During 1988 the US Congress became very interested in promoting an effective national as well as international anti-drug policy. Polls taken around the nation showed that from early to mid-1988 nearly half of the American people felt that drug trafficking was the nation's number one problem. (Perl 1988: 24) Congressional activity began to reflect the people's concern and of the one thousand bills introduced into the House of Representatives, roughly one out of five dealt with some aspect of the drug issue. (Perl 1988: 45) To this end the House and Senate passed the Anti-Drug Abuse Act of 1988 (Public Law 100-690, HR 5210) which, in its Section 4303, singled out Peru, stipulating that USAID programs for developmental assistance for the UHV would be conditioned on the effectiveness of the US programs there in reducing coca and cocaine production, distribution and marketing. Likewise special consideration was to be given to the progress made in meeting eradication targets similar to those established in 1985. (Perl 1988: 38) President Reagan had certified in his 29 February 1988 Presidential Determination No. 88-10 that Peru had "cooperated fully with the United States" in the anti-drug effort in the Andean Ridge and therefore merited continued aid and support from the US government. Since some members of the US Congress did not fully agree with Reagan, they had moved to ensure that aid for Peru was based on some form of measured or observable progress.

To help facilitate the US anti-drug policy's progress in Peru, US Attorney General Edwin Meese met Alan Garcia in April 1988 in Lima and reached a tentative agreement with the Peruvian President on the use of herbicides to help win the war on drugs. This involved more specifically a herbicide chemical called *Tebuthiuron* or "Spike" as part of an aerial spraying program which was to focus on the UHV. Spike, produced by the Eli Lilly & Company as the sole US manufacturer, is a highly potent toxic chemical that kills both trees and shrubs as it makes contact with their respective root systems. Garcia was both amicable and impressed with the new US concept. (Que Hacer 1988)

Testing on herbicides in Peru by the Country Team had actually begun in October of 1987 and was originally based on a September 1987 meeting between the Minister of the Interior, Jose Barsallo Burga, and INM Assistant Secretary Ann Wrobleski. (NAS 1990: 4). Four separate test phases were conducted with the last one finally terminating in March of 1989. During the first phase six distinct types of herbicides were tested on a quarter acre plot of coca at the Santa Lucia base. The Herbicide Technical Team (HTT), made up of US, Colombian and Peruvian technicians and led by Dr Peter W. Jacoby of the University of Texas's School of Agriculture and Mines, followed up the first tests with two more phases. These phases saw a manual application of the herbicides over a one-hectare plot of land and then over a two-hectare plot of sloped terrain to evaluate herbicide run-off. (NAS 1991: 4-5)

According to the tentative US-Peruvian herbicide agreement, an initial 100 ha to 200 ha of coca fields were to be sprayed with Spike. Experimental in nature, aerial spraying with Spike was viewed by the

US as both an economical and thorough way to force the eradication process through to a successful completion, destroying the entire coca crop in the UHV without having to unnecessarily endanger the DIPOD or ENACO personnel in confrontations with the campesinos, the SL or MRTA guerrillas or even hostile narcotraffickers. (SOUTHCOM J5 1989) After a year of inspections and evaluations of its test sites, the HTT determined that Spike had proven 95 percent effective in killing mature coca bushes. Soil and water samples collected during this time, as well as inspections of surrounding vegetation, were said to have had a "minimal impact" on the environment. (NAS 1991: 5) Spike had also been certified in US Congressional hearings as killing only coca and not the surrounding vegetation. (Senate 1990a: 21-22) While this appeared to be a stroke of good fortune for the US anti-drug policy in Peru, it quickly came to naught.

Eli Lilly, fearing narcotrafficker reprisals against its multi-national South American operations and the possibility of being held liable for damages to both the people of Peru and the ecology of the UHV region, suddenly announced that it would not sell its herbicides to the Department of State for use in any coca eradication programs. (House 1990c: 23; and Que Hacer 1988) Eli Lilly's concern was based on the fact that Spike's use in wetland areas similar to the UHV was potentially conducive to contamination of the environment. This, in turn, might produce a poisoning effect on the animal and fish life, which, when eaten by the people living in the region, could cause birth defects and even cancer. (House 1990c: 23-24; Eli Lilly Letter 1993; and Barsallo 1988: 155-157)

US environmentalists delivered warnings too. Dr Peter Kurtz of the California Food and Agriculture Department warned that Spike "creates deserts where it is used in sufficient quantity." Dr Richard Wiles of the National Academy of Sciences also warned of the devastating ecological effects that spike could have. (Lee 1989: 207) But not all people agreed with this perspective and some Peruvians argued that without the use of Spike it would take as long as 70 years to eradicate by hand the 200,000 ha of illegal coca then thought by some to be in existence. (Barsallo 1988: 157) Even the SL guerrillas entered the debate, but on the side of the coca farmers and narcotraffickers where they circulated leaflets decrying the potential detrimental effects that Spike might have on the livelihood of the UHV's population. On one occasion in its protest against Spike, the SL staged a three day "armed strike" which effectively shut down all transportation into and out of the UHV. (House 1990c: 24) On this note the debate about Spike ended. It was an obvious setback for the US Country Team's plan for a quick and simple resolution of the drug war in Peru. As a result, it now had to rely on the slow, manual eradication strategy with all the problems of potential confrontation and conflict that it entailed.

On 19 December 1988 Peru became one of the 77 nations which agreed to adopt the United Nations' Convention of Vienna against trafficking in illegal drugs. While agreeing entirely with most of the Conventions 34 articles such as those dealing with control of precursor chemicals, extradition, and prosecuting specific acts of narcotrafficking by individuals, the Peruvian legal system and its associated jurists debated the significance of the details of the Convention for some time thereafter. (Soberon 1992: 37-46) Nonetheless, signing the Convention displayed a continued willingness on the part of the Peruvian government to support the anti-drug initiatives and the US policy in play. This was significant since Alan Garcia was having problems.

At the end of 1988 President Garcia's popularity was plummeting. His entire economic recovery strategy for stimulating the economy and reducing poverty had failed and inflation was running at 1,722 percent. (Palmer 1990: 269) Moreover, his government was failing in its counter-insurgency efforts against the SL guerrillas who appeared to be gradually expanding their operations and gaining influence and control over ever more territory. In addition, Garcia's approval rating in Washington, D.C. was not very high ever since he had established the 10 percent ceiling on Peru's international debt payments. A general perception began to take place inside Peru, as well as among the international community, that Garcia was anti-banking and business and anti-American. Even elements within his own party had rejected his policies and were turning their backs on him. (Interviews NAU-PE 1988 and Cabezas 1992)

As 1989 came on President Alan Garcia began to rail against the US approach to resolving the narcotrafficking problem in Peru, terming it inadequate and failing to provide the campesinos with sufficient incentives to stop growing coca. He suggested that, because Peru did not have the resources, the Country Team should approach the problem by emphasizing crop substitutes such as coffee, cacao and a vegetable similar to a squash or potato called achiote. Chocolate was another industry deemed as having the potential to provide a reasonably good profit as a substitute for coca. (Pais: 28 Sep 1989) Due to the consternation and fear that was being produced among the farmers by the operations of the DIPOD, the narcotraffickers and the SL and MRTA guerrillas in the Huallaga Valley, some *campesinos* were beginning to have doubts about the viability of growing coca as long term livelihood. A United Nations survey indicated that crop substitution ideas were being viewed with favor by a number of the coca farmers who were reported as being fed up with the guerrilla violence and perceived excessive taxes as well as price gouging on the part of the narcotraffickers and paste makers who only paid the minimum price possible for the coca leaves. Here the farmers were looking for a way out of their coca crop dependency situation. (Senate 1989-1990: 97; and Stevenson 1989)

The Country Team and the Department of State, now attempting to achieve an eradication goal of a 10 percent reduction in coca over a two year period of time, were well aware of President Garcia's criticisms of the US anti-drug policy, but had been able to convince the US Congress to allocate $52 million in support of the USAID economic assistance programs in Peru. US objectives in Peru included the continuing support for the constitutional and democratic processes which had been in play since 1980, as well as the strengthening of the anti-narcotics effort and assisting in Peru's economic and social development. Specific Country Team activities were to:

1. Assist legal-income earning opportunities for farmers willing to shift away from coca production in the UHV.
2. Expand the drug awareness program.
3. Improve the efficiency of the criminal justice system.
4. Improve the agricultural sector and provide food to alleviate hunger.
5. Provide scholarships to Peruvians to familiarize them with the democratic processes in the US.
6. Support a medical immunization (measles and polio) program.
7. Reduce barriers to growth and access to credit from Peru's ever larger informal sector. (Senate 1989-1990: 161; and Henson 1992)

Yet it would be technically difficult for Peru's Congress to fund to any extent the above ambitious projects since Peru was now more than a year behind on its international debt service payments. The US Congress decided that, under the Brook-Alexander Amendment (Section 620Q) of the US Foreign Assistance Act of 1961, amounts of aid over and above what was already authorized were prohibited when a country became more that a year behind in its debt service payments. As a result of Garcia's policies, Peru fell into this category. Ironically the Peruvian economic policy, in conjunction with US Congressional prohibitions, was undermining the US anti-drug policy. Nonetheless, the Country

Team was able to have the Brook-Alexander restriction waived for fiscal year 1990 so that assistance could be increased. (House 1990c: 27) Always tainting the Peruvian government's attitudes on the eradication-interdiction aspects of the US anti-drug policy was the considered appreciation by most parties concerned that the government did benefit from the estimated $1.5 billion in foreign exchange (about equal to half of its legal exports) that the illegal coca crops were still bringing Peru. (Washington Post: 5 Aug 88) This was important since the Peruvian GDP was said to have contracted 24 percent in early 1989, with manufacturing falling 13.8 percent, and an annual rate of inflation being recorded at about 5,000 percent. (Economist 1989: No. 2)

Another factor tending to inhibit economic growth were the ubiquitous SL and MRTA insurgencies. As an example, in one incident a reported 250 guerrillas ambushed Army troops on a road killing thirteen soldiers. In another, nine civilians were tried by SL "people's courts" in Ayacucho and then summarily shot by the guerrillas. Assassinations and ambushes continued throughout the country and in Lima itself ten buses were burned by guerrillas whose personel included a number of women. (Presencia: 25 Oct 89) The threat of guerrilla violence as well as the actual violent acts often disrupted transportation for hours if not days and even weeks. The lethal aspect of the insurgencies was very intimidating and foreign investment in Peru was almost non-existent. (Hengle 1992) The Peruvian military found that its counter-insurgency operations only had a temporary impact on the presence of the SL guerrillas. Unless there was an overwhelming government troop presence in a particular area that forced the guerrillas to move away, the SL eventually returned to reassert its influence and control.

By the end of 1989, with coca cultivation increasing by an estimated ten percent each year, it was estimated by the Country Team that as much as 200,000 metric tons (mt) of coca leaves or the equivalent of 370 mt of cocaine were being produced annually or enough to satisfy four times over the US cocaine market. Of this amount only 15 percent or about 18 mt was considered to be legally authorized cocaine production by the Peruvian government. (DOS-INM 1990: 19-20) It was also reported at this time that SL and narcotrafficker activities had expanded from the UHV to other similar growing areas around the Maranon, Ene, Apurimac, and Urubamba River complexes. This virtually doubled the potential coca growing area available to the narcotraffickers. (House 1990c: 18; and New York Times: 14 May 89) Despite this report, it was already known that illegal coca production had been going on in the high-Andes' valleys since the early 1980s in small *cocales* (coca plantations). The relatively vast distances of the Andean highlands and the widely distributed nature of the *cocales* compared to the highly concentrated UHV coca crop lands made the former less attractive for anti-drug operations even though they were producing up to 50 percent of the total Peruvian coca output. (Barsallo 1988: 123-125) An earlier USAID report had commented on this possibility stating: "A decrease in production in the Upper Huallaga Valley could be compensated for by increases in other areas unless control efforts occurred nationwide." (USAID 1986: 16) The warning went largely unheeded by the Country Team and its DEA-DIPOD effort.

The Country Team's eradication goals for 1989 had been 11,250 ha of coca bushes and the destruction of some 15,000 ha of coca seed beds or a grand total of 26,000 ha. This was to have been done both by hand using bush trimmers and machetes and was to take place by exploiting Santa Lucia as a forward operating base for the CORAH workers. (House 1990c: 39) Only a little over ten percent (1,285 ha) of the targeted 11,250 ha of coca or less than one percent of the total Peruvian coca crop were actually eradicated by CORAH in 1989. The new coca cultivation effort of some 4,785 ha was found to have out paced the US sponsored CORAH eradication effort with an overall estimated four percent increase in favor of the traffickers. (House 1990b: 18-20; and House 1990c: 39) This was in large part due to attacks on the eradication workers by the SL guerrillas and the narcotraffickers which resulted in some forty workers being killed, forcing a suspension of the DEA program from February 1989 to March 1990 or more than a year. (Taft-Morales 1990: 21)

The Peruvian government suggested to the US Congress that to avoid further complications in the anti-drug effort the US simply purchase the entire annual coca crop as a first step towards crop substitution and the formation of an agro-industrial infrastructure. As this was estimated to cost around $800 million, the Congress balked at the idea of a US subsidy for Peru with no guarantee for success. (Senate 1989-1990: 65 and 169) In the meantime DEA intelligence sources were indicating to the Country Team that more and more Colombians were becoming involved in the Peruvian trafficking operations and that their physical presence at the processing sites inside Peru had been on the increase since 1989. In this case up to 150 Colombians were reportedly operating in Peru, insuring that the coca paste and cocaine base/HCl produced were quality products and that timely deliveries were being made. Both the Cali and Medellin cartels were said to be well represented in all cases. If nothing else, by controlling the international transportation and distribution networks and keeping a presence in Peru as the primary source for coca-cocaine products, the Colombian narco-mafia could ensure that the Peruvian traffickers, such as Reynaldo Rodriguez, would not be able to readily bypass the cartels to the north and deal directly with the US market. (House 1990c: 38; and Lee 1989: 109)

By this time some 75,000 additional people had migrated to the UHV over the previous several years, bringing the total population of the area to roughly 250,000 of which less than ten percent were indigenous UHV residents. (House 1990c: 19) There was now a rough balance established between the number of people in the UHV and the amount of coca grown to the degree that there was in theory about one hectare of coca for every person living and working in the UHV. The coca trade was providing a considerable stimulus to the local economy and also providing a myriad of jobs, including those for carpenters, electricians, roofers, and merchants selling food, wares, tools, spray equipment, herbicides and fertilizers etc. needed to manage the coca crops. It was estimated that 95 percent of the UHV's economy revolved around the production of coca and its cocaine related products. (House 1990c: 19-20)

Yet it was the debate over the issue of which focus, the guerrillas, or the coca growers, or both, should be the priority for the armed forces that finally brought things to a head in the UHV. The Peruvian Army commander on the scene, General Alberto Arciniega, was named to his position in August 1989 after the SL guerrillas overwhelmed and captured the police station in Uchiza. In addition, some 27 INM-paid coca eradication workers were killed while attempting to destroy coca crops growing on illegal or unregistered plots of land. (DOS-IG 1989: 6) Arciniega's approach to the problem was to give first priority to attacking the guerrillas through a counter-insurgency campaign. To gain the critical support of the people required to defeat the guerrillas, he found it necessary to befriend the coca growers. By severing the informational and logistical links between the population and the guerrillas, the General reasoned that his forces could isolate the guerrillas and eventually clear them from the UHV. For this reason the Army refused to countenance any action which might deny it the people's support, including any actions against the coca farmers. As a result, Arciniega directed that forced eradication of coca should cease immediately. (Campodonico and Zapata 1992)

Overcoming the heretofore general distrust of the population of the government and its programs, the General and his men made slow but steady progress in an often bitter fight against both the SL and the MRTA. No quarter was asked and none given in this relentless and vicious struggle against the guerrillas for the control of the UHV. (Bailetti 1992; and Gonzales 1992: 115) As the security situation gradually improved, *campesinos* from 42 of the roughly one hundred communities in the UHV indicated that they were ready to begin in many cases to switch from coca crops into other more legitimate produce, provided that they would receive a reasonably fair and comparable price. Citing police corruption and abuse, the SL's strict political and moral agendas and taxes, and the threats of retribution from both the narcotraffickers and the Peruvian government's CORAH if cooperation was not forthcoming, the coca farmers were looking for a way out of their highly stressful situation. Yet winning against the guerrillas was to ignore the anti-drug struggle in the UHV which was the priority interest of the US government and its Country Team in Lima. (Gonzales 1992: 115; and WOLA 1990: 20-21)

Taking issue with the Peruvian policy in the UHV was the US government's Assistant Secretary of State for International Narcotics Matters, Melvyn Levitsky, who accused the popular General Arciniega of being involved in narcotrafficking. Pressure was accordingly placed on the Peruvian government and in December 1989 General Arciniega was transferred to the Ministry of Defense. (Senate 1989: 170) Nonetheless, Arciniega's successor, General Mario Brito Roman found that to defeat the guerrillas he would also have to follow essentially the same policy used by his predecessor. This placed the Peruvian military at loggerheads with the US anti-drug policy and the DEA-DIPOD forces who were interested primarily in pursuing their top priorities of interdiction and eradication - a focus which often brought them into a confrontational situation with Peru's military as well as with the coca farmers. (WOLA 1990: 21-22) By this time police-military relations had deteriorated considerably as each organization, the Peruvian National Police (PNP) and the Army worked to achieve their now mutually contradictory goals. In the remaining areas of Peru during September and October of 1984, the SL had assassinated eight mayors and forced the resignation of fifty others, leaving up to 90 percent of the country without governing, local civil authority at the small town level. Voter turnouts were also reported at only 30 percent and much less than expected. (Gonzales 1992: 125)

Other factors also played a part in the less than successful anti-drug effort now being played out. These for the most part involved US interagency squabbles over how to approach the anti-drug problem in Peru and what strategy to use. DEA wanted to use the Santa Lucia based helicopters for interdiction operations against laboratory sites, while the NAU wanted to use the helicopters in support of the Peruvian eradication campaign. Friction also developed between DEA personnel and the Peruvian anti-narcotics police and naval riverine force personnel. Beginning in 1989 the US Army's Special Forces' Mobile Training Teams (MTTs) had begun training the DIPOD forces as part of the US Southern Command's (SOUTHCOM's) *Operation Blue Venture* training mission. (WOLA 1989: 84) After the DIPOD personnel had been trained by the MTTs, it was found that the Peruvian police were complaining that they were not being employed by the DEA in accordance with their newly acquired capabilities and that the DEA directors were unfamiliar with the new DIPOD tactics and operational techniques. In addition, the DEA agents, all too frequently on ninety-day rotational assignments from the US, could not always speak Spanish. This lack of training and communication problems on the part of the DEA tended to inhibit the coordination and effective employment of the DIPOD forces. (House 1990b: 24-25)

That the DEA-DIPOD airmobile strike forces could not carry out nighttime counter-narcotics operations was also an inhibiting factor which was mitigating the success of the US anti-drug programs in Peru. Here the lack of night vision goggles for the pilots and forward looking infrared radar (FLIR) were cited as reasons why the narcotraffickers, who usually flew at night, were able to conduct their business in a relatively unmolested manner. An ominous sign that the narcotraffickers were anticipating enhanced DEA-DIPOD aerial capabilities for the future was the way they tried to circumvent future US-Peruvian operations by shifting the locus of their laboratories and even coca growing areas to points north out of range of the helicopters then operating from Santa Lucia. (House 1990c: 42)

There were other shortcomings as well which tended to work against the successful execution of an anti-drug policy in Peru. Problems were noted in the support and maintenance rendered to the DEA. INM had leased a number of helicopters and pilots from the Evergreen, Inc. but, because of delays in entering the country due in the main to bureaucratic Peruvian customs procedures, INM only received 14 days of operation out of a 98 day lease. (DOS-IG 1989: 10) Special communications equipment on loan or even purchased from the Department of Defense often took over a year to arrive in the DEA's hands from the time it was ordered. Apart from this, equipment maintenance deficiencies at Tingo Maria led to a May 1989 crash of a Country Team aircraft resulting in the deaths of six Americans. (House 1990b: 24-25) As a result of the problems noted, Operation Snowcap fell short of its goal of doubling the 75 laboratories destroyed, 8 mts of cocaine base/HCl and 142 arrests made during 1988. Snowcap's 1989 tally showed 34 laboratories destroyed, less than one metric ton of cocaine base/HCl captured and 44 individuals arrested, or considerably less than the previous year. (House 1990c: 40-41) The US thus found itself disrupting to some degree the operations of the narcotraffickers but not able to reduce in any significant way their output. Coca production and the availability of coca products for processing and export continued unabated.

An INM study indicated that the narcotraffickers were so confident of their operations that couriers carrying lots of $20 million would arrive in Lima and other major towns in Peru and launder their money through the six dozen or so exchange houses which then made the required transfers to local or to international banks as desired by the traffickers. (DOS-INM 1991: 337) The Central Bank of Peru was said to be purchasing between $4 million and $13 million narco-dollars per day. (Andreas and Sharpe 1992: 78) During the mid-1980s an estimated up to $1.9 billion in narco-dollars were processed by the banking systems in Peru. (Briceno and Martinez 1989: 269) This was reportedly facilitated by the lack of government regulation of the parallel market through which half of the Peruvian economy was then estimated to flow. (Latin American Times: Apr-May 91) The amount of narco-dollars entering the Peruvian economy was now said to be somewhere around $400 million per year. (Si: 28 Aug 91) Other studies showed that, while an influx of dollars into the Peruvian economy might appear beneficial, cheaper dollars tended to cause Peruvians to consume more imported food and less domestic produce. In this case a *Dutch disease* affect was taking place in which for every ten percent decrease in the value of the dollars circulating in Peru, it was estimated that there was a corresponding 4.8 percent decrease in the price of potatoes with the end result that the poor potato farmers were earning less money and becoming even poorer still. (Clawson and Lee 1992: 13)

Despite all the efforts to the contrary by both the US and Peruvian governments, the supply of cocaine coming into the US and its attendant consumption remained steady as did its price and availability on the street. The US Senate Judiciary Committee was reporting that some 2.4 million Americans were cocaine addicts (one out of every hundred citizens). Up to ten percent of the US population indulged in some form of cocaine product or other illegal narcotics (Peru was reported at about 2 percent). If this was not alarming enough, it was found that during the period of little more than a year some 400,000 "crack babies" (crack being a derivative of cocaine) had been born in hospitals throughout the nation. (Senate 1991a: 1; and Lee 1989: 195) With public opinion polls reflecting drug abuse as the priority concern among Americans, a newly elected US President, George Bush, decided in 1989 to take the initiative to resolve the issue decisively.

Chapter 7

George Bush and Alberto Fujimori

Coordination was made by US representatives from the Office of National Drug Control Policy (ONDCP) during 1989 to develop policies and strategies which would disrupt and destroy trafficking groups throughout the Andean region, improve close collaboration between local police and military forces, and inflict as much damage as possible on the narcotraffickers in general. Once this initial coordination was accomplished, President Bush announced his new strategy called the Andean Initiative (AI) as part of his own national security imperative (National Security Directive or NSD 18). This was now the driving force behind the US anti-drug policy for Peru. (Quainton 1990: 26, 29 and 31) In mid-February 1990 at Cartagena, Colombia, Bush met with the presidents of Bolivia, Colombia and Peru in an anti-drug summit to attempt to cement a formal agreement on how to approach and combat the drug problem in the Americas in support of AI.

President Garcia had threatened to boycott the meeting in protest of the US invasion of Panama. Without Peru, the summit would be incomplete and lack the show of hemispheric solidarity and cooperation which Bush very much wanted to have. To deal with Garcia and cause him to reconsider his position, Bush declared in mid-January that the US would begin to withdraw its troops from Panama prior to the summit. Garcia attended the summit, but his own, highly vocal nationalistic attitudes concerning economics caused Bush to emphasize developmental aid as one of the primary strategies for ameliorating the disruptive effects of the drug trade on the Andean economies. (Miami Herald: 17 Jun 90; and Gamarra 1993) Garcia's economic nationalism and activist approach in inserting himself into the anti-drug policy making process was part of the legacy which he left for Peru's future president, Alberto Fujimori.

President Bush's Andean Initiative proposed that a joint effort be made to accomplish four objectives:
1. Disrupt and dismantle drug trafficking organizations,
2. Isolate major coca-growing areas by air, land and sea,
3. Block delivery of chemicals used for cocaine processing, and
4. Destroy the cocaine laboratory systems. (Taft-Morales 1990: 20; and ONDCP 1990: 49-51)

To accomplish the objectives above, the Bush administration announced a $2.2 billion economic, law enforcement and military logistics and training aid package for Bolivia, Colombia and Peru. Peru was to receive roughly a third of the monies planned for in the Andean Initiative (Appendix F)

The increased economic aid to assist crop substitution programs was conditioned on the acceptance of the military aid package involved. (Gamarra 1990: 4) In the case of Peru, from FY 1990 to FY 1994 or a period of about five years, it was to receive some $701.8 million. Of this amount roughly $376.7 million would be for economic assistance, $196.1 million for military assistance, $95 million for law enforcement and $34 million for DEA support. (House 1990b: 17) For Peru this was a yearly average of several times what it had received in 1989 alone. The US agreed to crack down on its own export of precursor chemicals such as acetone and ether and the sales of weapons coming out of the continental USA. In addition, those US troops involved in the drug war in the Andean Ridge were to be involved in training only and not have an active operational role. (Newsweek: 19 Feb 90)

On the basis of the Cartagena conference, it was decided by the US government that Operation Snowcap in the UHV was to be enhanced with a special emphasis on destroying cocaine (HCl) laboratory systems. (Taft Morales 1990: 20) In addition, some ten DEA agents and other Country Team personnel would continually serve as advisors to about one hundred DIPOD police and between two and four hundred eradication laborers working for CORAH in the UHV. All units were to operate out of the Santa Lucia base. To support these efforts eight INM provided helicopters and one cargo aircraft, as well as a DEA aircraft would provide the required air mobility. (House 1990b: 15) All these aircraft were to be piloted by 57 contracted American and seven Peruvian aviators and mechanics. (House 1990b: 15; and NAS 1991: 3)

As in Bolivia, SOUTHCOM, under the direction of General Maxwell Thurman, began to take a special interest in Peru. (Bagley 1991: 22) Intelligence and operational planning cells (TATs) as well as trainers were to arrive in Lima to enhance the Country Team's efforts. As such, a US Special Forces MTT, as part of Operation Blue Venture would train all DIPOD personnel in small unit tactics, air mobile operations involving the use of helicopter tactics and techniques, and base security. Throughout other portions of Peru to include Cuzco and its adjacent regions, sixteen DEA agents and a staff were to support some thirty thousand civil police and ten thousand investigative police in a nation-wide anti-drug effort. (House 1990b: 15) In addition the US and Peru reaffirmed the 1899 United States-Peruvian extradition treaty covering narcotics related offenses. (House 1990c: 37) This was to serve as part of the cutting edge of the US Andean Initiative (AI) and strategy for Peru.

Yet central to AI for its first year was the required direct involvement of the Peruvian military as well as the police in the anti-drug effort. For FY 1990-91 some $6.6 million in military and $19 million in police aid was appropriated, while economic aid remained for the moment at the relatively low level of $4.3 million (Peru was still getting the $52 million in economic aid allocated the previous year). (Senate 1989-1990: 161) INM funding now supported up to 750 men assigned to the DIPOD which, in conjunction with 425 members of CORAH, formed the core of the anti-drug strike forces employed by the Country Team. DIPOD and CORAH were further supported in turn by some 250 persons from the National Police Investigative Division (DINTID). Field equipment, rations, uniforms, boots, meals and medical supplies were provided by INM through its NAU office to maintain the forces. All Peruvian members received a special INM provided salary in addition to what they were receiving from the Peruvian government. In short, at any given time up to 1,425 Peruvian police personnel were operating in the pay and support of or under the direction of the NAU or DEA. In addition, anti-drug field operations training which included instruction in human rights was provided by US Army Special Forces teams for the DIPOD personnel. (NAS 1991: 2 and 6)

The US funding for the military was to finance, equip, and train six Peruvian Army battalions (5,500 men) and enable the purchase of six riverine patrol boats and the reconditioning of twenty A-37 fighter-bombers as laboratory attack aircraft. (New York Times: 22 Apr 90; and

House 1990b: 59) In addition plans were formulated and under way to construct other bases further north of Santa Lucia. (Taft-Morales 1990: 24) Again very seriously considered for employment by the INM and the Country Team in the drug war was the use of herbicides such as "Spike". (Taft-Morales 1990: 21) Nonetheless, factors of potential environmental contamination and the possibility of destroying the livelihood of the campesino growers, thus possibly driving them into the arms of the guerrillas, finally caused the herbicide portion of the plan to be discarded. (House 1990b: 61)

Anti-drug operations, however, were spotty in terms of success. During the first four months of 1990, there were two interdiction raids on the town of Uchiza. In each case DEA agents and their accompanying Peruvian police were stoned by irate campesinos as the former conducted their search for illegal drugs and precursor materials. There also appeared to be complicity if not encouragement on the part of the military personnel stationed at Uchiza to incite the campesinos to violence. It was also found that from February of 1989 to March 1990 or the period of the lapse in eradication and interdiction due to the intensification of the counter-guerrilla war, both coca producers and traffickers had relocated a number of their laboratories and production centers further north in the UHV into Tocache and Uchiza. There, with the complicity of bribed Peruvian officials, they redesigned and rebuilt their centers of operation to resemble harmless houses and gardens from the air. (House 1990b: 60)

The *campesinos* were also found to be eradicating only the least productive portions of their crops and then using their AID/DEA eradication compensations to purchase and replant new coca crops. They were also noted as having dispersed their crops and refining industries to remote jungle areas far from the US and UMOPAR bases. (House 1990b: 36-37) As in the case of Bolivia, it was noted that the *balloon effect* was also in play with narcotraffickers moving their operations over the international border into Brazil with its own immense Amazon River region which, because of sparse government control, was essentially wide open to narcotrafficking or any other type of contraband operation. (WOLA 1991: 105)

In April of 1990 the Santa Lucia base itself came under attack from an estimated two-hundred well armed guerrillas using rockets, mortars and machine guns (House 1990b: 63) One Special Forces trainer was noted as saying: "Between the G-forces (guerrillas) and the D-armies (narcotraffickers) and sometimes even hostile host forces, it's very hard to keep up with who's trying to blow you away." (House 1990b: 27) As such, it was noted that between the DEA and DIPOD some frictions continued to develop. Having been recruited out of the UHV a number of DIPOD personnel were being asked to not only wipe out the livelihood of their own families but also fight the SL guerrillas which offered to protect those very families. (Pais: 25 Oct 89) If this was not all, the factor of corruption on the part of DIPOD personnel came into play to plague the US anti-drug policy.

While Alan Garcia had dismissed some 1,700 corrupt officers, including over one hundred police generals and colonels, corruption remained a factor, if for nothing else, because of the relatively low pay scales for the police. (Werlich 1987: 32) One police Colonel in the Lima area, earning a monthly salary of $500, was reported to have said he had the opportunity to earn up to $70,000 a year by merely looking the other way when narcotrafficking was going on. (House 1990b: 61) Since police retirement pension plans suffered considerably under the hyper-inflation that often affected Peru and were, as a result, not worth very much, there was obviously an overwhelming temptation to supplement one's income with narco-dollars. The endemic police and military corruption in the face of ever increasing narcotrafficking operations and the inability of the government to afford to pay judges and law enforcement personnel high enough salaries to resist the temptations to accept bribes caused INM at this time to conclude: "Corruption will continue to be a major impediment to curbing the drug trade." (DOS-INM 1990: 151)

During February of 1990 a number of judges serving in the Loreto Department's Supreme Court were charged with having accepted bribes from members of the Colombian Medellin cartel. Singled out was one judge in particular who headed a group set up to manage some $50 million in cartel "investments" inside the Loreto Department itself. (House 1990c: 37-38) But corruption was not endemic to the police and judicial systems in Peru alone. A Navy Captain, based out of the port of Callao near Lima was arrested for having been in command of a Navy ship transporting over 400 lbs. of cocaine (HCl) to San Diego California where he was to have received $400,000 in payment for his services rendered. In March, when a DEA-DIPOD helicopter disrupted an attempted landing and pickup of coca products from a contingent of Army personnel by a narcotrafficker Cessna aircraft in the vicinity of the town of Ramal de Aspuzana, it was fired on by the Peruvian military personnel. (House 1990c: 37-38)

Since the SL threat in the UHV was such that the region had been classified by the Peruvian government as an emergency zone and therefore under Army control, led to other problems. The military had imposed a "prior notice" notification requirement on all police operations throughout all emergency zones in Peru. In the UHV and other coca growing areas this resulted in leaks of information by the military on impending anti-drug operations by the police. With this advance notice allegedly on the part of the military, the narcotraffickers were able to take appropriate counter-measures which usually involved escaping from and evading the police. (Senate 1992: 89)

Another factor inhibiting the success of the US anti-drug effort in Peru was the Peruvian judicial system and what was considered to be legal evidence admissible in a court of law. The confusion lay in determining precisely if a coca grower was "illegal". Likewise precursor chemicals could not be judged illegal and be subject to interdiction and confiscation until they had reached a laboratory site and were actually being used in the production of coca-cocaine products such as paste or base etc. Was a *campesino* carrying a bundle of leaves a "trafficker," a salesperson, or just a humble peasant taking some leaves to market for sale to satisfy the traditional demand for chewable coca. (Soberon 1992)

For the Country Team the issue of concern was the fact that the system did not facilitate the arrest and prosecution of high level narcotraffickers as well as the low level ones. For the most part this was due to the legal technicalities of the Peruvian law which held it illegal to work under cover to gather evidence against a person. This was the very essence of the DEA related detective work which often lead to the arrest and conviction of narcotraffickers in the US. Such was not to be the case in Peru. In addition, conspiracy statutes did not exist in Peru and any seized narcotics under Peruvian law would have to be directly linked to the apprehension of a specific individual in order that a case could be made. The result was, much to the consternation of the Country Team, that this made it especially difficult to prove a case in court against the managerial levels of the narcotrafficking organizations operating inside Peru since they did little or no actual handling of the cocaine products. (House 1990c: 37)

Interestingly enough at this time, as had happened in Bolivia, there was a noticeable drop in coca leaf prices for the first half of 1990 to an all time low of $10 per hundred weight. (House 1990d: 54; New York Times: 15 Feb 90; and Miami Herald: 14 Aug 90) This reflected the Colombian government's all-out efforts to counter-attack an on-going narcotrafficker political violence campaign which was attempting to intimidate and disrupt the national government in Bogota. (Smith, P.H. 1992: 13) As a result, instead of the previously noted five or six narcotrafficker flights per day into Peru, there were now no more than about five or six per week or an 85 percent drop in the flow of trafficking aircraft. This did cause a temporary glut of coca leaves and paste on the Peruvian market, lowering the price per hundred weight enough to reduce the incentive ($30 per hundred weight being the estimated point below which coca profits allegedly could not be made) of the *campesinos* to grow coca in Peru. Indicative of the effect was the estimated less than $300 million coca-dollars which were reported as having entered the Peruvian economy during 1990. (Si: 28 Apr 91) Nonetheless, over the long run it was not enough. (House 1990c: 43 and 62)

The absence of sufficient funding for truly viable economic alternatives on the part of the US government merely caused the coca farmers to wait out the situation rather than take a chance on a risky abandonment of their primary source of income. By recycling their kerosene and using their newly acquired vertical integration production techniques, the coca farmers were able to salvage much of what would normally have been significant losses by converting their coca leaves into paste, cocaine base and *agua rica*. (Alvarez 1992: 76) By mid-October it was reported that the price of coca had again risen back to an average of $40 to $80 per hundredweight with some prices in outlying areas exceeding $100. (DOS-INM 1991: A-2; and House 1990b: 66) During this time or over a period of a year, it was reported that some 900 mt of refined cocaine had been detected entering the US. (Miami Herald: 13 Mar 91) The total amount of cocaine base seized throughout Peru in 1990 was reported as about 4 mt or the equivalent of about one week's production by the narcotraffickers. (GAO 1991a: 20) The Country Team reported 8.5 mt of cocaine base and HCl combined along with 151 laboratories captured by the police as the considered total results for the year. (DOS-INM 1991: A-2)

Despite the US-Peruvian effort, 121,300 ha of coca were recorded as still under cultivation or about the same amount as in 1989. The only difference was that a certain leveling off had taken place in respect to the usual annual expansion of coca throughout the 1980s. Nonetheless, using INM ratios to calculate cocaine yields per hectare, if one hectare was rated as producing 3.3 kilograms (7.3 pounds) of cocaine HCl, the 121,300 ha of coca then growing in Peru were said to be capable of producing around 570 - 610 mts of cocaine. (DEA 1992: 15; and DOS-INM 1991: A-2, B-4 and C-1) This was somewhat dismaying to the Country Team which had been supported since 1987 by an average of $50 million per year in economic aid to strengthen the anti-drug effort in terms of increasing eradication and halting the proliferation of coca bushes. (Senate 1989-1990: 161) All the while this was going on the democratic process in Peru was taking its due course with the election in June 1990 of the new President, Alberto Fujimori. The US was not sure how the new Peruvian President would react to the anti-drug initiatives then in play in Peru but it would soon find out.

During his election campaign for the Peruvian presidency, Alberto Fujimori had been critical of the US anti-drug policy in Peru. His position was very unequivocal and to the point: "Repression has not produced any result in the fight against drug trafficking." (Washington Post: 12 Jun 90) After assuming his new position as President, he made the sudden and surprise announcement on 12 September 1990 that his government would not sign the agreement with the US accepting the $36 million aid package for Peru. Side-stepping the US strategy of using suppression as a stick to pave the way for the carrot of crop substitution, Fujimori opted for a different approach involving general economic development as the appropriate solution to Peru's drug problem in general. (Gamarra 1990: 5) Describing the US anti-drug strategy as "inefficient", he said: "The United States is just fooling itself.... You have to give the peasants an alternative. Otherwise, they will die of hunger or join the ranks of the guerrillas." (House 1990b: 60)

There was considerable truth in this as even the Peruvian government was finding out. Lacking the resources to provide adequate credit to the farmers to finance the growing of food crops and pay them for crops already grown through the national food marketing agencies, the government found itself in a situation where many farmers faced bankruptcy and starvation. Some farmers, out of desperation, had turned to growing coca which was still the most profitable crop grown in Peru. (DOS-INM 1991: B-2)

Fujimori, trained as an agricultural engineer and having served as the Rector of the National Agrarian University, had campaigned for his presidency under the political slogan of "Work, Honesty, and Technology." (Taft-Morales 1990: 3-4) The situation which he inherited was grim from any perspective. The previous Alan Garcia government's lethargic debt service policy on its $22 billion debt had resulted in the cutting off of foreign loans, assistance and investments in Peru. Hyper-inflation of some 3,500 percent was a domestic reality and both the SL and MRTA insurgent groups had exploited this situation as part of their propaganda campaigns against the government. (Werlich 1991: 61-62; and House 1992b: 14) In addition some 21,000 persons had been killed by this time or since the SL first openly initiated its insurgency in 1980. (El Nuevo Herald: 17 Apr 91) Dozens if not hundreds of other persons had simply disappeared and never been heard of again.

While the SL guerrillas had caused a great many of the human rights violations noted over the decade, including the forced production of coca by the local Indian population in the Ene River Basin (Miami Herald: 31 Oct 90), the Peruvian military and police were also repeatedly implicated in killings, torture, and the disappearances of numerous civilians labeled "subversives." (Soberon 1992) The report of the Inter-American Commission on Human Rights (IACHR) of the Organization of the American States (OAS) contained 175 pages of human rights violations by the Peruvian Army alone. (IACHR 1991: passim) That the Peruvian justice system had proved itself incapable of investigating or prosecuting these cases caused some appropriations committees in the US Congress to recommend that no military assistance funding be provided Peru until the military and police were brought under control and respect for basic human rights was properly enforced. (Senate 1990: 20-21) In some cases it was also suspected that the murder of coca grower association leaders was being done at the behest of corrupt government officials who did not want to see the coca farmers switch to alternate crop substitutes as they would then lose their "protection" money which many farmers paid to these officials to keep from being harassed. (New York Times: 17 Feb 92)

Adding to the problems above was the acknowledged fact that some forty percent of the population did not have access to potable water; a situation which was now contributing to a national health problem so severe that Peru experienced a major outbreak of cholera in early 1992 which extended to all parts of the country, affecting over a quarter of a million people directly and threatening another ten million indirectly. (EL Nuevo Herald: 21 Jan 92) The economic impact of the cholera epidemic was serious as its alleged contamination of the fishing industry and the resulting collapse of Peru's fish export market threw an estimated one million persons out of work, further exacerbating the adverse economic situation confronting Peru. At this time it was estimated that 80 percent of the Peruvian people were either without work or were underemployed. A number of the former fisherman now sought work in the UHV's coca markets. (Taft-Morales 1990: 13; and House 1991b: 23 and 25)

Yet during all the pains of Peru's economic recession and essentially bankrupt economy, the foreign exchange generated by the production of coca was greater than any other specific source of legal export. In fact, the Country Team's Narcotics Affairs Section (NAS - formerly the NAU) and the DEA were estimating that cocaine was worth $600 to $700 million per year to the Peruvian economy. Others at the US Embassy in Lima thought it might actually be in the realm of $1.2 billion. Still others thought it varied between $400 million and $1.5 billion. If nothing else the *campesino* coca farmers were said to be earning as a group between $60 million and $150 million annually, depending on the fluctuation in coca prices in the narcotrafficker market. (GAO 1991a: 28; and Cabezas 1992)

To deal with the various crises confronting Peru, Fujimori laid out his priorities and courses of action. Perceiving the deflated economy as Peru's most pressing problem, it became his number one priority for resolution. This reflected a poll conducted in Lima which indicated that about 80 percent of the people saw the economic crisis as the nation's most pressing problem, followed by insurgency threats and drugs in that order. (House 1990b: 55) Generally speaking at this time the use of illegal, refined cocaine in Peru was reported at about 1.2 percent of the population. (CEDRO 1991: Grafico 73) Fujimori's perception coincided with and had the support of the national consensus.

Fujimori's government was essentially bankrupt, hyperinflation was running at 3,039 percent through the first half of 1990, unemployment was rampant, investments were being withdrawn from the country and the productive sector was unable to satisfy the needs of the consumer. The SL guerrilla war contributed its part by placing in jeopardy the exploration of the large oil and gas deposits suspected to lie along the base of the eastern Andes. By fire-bombing and dynamiting oil drilling equipment and records of companies such as Mobile Oil, the SL had managed to reduce Peru's crude petroleum export earnings from an average of $210 million in the early to mid-1980s down to lows of $18 million by the end of the decade. (Strong 1992: 196; and IMF 1990: 424) As Fujimori saw it, only by means of a series of long, arduous and often unpopular austerity measures could the dire economic situation be reversed. While his first priority was rejuvenating the economy, this did not mean that he was ignoring the problem of drug production and the US anti-drug policy in Peru. (Chiri 1992: 9)

At the order of the Peruvian government the activities of the Peruvian Air Force (FAP - *Fuerza Aerea Peruana*) operating from the Santa Lucia base were cut back in early February 1991. For the Country Team and its anti-drug policy this was a setback as two FAP aircraft had just the week before shot down a narcotrafficker aircraft and forced another to ground, capturing in the process some 2,000 pounds of cocaine destined for Colombia. The shoot down reflected the highly successful integration of SOUTHCOM's ground and aerial (P3 aircraft) radar intercept activities as part of its Operations Support Justice I and II and the FAP's quick reaction operations which enabled Peruvian Tucano fighters to make accurate intercepts of suspected narcotrafficking aircraft. This was the result of the previous year's SOUTHCOM surveys and assessments to determine the feasibility of employing radar in Peru (SOUTHCOM J3 1993; House 1991a: 6; and Maimi Herald: 11 Feb 91) Nonetheless the Peruvian change in policy now reflected the Fujimori shift in emphasis from repression to assisted development of the coca farmers as an anti-drug strategy.

President Fujimori's initial action to deal with the drug problems in Peru also reflected his anti-corruption campaign motto. He abruptly and swiftly purged over a hundred top ranking police officers, including the commander of the DIPOD, General Juan Zarate. The total eventually reached 246 majors, colonels and generals from the national police. To reform the image and activities of the armed forces, human rights training programs were begun for Army officers and cadets. (House 1991b: 41-42; and Miami Herald: 5 Aug 90) At the same time the Peruvian President directed that 200 additional police be transferred to duties in the UHV, a long sought Country Team objective. (House 1991b: 13)

Fujimori also initiated the beginnings of a plan formulated by his principal advisor on drug issues, Hernando de Soto, which he hoped would ultimately become the basis for dealing with the *campesino* coca farmers. To create a unity of effort and maximize to the extent possible the focus of the government, he directed in November 1990 the establishment of the Autonomous Authority for Development Alternatives (AADA). The focus of this organization was to be on development, as well as some supporting police and military activities, with a goal of creating viable economic alternatives for the estimated quarter of a million campesino farmers and their families who were providing for their livelihood through the growing of illegal coca crops. (DOS-INM 1991: A-2; and Miami Herald: 19 Mar 91) This plan was delivered to the White House in January 1991.

The key to the "Fujimori (de Soto) Plan," as it was called, was said to be incentives and resources. This entailed bringing into play a variety of alternative crops with export potential and suitable access to international markets. The critical aspect of the plan was that each alternate crop had to be able to compete with coca's profits. Advocating a Free Trade Agreement between Peru and the US, the plan hoped to eliminate tariffs and other barriers that would adversely affect the free flow of products between the two countries. (Embassy of Peru 1991: 1-2) Exploiting the then innovative, US sponsored Brady Plan for reducing, swapping or even forgiving debts, Fujimori hoped to eliminate as much of Peru's debt to the US and use the debt service interest monies saved to stimulate structural readjustment and alternative development initiatives. (Embassy of Peru 1991: 2) This was not new by any means and had been proposed by the Peruvians towards the end of the Alan Garcia administration. (Senate 1989-1990: 72-74)

Another reform the Peruvian government wanted to undertake was the deregulation of its internal markets to the degree that farmers in the coca growing regions could get their produce to market and sell their alternative crops competitively. This reflected Fujimori's own personal understanding of the internal situation within Peru whereby there was a myriad of rules, regulations, laws and other impediments from a highly bureaucratic and overregulated economy which was inhibiting farmer access to markets. To deal with this in part, de Soto conceived of a major land reform based on securing property rights for farmers in the coca growing regions and granting them title to their respective lands. At the time only some ten percent of rural Peru was said to be properly titled. (Embassy of Peru 1991: 3) A US General Accounting Office (GAO) study had made the same observation. (GAO 1991e: 23) The Property Registry Law was also established by Fujimori to ensure that all communities, encompassing up to some 92 percent of the land in Peru, would be able to recognize and legitimate the traditional, yet unofficial land holdings involving the boundaries and tenancy customs of all the campesino peasants in Peru. This of course included the coca farmers. (Vision: 11 Mar 92)

By deregulating the Peruvian markets Fujimori and de Soto hoped to be able to reduce considerably the 45 days usually required to work through some 36 administrative steps involving seven distinct agencies to obtain the proper permits to export a crop. This administrative quagmire was in itself considered so daunting to the farmers, most of whom were unable to read or write, that, unless the government provided a solution, there was no possibility of reasonably insuring that a timely farm to market, international export regime could succeed. The loss from spoilage while awaiting the processing of export permits was seen as being too prohibitive to have a farmer risk the effort with an alternate crop. (Embassy of Peru 1991: 3) Fujimori summed up his position by stating that secure property rights and access to deregulated markets and democratic institutions were nothing more than the components of a functioning market economy and, without these, the Peruvian farmers would have no viable alternative to the continued production of coca. (Fujimori 1990: 5)

As part of his plan to eventually win over the coca farmers throughout Peru and defuse the potential for a civil war in early 1991, the Peruvian President decriminalized the growing of coca leaves in general. It was, however, still illegal for anyone or an organization outside of the government to purchase coca leaves for use in the production of cocaine. (GAO 1991a: 20) While this was promulgated under Penal Code 296 (1991) as an adroit political move to avoid civil war between the campesino coca growers and the government, it only added further confusion to the already distorted criteria for court admissible evidence dealing with narcotrafficking. An example of this confusion was the fact that even under the old law the government could not place a coca grower in jail for growing illegal coca (the crop to be sold to narcotraffickers), but could seize the coca grower's land and coca crops. Now it could do neither one nor the other. (Soberon 1992)

The US government adjusted to the Peruvian government's plan by shifting away somewhat from the purely law enforcement oriented eradication and interdiction approaches of reducing the amount of cocaine base and dismantling and disrupting drug trafficking organizations and operations, to a more integrated solution with considerable emphasis on economic assistance for developmental purposes. Bush's AI did have a major emphasis on this aspect in the out years and this helped the US adapt its anti-drug policy to Fujimori's new course of action. The Bush administration's Enterprise for The Americas plan and the Andean Trade Preference Act (ATPA) emphasized "trade not aid" as the approaches to be taken. Through the ATPA the US agreed formally to purchase Peruvian and Bolivian products with reduced tariff rates as a way to stimulate the Andean economies. Obtaining support in the US Senate, the Fujimori proposal was destined to become implemented as part of the "new" US strategy for winning the drug war in Peru. (Senate 1991a: 27-29; GAO 1991a: 14; and El Nuevo Herald: 16 Apr 91) To this end USAID now became a primary actor in the US anti-drug strategy as never before.

The expressed objective of the US alternative development strategy in Peru was to "revitalize the Peruvian economy and provide viable alternatives to the illegal coca economy." (USAID 1992: 20) To achieve its objective, the strategy had several major components. One was to stabilize the economy through the encouragement of macro-economic adjustments that would reduce inflation, balance its fiscal monetary accounts, and increase trade. Another was to open up the economy so that expanded, efficient non-traditional exports and production for the domestic market could replace coca as an export crop. Lastly it was hoped that economic revitalization would promote sufficient legal employment opportunities so as to attract the labor force away from the coca industry. (USAID 1992: 20-21)

For the strategy to succeed the following conditions would have to take place. First, the Peruvian government would have to successfully implement comprehensive macro-economic reform, implementing a market-oriented system. Second, counter-narcotics control efforts would have to result in the fall of coca prices making coca production less attractive. Finally, military, police, or some form of government authority or security would have to be reestablished throughout the Huallaga Valley and along all roads leading into and out of the Valley to protect the farmers from the SL. (USAID 1992: 21-22) By providing farmers with the appropriate technology, equipment, credit and the rural infrastructure to make alternate development crop opportunities viable, it was thought that, if the above conditions were met, the coca industry would be undermined and neutralized. To assist in the accomplishment of the strategy, the Selva Coastal Road Rehabilitation project was conceived of to solidly link the UHV to the coast with an all-weather road which would considerably lower the marketing transportation costs of the alternate crops. (USAID 1992: 22)

Yet at this time there were significant disagreements between US and Peruvian officials over what constituted viable, legal competitive crops in contrast to coca. While US officials wanted to focus on asparagus, mango, tomato paste, garlic grapes and beans, the Peruvian Ministry of Agriculture wanted to invest in citrus fruits, especially oranges, as an export crop focus. US officials argued that initial investment costs to build the necessary processing plants and acquire the large tracts of land to make the citrus economy feasible would be prohibitive. This debate continued among Peruvian business men and the National Agrarian University. Despite oranges being rated by AID as competitive and earning a profit of $4,280 per hectare compared to coca earning $5,059 per hectare (assuming that coca was earning not much more than $50 per hundredweight), the issue was dropped in favor of a non-citrus focus. (GAO 1991e: 18 and 56-57)

Soy beans were considered by USAID as an alternate crop for Peru but rejected as the soils and climate of the UHV and other coca growing regions in Peru were not considered conducive to this type of crop.

Palm oil had been given some consideration with the idea that a processing plant could be constructed in the vicinity of the Santa Lucia base. Nonetheless, the prohibitive costs of transportation made this alternative generally unfeasible as it was found that the city of Lima could obtain its palm oil more cheaply by merely purchasing it from Malaysia rather than making it in Peru. (Hengel Interview 1992) Finding suitable alternative crops to coca was difficult at best for the Country Team and USAID.

On May of 1991 President Fujimori proceeded to sign an umbrella agreement on counter-narcotics with the US. The process initiated in November 1990 leading to the agreement had not been easy and had even broken down on several occasions over technical points involving human rights, the investigation of corruption and legal perspectives concerning the coca farmers. In agreeing to improve military and police human rights performance and reduce corruption, as well as intensifying counter-drug eradication, alternate development, drug interdiction and counterinsurgency operations, Peru was to receive enhanced economic and military assistance. (US Embassy 1991: passim; and WOLA 1991: 150-153) As most of this had already been programmed under AI, the US government's portion of the agreement was relatively easy to fulfill. The results of the agreement were noted over the remainder of the year. The US for its part agreed with Fujimori to not officially view the coca farmers and their 180 coca grower association committees or federations as criminals. (Vision: 11 Mar 92)

In the UHV the FAP, using *Tucano* interceptors asserted itself in an effort to regain control of the air space. In the UHV itself the former seven distinct police and military commands were reorganized under one central headquarters. This was to avoid further incidents such as had occurred earlier at Uchiza where a local police garrison under attack by the SL guerrillas was overrun because the nearby Army unit refused to relieve the police until such time as it could obtain permission from a higher headquarters as far away as Lima. The beleaguered police detachment was wiped out to a man. (Bailetti Interview 1992)

At this time SOUTHCOM was maneuvering four ground based radars around the Iquitos and Andoas region of northern Peru as well as a series of AWACs and US Customs P3 search aircraft to help identify and hand off suspected narcotrafficking aircraft to the FAP interceptors. There were estimated to be several narcotrafficker flights per day or about 70 to 90 per month into and out of the northern Peru area. (SOUTHCOM J3 1993) Working in conjunction with the US operated ground radars, AWACs and P3s, as part of SOUTHCOM's

Operation Support Justice III (October 1991 to May 1992), the FAP intercepted some 55 unscheduled aircraft, forcing most of these down, including six narcotrafficker planes enroute to Colombia. This continued on into January 1992 when nine aircraft were forced down in that month alone. Yet mistakes were made and one civilian aircraft on 9 July 1991 was shot down, resulting in the deaths of 17 people. The Peruvian police were later reported as having rummaged through the wreckage of this aircraft, robbing the dead of their personal possessions. (House 1991b: 105-106; and DOS-INM 1992: 125)

Nonetheless, by this time Coca prices again dropped and overall cultivation was said to be down by about 500 ha. This was thought to be in part due to the emphasis that CORAH was placing on the destruction of coca-seed beds, which were estimated to be equivalent to 13,000 ha of mature coca and took only one-tenth the time to destroy compared to mature coca bushes. It was hoped that this effort would at least stabilize or level off the expansion of the coca crop and even contribute to a substantial reduction over time. (NAS 1991: 2; and DOS-INM 1992; 126) By the end of 1991 over half of the Peruvian population, including most of those in the coca growing areas, now lived in the emergency zones or those regions which, because of a perceived deteriorating security condition, had been placed under the direct control of the Peruvian armed forces (mainly the Army). Here civil rights and due process were suspended and Army colonels and generals in charge of the zones dictated a martial law in the name of the Peruvian government. (House 1992a: 34)

The narcotraffickers reacted to the US-Peruvian interdiction operations by flying only at night or by using more circuitous routes into Brazil and Ecuador to avoid the US ground based radars. (Interview CT:PE 1992) The MRTA, numbering at this time up to about a thousand guerrillas of its own in the Huallaga Valley, asserted its presence by simultaneously attacking five police posts in the UHV and cutting the electricity to four towns. (El Nuevo Herald: 13 May 91) The police fought back as best they could and, in conjunction with the DEA, launched an operation which resulted in a 6 June capture of a fully operational Cocaine (HCl) laboratory in the vicinity of Aguaytia which was capable of producing up to two metric tons of cocaine per month. This operation was a joint effort on the part of the DEA and the Peruvian National Police (PNP) and was the first confirmed HCl laboratory to be captured inside Peru. (Harmon 1993: 31; Senate 1992c: 11 and 20; and House 1991b: 19 and 57) The laboratory, located at Boca Santa Ana, was the largest cocaine HCl production facility up to that time encountered outside of Colombia. (DEA 1992: 15)

The Colombians, feeling some pressure from the government's operations, had been teaching the coca farmers not only how to make coca paste but also how to operate small cocaine base preparation laboratories inside their homes and businesses. This vertical integration of the Peruvian cocaine processing infrastructure was an obvious attempt to cut costs and avoid potential losses when government operations successfully targeted major laboratories, creating a temporary glut of coca leaves on the market. In this case the coca farmer could preserve his investment by processing his leaves into *agua rica* (liquefied cocaine base), going well beyond the coca paste stage of the production process. In addiction the situation found the traffickers more and more moving some laboratories out of remote jungle areas into the vicinity of towns and villages where they apparently thought their security would be better enhanced through the presence of "friendly" people and corrupted government officials. As it was, much if not all of the economy of these small towns was based on the cocaine industry to one degree or another. (DOS-INM 1992a: passim)

During this time over 500 police and 61 members of the military were purged by Fujimori for abuses of authority and other crimes. (House 1991b: 17) Still the situation was very difficult for the US anti-drug policy and its interdiction strategy in play. Peru was known to have up to 396 airports (356 registered airports and some 40 privately owned, unregistered airports) of which 58 were actually controlled by the government's civil aeronautics agency and the other nine by the FAP. This meant that over 80 percent of all airports in Peru were not under any government control at all. (GAO 1991a: 23) That the FAP controlled only nine of these gives one an indication of the magnitude of trying to catch infiltrating narcotrafficker aircraft in-bound to any of the other 319 airfields not firmly under government control and otherwise open to drug trafficking operations. In addition, despite Fujimori's specific orders to have the FAP take control of the airfields in April of 1991, it was reported late that next July that trafficking aircraft routinely continued to use even the government controlled airports in the UHV with little or no restraint on the part of the military or the police. (GAO 1991a: 23)

Very typically narcotrafficker aircraft would leave Colombia around 3 to 5 PM enroute to Peru. Communicating by radio to a ground station in Colombia and one in Peru, they would receive final approval and routing instructions for the often up to six hour flight ahead. Landing sometime between 10 PM and 2 AM at the destination airfield, the aircraft would then load between 1,000 and 2,000 pounds of cocaine base or HCl, refuel and take off. While this happened an estimated up to 70 times a month, the FAP, having little or no night fighting capability, was reduced to trying to make its intercepts during periods of daylight and at dusk or dawn. (Interview DEA:PE 1992)

Indicative of the expansion of the narcotrafficking activity was the police report out of Palma Pampa located in the vicinity of the border between the Ayacucho and Cuzco Departments. Here some 300 miles south of Santa Lucia it was confirmed that cocaine production and export operations were well established and functioning in a radius extending out some six miles in all directions from the town. This site now became the focus of a two-day DEA and PNP interdiction effort. In addition to some weapons and precursor chemicals, the operation captured 169 kgs of cocaine base and the radios by which the narcotraffickers were coordinating their shipments. (DOS-INM 1992: 125; and INM 1992a: passim) Nonetheless, as the traffickers found their operations disrupted or blocked through northern Peru into Colombia, they used air, land and riverine routes into and through Brazil and Ecuador to link up with their appropriate cartel buyers. From time to time it was reported that the refining of cocaine base and HCl was also taking place in those countries. Some Peruvian based traffickers managed to avoid the Colombian connection completely and established direct links into the US and Europe via Brazil and Venezuela. The precursor chemicals for all these operations was moved with relative ease by boat and truck, exploiting the Amazon River tributaries over which there was little or no police control. (INM 1992a: passim)

Despite the problems with interdiction, USAID was noted as having made some progress. The increased presence of the Peruvian military and police in the UHV enabled a number of coca growers (eventually totaling some 14,000 former coca farmers over the period of a decade) to receive technical assistance, agricultural loans and some 4,700 land titles. This also came about as coca growers grudgingly admitted that they did not feel a sense of personal dignity knowing that they were looked down upon by their peers and society at large as being involved in an illegal activity. (Cabezas 1992) As a result, in June some 126 coca farmers approached USAID representatives in the field and agreed to a formal involvement in the alternate crop substitution program which they had heard about. Unfortunately for the US anti-drug effort, AID was not fully prepared and little support was forthcoming. This caused the US programs to lose some credibility. (Cabezas 1992)

USAID's other programs appeared to be more successful with about

1,256 kilometers of roads and twelve bridges being rehabilitated, improving the direct road link and ground access from the UHV over the Andes to the coast. In addition AID sponsored projects provided 38 potable water systems and 88 water pumps. At this time it was estimated that the PL 480 assistance program was feeding one Peruvian in seven or just under 15 percent of the total population. (Senate 1992c: 21) A US Information Agency (USIA) poll (1201 respondents) conducted in June indicated that the population as a whole or about 58 percent still considered the economic situation as the worst problem facing the country and only 6 percent felt that drugs and drug addiction and narcotrafficking were real problems for Peru. (USIA 1991a: 9) Nonetheless, the anti-drug alternative development programs contrasted significantly with the 1.6 million acres of Peru's Amazon rain forest which had been lost due to pollution and contamination caused by the tons of toxic waste involving gasoline, kerosene, sulfuric acid and toluene as well as insecticides which had been continuously dumped into the soil and waterways as part of the cocaine production process. (Senate 1992c: 19; Dourojeanni 1989: 283-294; and Cabezas 1992)

Yet by the end of 1991 US Congressional committees still felt that the Peruvian government did not have effective control over its military and police units and that human rights abuses abounded. Of the 86 cases of human rights abuses ascribed by the Organization of American States (OAS) to countries in South America, almost two-thirds or 55 cases involving some 500 persons were reported as having occurred in Peru. (Senate 1992c: 114; and House 1991b: 81) Political violence related deaths were also reported as commonplace in Peru. Of some 3,452 deaths reported in 1990 over half (1,766) were attributed to the military, police and paramilitary civil defense groups. The remaining were attributed principally to the SL guerrillas. Reflected in 1991 was a similar pattern. In June alone of that year it was reported that an average of 18 persons per day had been murdered for political reasons. (House 1991b: 107) In addition it was also noted by the Congress that there was still a lack of coordination and cooperation between the military and the police, a failure to consistently control the national airports, continued corruption, and the still ubiquitous SL and MRTA guerrillas whose presence in the UHV and other parts of Peru continued unabated.

The Congress had based its appraisal in part on a report rendered by the US General Accounting Office (GAO) which commented on the situation at that time, stating: "U.S. counter-narcotics programs in Peru have not been effective, and it is unlikely that they will be until Peru overcomes serious obstacles beyond U.S. control." (GAO 1991f: Summary) Congressman Charles B. Rangel, fresh from a trip to Peru commented that while Fujimori was committed to economic reforms, the security situation in the UHV and the presence of the SL guerrillas was such that eradication and alternate development could not go forward. Reflecting on the situation he concluded: "Until this situation is brought under control, narcotic control efforts in Peru will be stymied." (Rangel 1991: 1) In early 1992, among some of its activities, the SL took credit for shooting down an INM helicopter in which several contract DEA agents were reported killed, dynamiting a freight train, a town hall, a government bank and ambushing a number of Army units. These actions were conducted to help the guerrillas build rural bases and then use them to "surround and asphyxiate Lima." To this end some 250 mayors had also been murdered over the previous several years. (Miami Herald: 9 Feb 92)

Despite the fact that President Fujimori had carried out wholesale dismissals of corrupt government officials, corruption was still seen by the GAO as "pervasive throughout all levels of the civilian government, the military, and law enforcement agencies." This observation also included numerous mayors and judges. (GAO 1991f: 10-11) That this was having an impact on drug production and narcotrafficking, there is no doubt. Coca cultivation for 1991 was reported as having increased some 500 ha to a total of 120,800 ha which was thought to be capable of producing 645 mts to 690 mts of cocaine base or refined cocaine. (DEA 1992: 15) The total amount of cocaine confiscated by the DEA-DIPOD forces was said to be equivalent to one week's production from only one town in the UHV (Miami Herald 30 Apr 92) and narcotrafficker flights between Colombia and Peru were reported to be averaging around 20 per day. (El Nuevo Herald: 6 Jun 92)

Yet when President Fujimori agreed to finally accept the $35 million US military aid package, it was then reduced to $25 million by the US Congress over the issue of unresolved human rights violations on the part of the Peruvian military. Corruption on the part of the military and its complicity with the narcotraffickers were also cited as evidence that Peru was not thoroughly committed to the drug war. (Senate 1992c: 113) According to the International Narcotics Control Act of 1990 which was part of the Congressional law supporting the AI, the US President had to assess the performance of each country including Peru in terms of its achieving counter-narcotics objectives and protecting internationally recognized human rights before US assistance was released. It was on this basis that the US Congress was withholding monies from Peru. (House 1991b: 1-2)

The Department of State, to no avail, took issue with the Congress maintaining that the $10 million cut would undermine the training and equipping of Army units which were needed to aggressively pursue the SL guerrilla columns in the UHV. As a result it was alleged that military control of airports and military-police cooperation would suffer unduly since the Army would remain weak and unable to campaign effectively against the guerrillas. (Levitsky: 23 Oct 1991) Nonetheless, the Congress maintained it position and also criticized the US anti-drug policy claiming that aid for anti-drug police operations was being diverted and used for counter-insurgency purposes in violation of the Department of State's own policy. (Miami Herald 26 Feb 92) For the Country Team in Lima the situation would only get worse.

President Fujimori, true to his promises during his electoral campaign, acted boldly and through some 126 decrees, involving national defense, labor, health, housing, commerce, industry, tourism, agriculture, energy and mining among others, implemented sufficient economic reforms throughout 1991 to enable him to balance Peru's budget. In addition he reduced the government payroll by some 50,000 employees, terminated price controls and subsidies, reduced the national tariffs roughly 75 percent (from an average of 80 percent down to 17 percent) and eliminated virtually all barriers to foreign investment. Inflation was now running at a relatively low 50 percent and the GDP grew during the period 2.8 percent. (House 1992b: 15; WOLA 1992: 24; and House 1991b: 31-32) During a visit to Washington, D.C. in September of 1991, Fujimori stated to the Congress he believed that his best chances for success against the narcotraffickers lay in a total reorganization of Peru's economic structure. To this end he was granting land titles, getting farmers better access to credit, and developing the means by which alternate crops could be brought to market in an efficient manner. (New York Times: 24 Sep 91) With the financial assistance of the US, Japan and other nations, Peru was in the process of reentering the international financial system. Nonetheless, the austerity measures were perceived as slow at diminishing the state of poverty which half the Peruvian population still found itself in, earning little more than an average of $15 per month (government officials received an average of $105 per month). (Cuanto: Jun 92; and McClintock 1993: 113)

Meeting at the anti-drug summit in San Antonio, Texas, on the 26th and 27th of February 1992, President George Bush was able to persuade President Fujimori, along with his counterparts or representatives from

Bolivia, Colombia, Mexico, Ecuador and Venezuela, to reaffirm their respective country's commitment to bilateral and multilateral cooperation in the Andean Ridge anti-drug effort. While Bush originally wanted to have Peru agree to tough narcotics controls which would reduce its cocaine supply by 50 percent by the year 2000, Fujimori rejected this approach stating: "We cannot get specific goals if we do not have the financial means to achieve them." His point, which was also echoed by both Bolivia and Colombia, was that trade and not aid was the ultimate solution for the economic and narcotrafficking problems facing Peru. (Miami Herald 27 Feb 92) Rising tensions over this issue were evident and Bush and Fujimori met privately in what was officially described as a "friendly" conference. Expressing fears that the UHV could turn into another "Vietnam" in Latin America with the 250,000 coca farmers siding with the SL guerrillas, President Fujimori further declared: "We want the coca growers to be our allies, not our enemies." (Miami Herald: 27 Feb 92) Fujimori had now injected himself into the US policy making process to secure an economic emphasis in the US Andean anti-drug strategy. In this he was supported by Bolivia and Colombia.

As the summit came to a close, the sharing of information on narcotrafficking operations, aircraft, airfield and landing strip controls, the strengthening of the administration of justice as well as economic issues involving alternate development were stressed by all those in attendance. In addition it was acknowledged by the US, at the insistence of Fujimori, that demand in the consumer nations also be acknowledged as a key factor in the drug problem, deserving equal emphasis. Peru agreed to expand its counter-drug cooperation with the rest of the Americas and, much like in the Vienna Convention, agreed to try and insure that essential chemicals which could also be used as precursors would only used for legitimate purposes. (DOS 1992a: 14-20) The US in turn modified its eradication goals for Peru and, instead of attempting to achieve a 10 percent reduction of coca over a two year period as had been the policy in 1989, would now seek to achieve a 50 percent reduction of coca over a ten year period. In addition it would pay the coca farmers $2,000 for each hectare eradicated as part of the incentive program to influence the latter to switch to alternate crops. (Hensen 1992)

As a result of the summit conference, using a series of decrees, Fujimori amended the criminal code to make narcotics-related money laundering a criminal offense. This also made anyone, including bank officials who participated in or facilitated money laundering, liable for prosecution. With this and Peru's 1991 agreement with the US to maintain records of all cash transactions in excess of $10,000, these were policy directions that the US wanted to see come into effect. Nonetheless, the lack of a system for identifying, freezing, and seizing narcotics related assets, undermined the potential success of the limited regulatory and enforcement capability capabilities that already existed. (DOS-INM 1993b: 128-129) In short Peru was woefully incapable of carrying out a money laundering prevention policy. Despite promises of aid, totaling some $2.5 billion in the form of loans and grants from the US, Japan, Germany, Canada, Spain, Chile, Colombia and Mexico, by early 1992 the impoverishment of the Peruvian people, the lack of viable solutions to the nation's problems from the country's leaders, and the general deterioration of the country's fundamental institutions were leading to increased serious questioning of the legitimacy of the Peruvian government and the established order in Peru. (Chiri 1992: 10-11; and North South 1992: 66) In April, President Fujimori made another surprise decision.

Chapter 8

Fujimori Reigns Supreme

On 5 April of 1992, citing legislative and bureaucratic inefficiency and a lack of cooperation, irresponsible politicians, inept and weak state institutions such as the judiciary, and state corruption as hindering the Peruvian nation's economic recovery and progress, President Fujimori abolished the national legislature and judiciary and suspended the Constitution, virtually giving himself dictatorial powers. This *autogolpe* or assumption of power by his own hand actually had the support of the majority of the Peruvian military, commercial business elites and most importantly the majority of the people. Promising a return to democracy in 1993, the government was now called the "Government of Emergency and National Reconstruction" and granted its authority under Decree Law 25444. At this time Fujimori enjoyed a 75 percent approval and popularity rating as many Peruvians were fed up with their socio-economic and security situations. (New York Times: 29 Jul 92; Caretas: 27 Apr 92; and McClintock 1993: 115)

The US, taking issue with the suspension of the democratic process, immediately reacted to Fujimori's actions by suspending its military and economic aid programs totaling some $236 million to Peru. Only the INM (Country Team NAS) budget for keeping the anti-drug policy in play was not affected. President George Bush called the Peruvian President's actions: "A regrettable step backwards for the cause of democracy in the hemisphere." (House 1992b: 16; and Miami Herald:

8 Apr 92) Some $164 million in future economic aid was also now suspended. Included in the suspended USAID projects were the economic stabilization, recovery, investment and import promotions, as well as the Selva-coastal road rehabilitation and small business employment expansion programs. (USAID 1992: 64) The Inter-American Development Bank (IADB) which had been lending money to Peru in 1991 suspended its $220 million in loans. (Miami Herald: 8 Apr 92) US military trainers and radar crews were directed to shut down their operations and leave country. (Miami Herald: 15 Apr 92) All this of course was setting the US anti-drug effort back considerably.

In the meantime Fujimori, declaring an *estado de emergencia* (state of emergency) in the UHV, directed in early April that the FAP assume full control of the airports in the UHV. In addition the FAP established a formal command post at the Santa Lucia base where Tucano and some A-37 counter-narcotics interceptors were stationed for immediate deployment against the narcotrafficker aircraft. By May, PNP (DIPOD) pilots and air crews were now generally manning the previously contracted positions in the INM owned helicopters. (DOS-INM 1993a: 123; and Miami Herald: 11 Apr 92) The Army was also ordered back in force to the remote portions of the UHV, securing the town of Uchiza so that the national police and the DEA could reassert the government's control. General Nicolas Barrios Hermosa, the Chairman of the Peruvian Joint Staff, was directed by Fujimori to develop standing operating procedures whereby the Army would conduct counter-insurgency operations against the SL and MRTA and the police would conduct counter-narcotics operations against the traffickers. Mutual cooperation between the two organizations was now thought to be assured through the centralized command structure. (Interview DEA:PE 1992)

In addition to the operational coordination arrangements demanded by the Peruvian President, human rights sensitivity training was implemented and some 28 percent of the Army, involving in the main officers and non-commissioned officers, received the instruction. While this was going on, the Army was further directed to prepare to send up to 50 percent of its forces into the UHV. (Interview Military:PE 1992) At this time, despite a decade of severe political violence and guerrilla operations in the Peruvian interior, only about one-quarter of the Peruvian Army was actually attempting to engage the SL and MRTA guerrillas. A full 70 percent or over two-thirds of the Peruvian ground forces were stationed in the vicinity of the northern and southern frontiers to defend Peru against the alleged possibility of "invasion" from Ecuador and Chile respectively. (House 1991b: 158)

The US intended to support the Army effort in the UHV, using up to $6 million of the INM funding still available to create an Army engineer brigade consisting of several road construction battalions. These were to build roads and construct bridges into the interior of the UHV to assist in providing security and fostering economic development and its related market infrastructure (House 1992b: 18-19 and 61; and House 1991b: 25) Only the Army engineers could do this, since civilian contractors refused to work in the region due to the high threat presented by the SL and MRTA guerrillas. (Henson 1992)

In addition to the above, some 135 judges and prosecutors implicated in corruption scandals were fired by Fujimori as part of a general housecleaning by the Peruvian President. (Miami Herald: 25 Apr 92) Ironically, the end result of Fujimori's actions had the effect of cutting Peru off from US and other international financial aid, such as that from the International Monetary Fund (IMF) and the World Bank (WB), as well as reducing his government's image of legitimacy relative to the SL and MRTA guerrillas. All this was happening while Fujimori was actually intensifying military and police operations in the UHV to comply with the US anti-drug policy's interests. While Fujimori himself was reported as being "stunned" by the general condemnations of the international media and world leaders (Miami Herald: 8 Apr 92), another action would prejudice his position even further.

On 24 April a US Air Force C-130 aircraft, returning to Panama after conducting a routine anti-drug surveillance mission in support of the DEA and DIPOD over the UHV, was fired upon by Talara based FAP Soviet manufactured SU-22 jet fighters some 60 miles off the coast of Peru in international air space. One US serviceman died in the encounter and several others were wounded. (House 1992b: 19-20 and 43) The lack of any apparent remorse on the part of the Peruvian military (the Peruvian pilots were awarded medals for their actions) made US-Peruvian military relations extremely tense for the remainder of the year and undermined US confidence in Peru as a loyal and trustworthy partner in their anti-drug relationship. Exacerbating the situation to a large degree was the $20,000 bill the Peruvian Ministry of Defense sent to the Pentagon via the US Embassy in Lima, demanding payment for the medical treatment rendered the surviving C-130 crewmen who had been forced to land in Peruvian territory (Talara). (Miami Herald: 28 Oct 92)

There is a point worth commenting upon in terms of the US-Peruvian military relationship which is pertinent to the case study and the C-130 incident. Some people contend that the pilots of the Talara based SU-22 squadron were unhappy about not being able to participate in the drug war to the extent that the Santa Lucia based Tucano pilots were and were thus anxious to play a role, leading to the unfortunate shooting incident. This may have unduly prejudiced the attitudes of the Talara based SU-22 pilots and served as a catalyst which apparently needed little prodding other than the order from the FAP General Headquarters in Lima to produce the incident. (Interview Military-PE: 1992) Whatever was the exact underlying motivation for the attack, the net result of the incident was that the US suspended all further US aerial surveillance activity in Peru for most of the remainder of the year, hampering to a considerable degree the effectiveness of the anti-drug aerial interdiction effort. (El Comercio: 28 Apr 92; and Interview DEA:PE 1992)

As 1992 wore on the US Congress rescinded all fiscal 1992 military assistance to Peru and capped economic support funds at $50 million, requiring that further disbursement be based on certification reviews demonstrating that the democratic process had been reinstituted and known human rights conditions inside Peru had been corrected. Criteria to this effect stipulated that the International Committee of the Red Cross (ICRC) would have full access to military and police detainees and that human rights groups, lawyers and family members would also have ready access. In addition the Peruvian government had to have acted to investigate and bring to justice those responsible for human rights abuses. (Senate 1992b: 40-41) In the meantime, Fujimori's Minister of Energy and Mines, Jaime Yoshiyama, announced that the government, in an effort to cut administrative costs, planned to sell off all remaining publicly owned companies and enterprises without exception, selling one per week on into 1994 as necessary. (Expresso: 27 May 92)

While the international community railed over the anti-democratic nature of Fujimori's ruling by decree, the internal security conditions within Peru began to take on an escalating dynamic of their own. In June the Tupac Amaru Revolutionary Movement's (MRTA) leader, Victor Polay Campos, was captured. This, in conjunction with the dissolution of the Soviet Union and the capture of other key MRTA leaders over the previous several months, reduced somewhat the morale and the intensity of the activities of this secondary, yet still very irritating insurgency. Nonetheless, at the same time the SL guerrillas began to intensify their own campaign in Lima which had actually gotten under way in 1991. Using dozens of car bombings and other brutal types of assassination and political violence directly against the seat of the Peruvian government. "Operation Conquer Lima" had now begun. (La Hora: 22 Jul 92; Miami Herald: 19 Apr 92; Christian Science Monitor: 31 Jul 92; and Bailetti 1992) Overall, the SL strategy was to make Peru ungovernable and then use this situation to allow the guerrillas to consolidate their position by blocking any further elections to keep the constitutional process from being reincorporated. If this happened, the government's illegitimacy could be further demonstrated which would reinforce the SL's contention that the government had to be overthrown. (Degregori 1992)

One SL car bomb detonated in June 1992 killed 21 people, injured 250 and damaged 6 hotels, 10 banks, 20 shops and some 400 homes in a Lima suburb. By the end of July alone 293 distinct attacks had taken place, leaving 179 persons dead. In August some 173 persons were reported as having been assassinated, including numerous shanty-town mayors on the outskirts of Lima. (McClintock 1993: 113, and 116-117) Erecting street barricades and covering windows with plywood, the Lima population responded to the fearful atmosphere of the SL's "total war." Reportedly with an overall strength of 100,000 persons which included both fighters and supporters and a war chest of some $30 million from its "tax collections", the SL extended its attacks nationwide, killing up to nine people a day over the first six months of 1992. (Miami Herald: 23 Jul 92; New York Times: 23 Jul 92; and Bailetti 1992) Concern for security within Lima was so great that the government canceled its annual Peruvian Independence Day celebrations. (El Nuevo Herald: 29 Jul 92) As part of its operations the SL attacked Peru's Institute for Liberty and Democracy (ILD) with car bombs. Besides its support for democracy, the ILD had publicly expressed its support of crop substitution in the coca producing regions. This of course the SL opposed since successful crop substitution on the part of the government would undermine the guerrillas' primary source of funding. The ILD was therefore a natural target. (Wall Street Journal: 31 Jul 92) The dynamiting of electrical power pylons and stations were frequent occurrences which left major portions of the city with out electricity virtually every day. The total cost of all the guerrilla activities and damages to the government and the people was estimated at about $500 million. (New York Times: 24 Jul and 1 Aug 92)

Despite the distracting guerrilla bombings and killings that were taking place and the otherwise now very strained relations with the US over the issue of democracy in Peru, the Peruvian government did reaffirm its 14 May 1991 agreement with the US and its commitment to the multi-national anti-drug effort based on the San Antonio summit earlier in 1992. Here again, at the advice of de Soto, Peru agreed to commit its national police, the police aviation regiment and the armed forces to the anti-drug effort, emphasizing the carrying out of eradication, alternative development, interdiction of precursors and drugs, the prosecution of narcotraffickers and the continuation of education and information programs for its people. (DOS 1992a: passim; and Gamarra 1993)

The most spectacular event of the year 1992 was the major setback given the SL guerrillas when their leader Abimael Guzman was captured on 12 September at a Lima neighborhood (Los Sauces), SL safe house by a special police commando unit (DINCOTE - Directorate Against Terrorism). Having watched Guzman's house and tapped his telephones, the PNP was able, after several years of trying, to move in and make their capture. In addition to Guzman, dozens of computers and some 200 diskettes and files were seized. These provided valuable information on SL operations, organization and the whereabouts of many of its members which led to another 1,200 guerrillas being captured by the police over the next several weeks. Included in this group were 19 SL Central Committee members or a significant part of the insurgency's senior leadership cadre. (Bailetti 1992; and New York Times: 15 Sep 92) Only a few scattered members of the original early 1970s SL cadre, such as Teresa Durand Araujo or Oscar ("Alberto") Ramirez Durand, the son of a Peruvian Army General and Teresa's husband, remained at large to reorganize and attempt to run the movement. In the meantime the SL's semi-autonomous regional cadres carried out violent attacks in retaliation for Guzman's arrest, killing over 170 persons throughout the country. (Nezavisimaya Gazeta: 24 Oct 92; and Bailetti 1992)

The Peruvian government exploited Guzman's arrest for propaganda purposes, trying to publicly humiliate the SL leader and what he represented, displaying him as a paunchy, middle-aged degenerate. Looking disheveled and lackluster in appearance with a ragged beard and thick glasses, Guzman now took on a less than inspiring image of what was a seemingly fearless and invincible leader. Even though the SL tried to rebound from its losses and reassert itself as a still powerful threat to the Peruvian government, the insurgency had definitely been hurt. Nonetheless, while the Lima Front was in disarray, the UHV commercial Front and the Ayacucho revolutionary Front remained intact. (Degregori 1992) During the month following the capture of Guzman, the SL and MRTA guerrillas generally appeared to have lost their continuity and fewer acts of political violence were reported. The campaign to conquer Lima had been frustrated. (Bailetti 1992; and Latin American Weekly Report: 8 Oct 92)

By the end of the year, exploiting their intelligence coup, Peruvian Army and Police commandos were able to storm SL and MRTA guerrilla sanctuaries throughout the Ayacucho and San Martin (Huallaga Valley) Departments. Over time, 2,386 guerrillas, mostly from the SL, were killed or captured and imprisoned. (El Comercio: 4 Dec 92 and 16 Feb 93; and El Nuevo Herald: 2 and 11 Nov 92) In Lima itself 712 persons were rounded up as SL and MRTA guerrilla suspects. (INIDEN: Oct 92) By this time Abimael Guzman himself had been convicted of causing the deaths of some 25,000 persons and sentenced to life imprisonment by a military court. (Caretas and Miami Herald: 8 Oct 92) President Fujimori himself expressed confidence that defeating SL terrorism and its political violence strategies would promote investment and increase production - all to the benefit of the Peruvian people. (El Comercio: 4 Dec 92) The question was one of whether this would actually happen. Other reports indicated that Peruvian exporters were slow in taking advantage of the lower European tariffs and the ATPA which had been deliberately adjusted downwards to help the Andean countries to better deal with the economic aspects of the alternate development programs in play. (El Comercio: 4 Dec 92)

Despite successes by the police against Peru's two foremost insurgencies working to bring down the Peruvian government, not all government security organizations and their members were content. That many Peruvian Army officers saw themselves as second class citizens economically was an undercurrent which strained the civil-military relationship in Peru, even within the officer corps itself. High resignation rates among the junior officers tended to be the norm. The author noted in 1980-81 that many officer students at the Peruvian General Staff and War Colleges as well as other professional schools often had to hold second jobs to supplement their income. Over the years the situation had not changed much and by 1992 the senior generals in the Peruvian Army were reported as earning the equivalent of about $350 per month with a sergeant earning about $30 per month (As a comparison, teachers were earning about $200 and judges up to $400 per month). (Miami Herald: 15 Apr 92; and Interview Military:PE 1992)

The discontent among the junior to mid-level officers over their correspondingly low salaries and the apparently failing battle against the SL and MRTA guerrillas had spawned a clandestine yet informal organization called "COMACA" ("Commanders, Majors and Captains"). Through this organization the members hoped to be able to protect their interests and rectify in some manner their less than happy economic situation. As such, the organization was feared by the more senior officers in the Peruvian armed forces. (Clarin: 28 Jul 92; and Miami Herald 21 Dec 92) In November a mixed group of around one hundred officers, for the most part from the Army and led by Generals Jaime Salinas and Marcos Zarate Rota (a former DIPOD commander who was then under investigation for narcotrafficking), attempted a coup against Fujimori. (Miami Herald: 14 and 18 Nov 92) While the attempt fizzled and failed, it did place some pressure on Fujimori to begin to change the authoritarian, anti-democratic structure and nature of control being exercised by his government. (Bailetti and Soberon 1992) To this end he announced that Constitutional Assembly Elections would take place on 22 November. In so doing he expected that the new Democratic Constituent Congress would help legitimize his government and enable it to break out of its international isolation. That the elections took place, despite SL threats to kill anyone who opened a business or left their home on Election Day, and were judged to be fair by international observers was a good omen. Even so the SL were able to kill a reported nine people as part of some twenty bombings which were carried out with the intention to coerce the public into staying at home. The election process helped Fujimori significantly in terms of regaining part of his lost democratic image. (McClintock 1993: 118; Miami Herald: 21 Nov 92; and USE-PE 1993a: 1 and 2)

The new 80-member assembly was potentially more manageable than the old 240-member Congress and eventually rewrote the Peruvian Constitution to allow Fujimori sufficient power to reform Peru's ponderous government and bring about the social-economic structural changes which he felt were necessary to bring the nation out of its various social, economic and political crises. (Economist: 28 Nov 92) With his party winning 44 seats in the new Assembly (Congress), the Peruvian President was fairly assured that his programs involving increased privatization of the economy, greater autonomy for local governments and his long sought death penalty for convicted terrorists could be achieved. The law concerning the death penalty was brought into effect in mid-1993 and a referendum held in late October supported Fujimori on this and the other issues. (Miami Herald 15 Sep, 24 Nov 92 and 5 Aug 93)

While Fujimori was unable to stimulate economic growth or employment in 1992, he was able to reduce inflation to its lowest level in 15 years or about 57 percent (3.6 percent per month at the end of 1992). (Economist: 14-20 Nov 92; and Campodonico 1992) The IMF declared that Peru had successfully completed an IMF-approved economic stabilization and adjustment program which now cleared the way for new negotiations with not only the IMF but also the World Bank (WB) and the Inter-American Development Bank (IADB). Loans of up to $222 million (IADB) and $100 million (Japan) were seriously being considered. (Interview CT:PE 1992) Peru's arrears on its international debts had been cleared or rescheduled. This caused the remainder of the international community in general to take note. The stabilizing of the economy and the reinitiation of the democratic process reflected the new confidence that the world financial community now had in Peru. (El Comercio: 25 Sep 92; and Financial Times: 13 Nov 92) While some economists predicted renewed economic growth and a bright future for the mid-1990s, the economy still remained essentially depressed with the GDP further declining during 1992 by 2.8 percent. (USE-PE 1993a: 1, 4 and 5; and Miami Herald: 5 Apr 93)

Overall, manufacturing had declined 6.2 percent, while textiles, electrical appliances, and paper outputs also showed declines of 14, 20 and 39 percent respectively. Mining was also reported as down 4.6 percent. Agricultural production was reported as down an estimated 5.7 percent with potatoes, cotton and wheat specifically showing declines in excess of 30 percent. Of note was the report from the Ministry of Agriculture which was released to the public indicating that there was a net loss of almost 7 percent of the legitimate cropland under cultivation during 1992 alone. (Actualidad: 4 Dec 92) This was despite the reported ten year cumulative totals of 33,000 ha of newly registered croplands which by 1991 included rice, corn, bananas and yucca as the leading crops and some 15,223 farmers who had also been formally registered as land owners. (USAID 1992: 50) Nonetheless, the end of the year found Peru importing rice from Vietnam and sugar from Chile. (Cabezas 1992) Only petroleum and gas production increased about one percent and this was mainly due to the decline in SL guerrilla attacks on the petroleum facilities towards the end of 1992 reflecting the loss of significant portions of the SL's leadership. (USE-PE 1993a: 6 and 7)

Fujimori was able to override the adverse economic situation to a degree and service enough of his government's international debts by selling off government owned mining interests (Hierro Peru), an airline (Aero Peru), a bottled gas company (Solgas), and a chain of gas stations (Petro-Peru) to private interests. These sales provided upwards of $1.5 billion with which the government could now begin to deal with its economic crisis. (USE-PE 1993a: 3) The Country Team estimated that the narcotics industry in Peru was still generating some $590 million which supported 226,000 workers but now represented only 4.2 percent of the Peruvian GDP. (USE-PE: Cable 9548) While the economy began to stabilize and there was now guarded optimism that Peru might be able to work itself out of its precarious economic straits, the situation for the Country Team in terms of its anti-drug policy for Peru looked bleak.

After the shoot-down of the C-130, SOUTHCOM had begun to reevaluate its situation in Peru and had taken a dim view of Fujimori and how the drug war was going in general. By September the previously positive attitudes held towards Peru (prior to April 1992) on the part of the SOUTHCOM joint staff at its headquarters in Quarry Heights, Panama, began to wane and Peru, for all intents and purposes, became a less important element in the SOUTHCOM strategy for defeating the narcotraffickers in the Andean Ridge. Even with the reinitiation of aerial surveillance flights and the use of ground based radar systems which began again in late 1992 and continued on into 1993 as part of SOUTHCOM's Support Justice IV operations in support of the FAP, it had been found that narcotrafficker aircraft from Colombia were guiding on the US radar beams to help navigate their way to and from Peru. This also held true for radars deployed into Ecuador to help fill gaps in the US search and detection pattern. (SOUTHCOM J3: 1993)

Also indicating that the UHV anti-drug aerial interdiction campaign was having problems was the SOUTHCOM estimate that, in addition to the several hundred formal airports in Peru, there were also up to 2,000 grass airstrips potentially available to the narco-pilots throughout the country. Besides the grass airstrips, the narcotraffickers had access to thousands of miles of rivers on which to land hydrofoil or seaplane aircraft. This meant that, even with the best of all-source intelligence inputs, the drug war in Peru was much like a gigantic shell game with the narcotraffickers more frequently than not able to outmaneuver their US and Peruvian adversaries. (SOUTHCOM J3: 1993; El Nuevo Herald: 14 Mar 93; and Miami Herald: 15 Dec 92) Nonetheless, it was reported that the FAP claimed that from 1991 to about mid-1993 that 124 narcotrafficker aircraft transporting cocaine had been intercepted or shot down. (El Nuevo Herald: 23 Jul 93)

Shifting from airfield to airfield and small town to small town, the traffickers utilized much of the Peru's territory extending from the UHV up into the Loreto Department and the convergence east of Iquitos formed by the Colombian and Brazilian borders with those of Peru. This area was known as the *Trapecio Amazonico* and was known as a virtual safe haven and secure shipping zone for the narcotraffickers. (SOUTHCOM J3: 1993; USE-PE: Cable 7416; and Drug Trafficking Update: 9 Nov 92). In the Loreto Department itself a variety of coca called *Ipadu* was now known to be cultivated and grown on a smaller scale than the *Erythroxylum* coca species found in the higher tropical zones of Peru. (Dourojeanni 1989: 281)

The SL guerrillas had correspondingly extended their protection operations north to the upper reaches of the Loreto Department and even along the Putomayo River frontier with Colombia. This was well over 200 miles north of the Santa Lucia base in the UHV and well outside the normal operational range of the some 4,000 Peruvian Marines and Army troops assigned to the UHV. (Joulwan 1993; SOUTHCOM J3: 1993; and Bailetti 1992) Besides this it was also noted that with most of the anti-drug activities taking place in the UHV region, very little attention had been paid to the other half of the coca-cocaine producing areas in the La Convencion and Lares Valleys in the Cuzco Department and the Huanta and La Mar areas along the Apurimac River in the Ayacucho Department as well as other coca production areas in the Pasco and Puno Departments. (DEA 1992: 29) Here production was going on virtually unmolested. (Cabezas and Pedraglio 1992)

Corruption continued apace throughout 1992 and Peruvian journalists reported that the Marine Corps forces were only interested in fighting the SL or MRTA guerrillas and not the drug traffickers. (Pedraglio 1992) Indications of this attitude were said to be reflected in the operations around La Libertad and Aguaytia where Marine units stationed in the region were reported as having been bribed in exchange for allowing narco-aircraft to come and go at will. If there were any doubts about the allegations being made, the Peruvian media published copies of the actual aerial surveillance photos which showed twin engine narcotrafficker aircraft at 4:57 AM landing at Aguaytia just several miles away from a Marine Corps outpost. Another photo taken on 21 October at 5:03 AM depicted a narco-aircraft landing in the vicinity of Sapososa or just three miles away from a major Army garrison. (Si: 16-22 Nov 92) In addition some Army forces were reported as actually protecting the drug shipments during pickup operations. In one example a drug trafficker known as *El Polaco* (the Polish one) apparently formally contracted the services of the Army unit in his area. Still another trafficker, Demetrio Limonel Chavez Penaherrera was reported moving some 5 mt of refined cocaine HCl per month or a total of about 60 mt per year out of Peru into Colombia for the Cali cartel group, earning a profit of $900,000. Timely tips from the Peruvian military were said to have enabled Chavez to escape capture by the police and to continue to conduct his refining and transhipment operations. (Miami Herald: 27 Mar and 27 Nov 92; and Drug Trafficking Update: 9 Nov 92)

Some things, however, did go well for the US anti-drug policy and demonstrated that close military-police cooperation was possible against the narcotraffickers. At Aucayacu in the Ucayali Valley in November, DEA and DIPOD elements using FAP helicopters responded to an intelligence report about a narcotrafficking operation taking place. The force flew to an Army outpost which provided a truck and security personnel for further movement towards the target site. At a short distance from the target site the force dismounted from the truck and continued its way on foot, capturing 500 kg of cocaine base and a narcotrafficker aircraft. (Interview DEA:PE 1992)

Ironically, an event took place which was to have a mixed impact on the US anti-drug policy in Peru. Not fully appreciated initially but noted over time by the coca farmers beginning in 1991 was the growth and spread of a plant fungus (*Fusarium Oxysisparum*) which was credited by the Country Team with the destruction of some 6,000 ha of coca plants. While the fungus appeared to attack with greater propensity that coca which had been growing for more than ten years, it had also attacked tangerines and other broad leaf plants in the UHV. Some farmers believed that it was a plot or secret US sponsored experiment aimed at destroying the coca. Since 1989 there had been reports of helicopter spraying (dusting) and the dropping of objects onto coca fields which produced a blight. There may have been something to these reports as the use of the fungus as an effective anti-coca herbicide agent had been reportedly verified by a number of scientists in Hawaii during the 1980s while they were conducting experiments with coca related plant life on behalf of the Coca Cola company. (Interview CT:PE 1992) In Peru the apparent experimental use of the fungus reportedly spilled over and contaminated banana, yucca and other citrus trees growing in the area. A United Nations development agency recorded receiving complaints from 72 farmers in the UHV over the issue. (Miami Herald 2 Jun 91; and Drug Trafficking Update: 13 Oct 92)

In response to the growth of the fungus, coca farmers from around the small villages of Los Angles, Bajo Porango, Puerto Huiete, Santa Fe, Nuevo Union and Tupac Amaru began to migrate out of the regions under attack by the blight and into the Central and Lower Huallaga Valleys to the north, as well as into the region along the Ucayali River to the east. Here again they began to plant new crops and begin the coca production process anew. In part the farmers were also reacting to a drop in prices for corn, rice, coffee, tea and cocoa. As credits and loans began to dry up due to the economic crisis confronting the government, the almost defunct state owned Agrarian Bank proved unable to provide more than a very limited amount of capital for alternate development. As private banks appeared not to be very willing to take the risk to make loans involving alternate crops, more farmers began to opt for coca as a supplemental, survival crop. (Drug Trafficking Update: 13 Oct 92; and Pedraglio 1992) This was not good for the US anti-drug policy. By this time numerous coca farmers only desired to have some tangible benefit or reasonable income for their efforts and a relatively secure legal situation. To this end they now saw themselves as very frustrated, gaining neither complete satisfaction from the coca trade nor a viable escape from their economic situation via the USAID and Peruvian government's alternate crop projects. (Cabezas and Lerner 1992)

Nonetheless, around 150 coca farmers in one community alone did commit themselves to developing alternate crops as part of a pilot program. Some 500 others expressed interest once funding was available and a viable marketing infrastructure was in place. Still, farmers told USAID officials that personal security and fear of SL and narcotrafficker retribution were factors which kept them from making a fuller commitment to the alternate development programs. A fully protective and reliable security presence on the part of the government was now becoming a key element to the success of the US efforts. (Interview AID:PE 1992)

To further the US anti-drug policy effort in Peru, a series of meetings took place in Washington, D.C. during October and November. These saw INM and the Country Team attempt to develop yet another strategy for winning the drug war in Peru. Called an *integrated* effort rather than a series of parallel programs, the new plan sought to strengthen local government in the coca growing areas of the UHV, providing social and physical infrastructure in the form of roads, irrigation projects, schools, bridges, potable water, electricity and the development of an environment which would enable farmer access to the national and international markets. To accomplish all this it was estimated that some $125 million (not yet appropriated) from the US Congress and about $60 million in local investment would have to be forthcoming. Private sector involvement was important. Technical assistance, advice and credits would also have to be forthcoming. The only expected obstacle was apparently the US Congress which still retained a dismal view of Peru's human rights record. (Interview AID:PE 1992)

The UHV was now noted as having increased its population to around 300,000. (DOS-INM 1993a: 121; and Washington Post: 28 Feb 93) To a large degree this was due to the traumatic pressures generated by the guerrilla insurgencies and civil war situation which the campesinos found themselves caught up in. That 600,000 people, mostly from the Andean highlands, had been forced to abandon their homes because of the repetitive violence and human rights violations by all sides and were now looking for work wherever it could be found, did not help the situation facing the US anti-drug policy. (El Nuevo Herald: 17 Apr 93; and Interview AID:PE 1992) Even coffee, an otherwise stable and lucrative crop, had suffered a 68 percent loss in the international market, causing some farmers to opt for coca in order to survive. (Drug Trafficking Update: 13 Oct 92) Despite the effects of the fungus and the destruction of 6,138 ha of coca seed beds, coca cultivation in Peru actually increased during 1992 by some 8,300 ha, representing a 7 percent increase from 120,800 ha recorded in 1991 to the estimated 129,100 ha recorded as still growing as of the end of 1992. Most of the expansion took place in the SL and MRTA controlled areas of the Huallaga Valley. (DOS-INM 1993a: 6 and 124)

The end of 1992 thus found the US anti-drug effort seizing about one percent (8 mt) of Peru's total production of approximately 700 mts of cocaine base and refined cocaine before it was shipped out of country to Colombia. (DOS-INM 1993a: statistical tables for Peru; and Interview DEA-PE 1992) This statistic also reflects to a degree the estimated less than one percent of all narcotrafficker flights which were being intercepted (124) enroute to Colombia. (INM 1993: Statistical tables for Peru; and McClintock 1993: 116) This occurred despite the fact that the INM in Washington, D.C. and the Country Teams's NAS had now hired one US Army Lieutenant-Colonel (Retired) Edward Hayes to assist in its operations at the Santa Lucia base.

Fresh from an assignment to Venezuela after his Bolivian escapades, Hayes went to work to try and rejuvenate the US effort and bring it to a level of maximum efficiency. Yet Peru was not Bolivia and Hayes viewed the UHV and the general situation confronting the US effort as "overwhelming" in terms of its complexity and daunting in terms of its magnitude. Nonetheless, both himself and other active duty US military aviators who were on loan to INM from the Department of Defense battled the SL guerrillas and narcotraffickers wherever they were to be found. The SL had shown no particular interest in Santa Lucia and Hayes concluded that this indicated that the base was largely ineffectual in terms of inhibiting narcotrafficking operations. He intended to change this. By coordinating the actions of several dozen maintenance technicians and pilots, Hayes was able to keep six of the 14 INM helicopters operational virtually every day. Using long range fuel tanks and sometimes repositioning fuel at locations known as forward area refueling points (FARPs), the DEA-DIPOD force was able to carry out a number of extended range operations against narcotrafficker targets well outside of the traditional 200 mile operating range of the Santa Lucia base. (Hayes 1992) Yet, after all was said and done, the overall balance in Peru continued to favor the narcotraffickers and weighed heavily against the US anti-drug policy.

Also not promising for the US policy was the popular reflection on the human rights situation in Peru where half the population thought that the Peruvian government did not respect the rights of its citizens. (IPEA 1992) This of course reflected a series of on-going accusations in the Peruvian press from various military officials during the year who took issue with the way the government was handling the security situation in Peru. (Interview CT:PE 1992) In other polls, 76 percent of the population thought that drug consumption was very serious within the Peruvian society. (APOYO 1992) Despite the increasing public awareness of cocaine abuse, it had now actually increased to well over 2 percent of the population. (DOS-INM 1993a: 124; and Vassilaqui 1992) In addition over half (58 percent) of the people thought the judicial system was incapable of prosecuting successfully drug trafficking cases. (APOYO 1992) This was despite the fact that 375 judges had gone through special training courses to enhance their performance and that 905 prosecutors had been trained in narcotics case preparation and implementation by the USAID programs. (USAID 1992: 53-55)

The INM Bureau in Washington, D.C. summed up its perception of the situation in Peru as 1993 began, stating: "The Fujimori government has not taken effective anti-drug action in the face of continuing insurgent violence, economic chaos and political uncertainty. Unless the Government of Peru takes more aggressive action, further expansion of the Peruvian coca crop will offset hard-won gains in Bolivia and Colombia." (DOS-INM 1993b: 5-6) Added to this grim perception of the US anti-drug policy's situation in Peru was a Country Team report out of Lima which stated that for the first time, gum opium was being produced, indicating that opium poppy cultivation and opium latex exports to Colombia for processing the heroin from the UHV and other parts of Peru were now taking place. This now added another dimension to the drug war in Peru. The cost per kilogram of the gum opium was said to be $750 or roughly equivalent to the same amount paid for one kilogram of cocaine base. (USE-PE Cable 7416; and DEA 1992b: 6) Both the SL and the MRTA guerrillas were reported as charging 25 to 30 percent of the opium's value as their special surcharge or tax. (Nacional: 25 Jul 92)

Despite President Fujimori's claim in early 1993 that 95 percent of the key SL leadership was in prison, the SL guerrillas appeared to be recovering and reasserting themselves. In addition some 70 SL and MRTA prisoners escaped from Cuzco's Quencoro Prison following a violent 15 minute attack from the outside that opened a breech in the facility's walls. (New York Times: 6 Apr 93; and Pais: 3 Mar 93) In addition the SL murdered the mayor of Tocache, Freddy Aliaga, who, since assuming the position in 1989, had been a prominent crusader for alternate development and self-help projects for the coca farmers. (USE-PE: Cable 7416; and New York Times: 20 Nov 92) That the SL was still very much present in the Huallaga Valley and other coca growing regions, meant that the overall security problem for the government, at least in the coca growing regions, was essentially unchanged. Private companies were generally reported as being afraid to invest in Peru with the security situation being as precarious as it was. To this end, even Peruvian bi-lateral commerce with Bolivia and Brazil was in doubt. (El Comercio: 3 Mar 93)

A serious question remained as to whether President Fujimori's actions had merely strengthened his own personal position as an authoritarian leader or whether they had undermined democracy to the degree that the SL insurgency could now capitalize on what had transpired and thereby increase support for its cause. While this was debated both inside and outside Peru, that the SL's influence and support now came from virtually all levels of Peruvian society was noted in the media. The PNP arrested the son of the Assistant Attorney General for being a member of the SL. In addition the director of a posh secondary school (Cesar Vallejo Academy), one of Peru's more famous ballet dancers and a nun were also captured as SL activists. The economy remained stagnant and over half of the population did not feel content with their bare subsistence existence. (Miami Herald; 23 Oct 92; and Caretas: 6 Jul and 17 Sep 92)

In Lima, up to half a million people forming part of the informal or parallel economy could be found out on the streets in ever denser numbers washing cars, shinning shoes, and selling matches and cigarettes etc. in an effort to earn something of a survival wage. (US News: 2 Aug 93; and author observation December 1993) In the rural areas the people coped as best they could with the ubiquitous SL guerrillas. As it was, about half of the population of Peru or some twelve million persons and double the number from several years prior were now said to be living in dire poverty. (Guillermoprieto 1993: 66)

In a number of cases where local villages tried to arm themselves against attacks by the guerrillas, their requests for equipment and munitions were rebuffed by the government and the Army. In other cases, the villages, unable to obtain formal support from the government and still fearing the SL, attempted to associate with the local Army garrison to obtain self-defense training and weapons. In the villages, including some of the shanty-towns around the outskirts of Lima, the local *rondas* (self defense groups) were armed with little more than sharpened sticks and whistles - hardly a match against the fanatical SL. (New York Times: 16 Sep 92; and Oiga: 19 Oct 92) Sometimes the situation found the Army attempting to exploit its association with a *campesino* village using it to attack other villages suspected of being in sympathy with the SL.

Nonetheless, the often indiscriminate use of repressive methods by the Army began to drive a wedge between the local populace and the state security forces which were ostensibly there to help protect the former. (House 1992a: 32-33) This further complicated the civil-military relationship and exacerbated existing animosities to the degree that another dimension to the Peruvian civil war was beginning to develop. (Leonhard 1993: 9-11) Yet villages that did not defend themselves ran the risk of meeting the fate that befell Huayllao located some 400 miles southeast of Lima where the SL guerrillas, not content with the village's support of the government, murdered 47 people, including 30 women and 12 small children. As misfortune would have it, the village's civil defense force consisting of most of the men was away celebrating a wedding at a nearby community. (Miami Herald: 21 Oct 92)

The Peruvian Army, attempting to enhance its counter-insurgency efforts against the SL had recruited, sometimes by force, members of the indigenous Indian population to serve in the civil defense *rondas*. These did provide a semblance of security and often deflected SL attacks, reducing the levels of recorded violence in he Ayacucho Department. (House 1991b: 109-111; and Miami Herald: 7 Dec 92) Nonetheless, in the Amazonian regions of the Ene River and the Pichis

Valley, the Ashanika Indians found themselves assisting the Army's counter-insurgency efforts and the SL guerrillas simultaneously. (Globe and Mail 19 Sep 92; Financial Times 11 Dec 92; and Miami Herald 11 Oct 92) Other Indians complained that narcotraffickers and petroleum companies were invading their homelands and that these invasions were forcing them to contemplate war against the intruders. (Pais: 16 Nov 92) While the complexities of everyday life in Peru did cascade in and around the US anti-drug policy, there were indications of some residual strength within the body politic itself.

The interest in the democratic process in Peru appeared strong and was suggested by the approximately 12,000 candidates that registered for the 29 January 1993 mayoral elections. Traditional, independent and government sponsored parties all fielded candidates, including the Ayacucho, Puno and Huaraz regions where SL influence and corresponding intimidation were quite high. Nonetheless, true to their word that anyone participating in the democratic process would be liable for extreme retribution, the SL proceeded to murder up to a half dozen candidates. The impact of these actions did cause another hundred to withdraw from the race or risk the same fate. (El Nuevo Herald: 18 Jan 93; Expresso: 4 Oct 92; and Latin American Weekly Report: 7 Jan 93)

With the social-political situation so polarized and the deterioration of agriculture becoming more of a problem every day due to the ongoing violence and natural causes such as droughts, the people of the high Andes became that much more interested in desiring to escape from their relatively dire situation. (New York Times: 5 Feb 93) But escaping to Lima as an urban center was not necessarily a good solution as the United Nations was reporting that several million of the city's 5.8 million lived in "absolute misery." (Miami Herald: 9 Feb 92) The thirteen years of guerrilla war had had an adverse effect on the countryside from which it would be difficult to recover quickly. Little or no construction or even repairing of roads, the building of clinics and the provision of water, electricity and sewer systems to rural towns had taken place. Government efforts to entice the formerly terrorized population of displaced peasant campesinos back to their original settlements through the use of free transportation met with uneven results. Farm communities were reported to be without sufficient seeds, tools and building supplies to make a new start and were reduced to eking out a survival existence. Some people in the Ayacucho region took the option of seeking work in Lima or growing illegal coca in the eastern jungles of the lower Andes. (El Nuevo Herald: 22 Nov 93) In short the basic cause of the violent Sendero Luminoso (SL) phenomenon, poverty and inequality, appear to have worsened for many as unemployment was significant and the state remained weak in its ability to support the rural population.

Farmers were vulnerable to SL operations which continued to terrorize communities in the Amazon regions of eastern Peru. (El Nuevo Herald: 19-20 Apr 94) Army efforts to capture Oscar Ramirez Durand led to increasing human rights violations. In the UHV itself ("Huallaga Front" to the Peruvian army), military forces attempted to defeat approximately 160 SL guerrillas and drive them from their heretofore "liberated" or guerrilla controlled zones which included coca and cocaine producing areas. In doing so, the operations and their violent exchanges of fire with the guerrillas caused hundreds of campesinos to flee the battle zone fearing for their lives. (Miami Herald: 25 Apr 94) The competing MRTA guerrillas also engaged the army as both forces battled to maintain their presence in the UHV. The SL responded to the operations by blowing up one of Petro Peru's oil pipelines, slowing down production for a few days. (El Nuevo Herald: 28 Apr and 18 May 94).

The military situation for the Peruvian government appeared to improve with Abimael Guzman's decision to negotiate a peace accord at the end of 1993 with the objective of ending formally SL operations in Peru shutting the organization down. This decision by Guzman produced a serious division or schism within the ranks of the surviving SL cadres still in the field. One faction opted for peace while another faction rejected Guzman's overtures to the government and opted for a continuation of the war. SL leaders of the peace faction which agreed with Guzman, such as Martha Huatay, Edmundo Cox and Osman Morote, were characterized as traitors to the revolutionary process. In the field there remained the war faction led by hard liner Oscar Durand Ramirez in control of the SL Central Committee. He fought back against the government with assorted terrorist acts in Lima at the end of 1993 and into 1994 while other cadres continued to operate in the rural areas. (El Nuevo Herald: 29 Jan 94) Countrywide, SL attacks had dropped in quantity with less than 1,700 reported during 1993 compared to around 3,000 for 1992. (Miami Herald: 5 Feb 94) Despite intensive military operations in the UHV, the SL maintained its effectiveness, albeit smaller in size. (Expresso: 18 Apr 94; Miami Herald: 5 Feb 94 and El Nuevo Herald 24 Apr 94)

Accused of death squad activities and other human rights violations, the army remained under considerable pressure from both human rights groups as well as from members of its own institution and the Peruvian government. (Miami Herald: 7 and 11 Feb and 18 Mar 94) Denounced by the US State Department, the Peruvian government's efforts to try military officers involved in a particularly malicious human rights case involving the 1992 murder of nine students and a professor at La Cantute teachers training college east of Lima came under fire. Fujimori acquiesed to military interests to use the latter's own military justice system rather than subject its offials to civilian courts. Having withheld $105 million from Peru because of previous allegations of human rights violations, the administration of US President Bill Clinton now considered also withholding the $30 million in economic support funding authorized for Peru. Eventually five officers and four other army personnel were sentenced to up to 20 years in prison, the harshest penalty ever dealt by a military court against officers accused of human rights abuses. (Miami Hearld: 12 and 23 Feb 94)

With US government funding for Peru reduced by the US Congress in the wake of the 1992 coup and alleged human rights abuses, the US aviation and logistical support involving some 20 DEA agents, pilots and mechanics at the Santa Lucia counternarcotics operating base was terminated (the PNP continued to use the base). A new mobile basing strategy was then developed whereby the town of Pucallapa in the Ucayali Valley (140 miles east of the UHV) became the anchor for a series of temporary bases deep in the interior of the coca-cocaine production zones. Fuel and other supplies were airlifted into these remote areas to support long range helicopter and small boat counter-drug operations. In addition the FAP and PNP coordinated their efforts to control ten official airports and other selected airstrips. Aerial interdiction continued and narcotrafficking aircraft were apprehended both in the air and on the ground. (DOS INM 1994: 119; and Miami Herald: 15 Dec 93) Concrete obstacles blocked a dozen roads to prevent their use by trafficking aircraft. In one case the narco-effort to construct a dirt airstrip in the Central Huallaga Valley came to naught when members of local USAID-supported alternative development project refused to cooperate and called for the army to expel the traffickers. In sum, during 1993 there were 4,824 drug related arrests reported. (DOS INM 1994: 119-120 and 123) There were other successes too.

In January 1994 Demetrio Limoniel Chavez ("The Vatican") Penaherrera was captured in Cali, Colombia, and deported to Peru. As a Peruvian, he had formed a powerful production and transshipping organization that became the principal supplier of Peruvian processed coaine base and HCl to the Cali cartel. Using a weak government presence and the local insurgencies to protect him, Chavez was well on his way to achieving "cartel" status within the narcotrafficking world. Paying off the SL and the MRTA guerrillas with money and weapons, he had received permission to allow his trafficking organization to operate inside guerrilla-held territory. This arrangement eventually worked against him as he was sentenced by a military court to life in prison for treason involving his pay-offs to the SL guerrillas. (DOS INM 1994: 2; and Miami Herald: 14 Jan and 20 Feb 94) Unknown to Chavez, the Peruvian congress had adopted stricter penalties, including life imprisonment for serious drug offenses. Despite the success in the capture of El Vaticano, Peruvian cocaine product processing continued unabated.

Greatly assisting the US anti-drug effort in Peru was the natural phenomena of the deadly anti-coca fungus, Fusarium Oxysporum, which took such a toll in the UHV during 1993 that by early 1994 the Country Team in Lima was reporting a 33 percent drop in UHV coca cultivation. This produced an overall reduction of about 16 percent for Peru in general. Coca cultivation was now estimated at 108,800 ha compared to the 1992 high of 129,100. (DOS INM 1994: 2, 17 and 118) This led to some optimism among US anti-drug officials as Peruvian anti-drug police, supported by the Country Team's 12-man intelligence and operations planning cell (part of Operation Snowcap) and contracted logistical support personnel, broke up trafficking rings and restricted somewhat the coca farmers' opportunities to market their crops. Under pressure, numerous farmers abandoned their plantations and moved to more remote areas.

Despite some success, seizures of cocaine base and HCl fell by 17 percent from 6.9 mt in 1992 to 5.8 mt by the end of 1993. This may have reflected the now decreased yield of the UHV in which the metric tonnage of coca leaf production was estimated to have fallen from 223,900 mt in 1992 to a six year low of 155,500 mt by the end of 1993. Nonetheless, the US sponsored eradication effort remained inhibited as Fujimori specifically banned the use of aerial herbicides (glyphosulfate) due to the continued lack of economic alternatives for the coca farmers. While CORAH did eradicate over 6,000 ha of coca seed beds, Peru remained the worlds largest source of coca as cultivation expanded well beyond the UHV, spreading out into the Central Huallaga and Ucayali Valleys and other areas of Peru. (DOS INM 1994: 118-119 and 121)

Corruption, endemic to virtually all Peruvian governmental institutions, remained a significant factor, adversely affecting anti-drug operations throughout Peru. In 1994 the Peruvian congress implicated some 100 officers from the army, navy and air force as well as 250 others of the national police as involved in narcotrafficking in one form or another. Low saleries were indicated as the reason why so many were susceptible to the temptations of the drug trade. That General Nicolas Hermoza, president of the Armed Forces Joint Command, reported that over 100 members of the army had received sentences for their linkage to narcotrafficking activities, indicated the severity of the problem. (DOS INM 1994: 120; and El Nuevo Herald: 4 Apr 94) On the fringes of the eastern Amazon jungles around Aucayacu, several officers and 18 other police agents were accused by a local judge of trafficking with 180 kg of cocaine base which had been confiscated from various traffickers. (El Nuevo Herald: 16 Apr 94)

In Peru, by far the largest source of coca in the world, the US anti-drug program's success was viewed by ONDCP as abysmal. The US anti-drug policy there was not making a difference after four years of effort. As a result the ONDCP wanted to terminate its programs in Peru, take whatever money was left over in the anti-drug budget allocations and apply it elsewhere in support of more successful efforts. (ONDCP 1: 1993) As it was, in reaction to Alberto Fujimori's 1992 coup and actions dissolving the Peruvian Congress, the White House and Department of State suspended the $164 million in economic and $39 million in military aid already allocated. In turn they called for an immediate restoration of democratic rule. Fundamentally, the US anti-drug efforts in Peru were perceived as only producing marginal results. The factors of corruption and the ability of the traffickers to outmaneuver and outfly the US and Peruvian anti-narcotics police and helicopters operating from the $25 million dollar base at Santa Lucia consistently undermined the US anti-drug policy in Peru. With the US anti-drug effort able to intercept only some eight metric tons or about 1.5 percent of the 640 mt of cocaine HCl and cocaine base being produced annually in Peru, even the Department of State's own Inspector General had misgivings and recommended that the Santa Lucia base be closed down as an ineffectual effort. (House 1993: 2; Senate 1990: 20 and 1992: 40-41; ONDCP 1 and Deering 1993; SOUTHCOM J3: 1993; and Washington Post: 27 Mar 93)

Spraying with herbicides was generally not acceptable to the Peruvian government, which was concerned that a quarter of a million people would be thrown out of work in the Upper Huallaga Valley region and become a further burden for the severely depressed economy which was reflected in the over 30 percent unemployment throughout the nation. People out of work in the UHV could even become guerrillas. The

Sendero Luminoso (SL) guerrillas were seen as an ubiquitous threat that was also confounding the eradication effort as much as the traffickers themselves. In addition Congress was placing human rights caveats on the monies allocated to the anti-drug effort in Peru due to the some 80 extrajudicial killings and 170 disappearances of civilians attributed to the government's military and police forces. The Peruvian military was characterized as having adopted tactics and engaged in human rights violations and atrocities that were indistinguishable from those of the SL guerrillas. For this reason ONDCP decided that Peru should be cut out of the US anti-drug strategy effort completely. DOD, still incensed over the Peruvian Air Forces strafing of a C-130 conducting an anti-drug intelligence mission, concurred. (Senate 1990: 20; and 1992: 40-41; House 1993: 2; and Interviews DOD and ONDCP 1: 1993) Yet, at this time other government agencies also became involved.

The Department of State's influence was such that the NSC and President Bush decided it was imperative to see Fujimori's coup reversed and democracy and the constitutional process restored to Peru. Because of this the ONDCP's efforts to cut back the counter-narcotics efforts in Peru were viewed as potentially threatening to the overriding policy of creating democracy once again. The ONDCP's efforts to extract itself from Peru had failed and the US remained engaged. (ONDCP 1: 1993) This was despite the fact that funding in support of the Peruvian military remained cut off. At this time reports were received indicating that the Peruvian military was competing for assignments to the UHV where they could quickly enrich themselves through liaison with the traffickers. (DOD 1993)

By 1993 the ONDCP itself was looked upon by the new, incoming administration of Bill Clinton as an agency with merely a one issue agenda. With the appointment of a new drug czar (Lee P. Brown, the former Police Commissioner of New York City) as its Director and the elevation of the position to cabinet level status, the ONDCP was now said to have improved its efficiency and ability to coordinate all national anti-drug policy throughout the federal government. Nonetheless, early in the year it was reduced from an authorized manning level of about 125 personnel to no more than about 25. This massive reduction in personnel curtailed its capabilities for detailed policy making worldwide and limited its operational focus. While it could now only cover about 50 percent of its portfolio of anti-drug issues and countries, it did remain firmly focused on the Andean region. (Clinton 1993a; and ONDCP 1: 1993) Despite the emasculation of the ONDCP, it officially remained the lead government agency for establishing policy, priorities and objectives for national drug control purposes. (Clinton 1993b)

The roughly $13 billion anti-drug budget authorized for 1993 was slightly less than the NASA budget of some $15 billion. Andean source country anti-drug funding under the Andean Initiative was reduced about 28 percent to a level of $78 million for the year. As a result of the budget cuts, all US personnel and aircraft in Peru were transferred from the Santa Lucia base to the town of Pucallpa in an effort to reduce operating costs. In addition, DOD announced that it was cutting some $200 million from its $1.1 billion anti-drug budget. In part this reflected the government's belt tightening process for all its offices. (ONDCP 2: 1993; and Miami Herald: 19 Apr; 29 Oct and 15 Dec 93)

Where the US anti-drug policy stands in Peru has been conditioned by the numerous countervailing factors which endlessly buffet it as it attempts to make its relentless journey to a fruitful end. For an indication of where the policy is going as it enters the mid-1990s, one need only note the Fiscal Year 1996 budget submission from the Department of State. Peru, the primary source and supply of coca leaves for the international cocaine narcotrafficking markets was requested to receive but $42 million for narcotics control activities or $18 million less than Bolivia which produces half the amount of coca leaves as the former. (DOS INM 1995: INCSR) During this time President Fujimori's new Congress approved a new Constitution which allowed the incumbent president the possibility of being reelected. He took full advantage of this and the ensuing democratic process in early 1995 when he again won the national presidential election.

Fujimori's re-election as president in April 1995, with about two-thirds of the vote in his favor, assured him a strong mandate to the end of the 1990's. Having stabilized the economy, which he showed GDP growth rates of 12.7 percent and 7.5 percent for 1994 and 1995 respectively, he had garnered the people's support sufficiently enough to take ever stronger measures in regard to both the SL and narcotrafficking in general. (Miami Herald: 1 Apr 1996) Declaring all coca growing areas "emergency zones" in early 1996, the Peruvian president promulgated a series of anti-drug laws which included the formation of an anti-drug commission (CONTRADROGAS). The mandate given the new commission was to stop domestic drug consumption and trafficking in illegal drugs in general. The police were directed to assert their control over all aerial and maritime ports of entry that could be used for the transshipment of drugs. The military, specifically the army, was ordered to wage an all-out fight to the finish against the Sendero Luminoso in the UHV and other coca producing regions of Peru. This fleshed out a major portion of Fujimori's plan to reduce by half the farming population economically dependent on coca by the year 2000. (DOS INM 1996: 100 and Nuevo Herald: 26 Apr 96)

Fujimori's optimism for dealing with narcotrafficking was based in large part on the success of the air force (FAP) which had shot down some 25 trafficking aircraft, closing air routes and disrupting to some degree the flow of cocaine into Colombia. The US-supported FAP air interdiction effort caused a drastic drop in the prices for paste and coca leaves. Whereas twenty-five pounds of coca leaves were selling for $127 in February 1995, they now were selling in some parts of the UHV for as low as $2. By mid-1996 a kilogram of paste had gone from $1,200 in price down to $230. Such was the impact the glut of these products produced on the local markets. This gave a temporary uplift to the otherwise stagnant AID alternate crop development program. (DOS INM 1996: 101-102; Miami Herald: 27 Oct 95; and Nuevo Herald: 5 May 96)

The ensuing crisis over the drop in prices caused some coca farmers to begin switching to palm hearts, earning about $3,000 per hectare per year. Nonetheless, it was noted that, as an agricultural insurance policy of sorts, rows of coca bushes were also planted between the palm cultivations. In addition, trafficking groups such as the Cachique Rivera brothers reacted to the new situation by having their coca farmer contacts store their respective products for eventual sale on Peru's Colombian frontier. (Nuevo Herald: 5 May 96) Throughout 1995 the SL remained a tenacious enemy for the Peruvian army which attempted to track down and destroy the former in the remote regions of the UHV. The SL often ambushed army patrols, inflicting heavy casualties on the latter. With coca profits as a lure, the SL augmented its forces in the coca growing regions to remain a contender with some units operating with up to 180 guerrillas in a single action. (Nuevo Herald: 22 Jul 95) US AID countered with a potato development program which it was hoped would create 150 thousand jobs for poor peasants living in and around the high Andean valleys. (Miami Herald: 5 Oct 95) Despite these efforts, traditional countervailing factors all continued to offset the US-Peruvian progress.

Corruption remained endemic throughout the mid-1990s, undermining all programs to one degree or another. In one case a group of some forty army and police officials, including two army generals, were charged with having protected aerial trafficking for the Cachique Rivera brothers. In return for ignoring the use of selected clandestine airstrips, the group's members received up to $7,500 weekly and up to $25,000 for each flight. (Nuevo Herald: 3 Aug, 4 and 8 Nov 95) The FAP was not immune either as one of its DC-8 aircraft was intercepted on the outskirts of Lima, enroute to Europe with approximately 380 pounds of cocaine (HCl), worth $40,000 on the European market. (Nuevo Herald: 13 May 96) Even when cocaine was captured by the police, there were doubts as to the integrity of the operation, as demonstrated by the 21 officials accused of absconding with 400 pounds of confiscated cocaine paste. (Nuevo Herald: 16 Apr 94)

With harvestable coca leaf production once again rising at a 6 percent rate (115,300 ha reported under cultivation for 1995, compared to 108,600 ha for 1994), the viability of the US eradication program for Peru remained in question. This, in conjunction with reported poppy cultivation taking place in the Apurimac Valley region (4 mt of harvested leaf were siezed during 1995), does not bode well for a US anti-drug policy success in Peru. (DOS INM 1996: 99, 103 and 105; and Nuevo Herald: 16 Apr 94) Despite an all-out US effort, Peru will remain the leading coca leaf producer in the world well into the 21st century.

Chapter 9

Observations and Conclusions in Regard to Peru

The US anti-drug policy in Peru tended to focus for the most part on the Upper Huallaga Valley (UHV). The relatively high concentration of the coca-cocaine production processes in the UHV made the coca eradication problem there appear deceptively simple to the US Country Team at the beginning of the early 1980s. In reality it was profoundly complex. The Peruvian government had already begun to find this out in the late 1970s when it tried to gain control of the coca growing areas by declaring them to be national enterprises (ENACO). That the Peruvian government was making the effort to control coca was a positive factor in favor of the US policy. Nonetheless, it was immediately confronted by a countervailing effect in the form of the *campesino* farmers who looked upon the land in the relatively remote UHV as available and rightfully theirs as part of the general thrust of the agrarian reform programs begun during the era of General Valasco.

In turn, the general poverty of the Peruvian population and its aspirations to break out of this depressing situation continuously propelled more and more people looking for a better livelihood into the UHV and the other high-Andean valleys. As word spread throughout Peru that substantial earnings could be had through the production and sale of coca, the coca growing industry became a nirvana of sorts for the poor, destitute peasants lacking productive croplands. As it was, only those people who were desperately poor, landless or disenfranchised to one degree or another tended to go to the coca growing zones. Most of Peru's population either stayed in place or gravitated to the urban areas such as Lima. Complicating the legalities of the government's program to control the now burgeoning coca industry was the Andean Indian culture and tradition of chewing coca leaves and the indigenous population's use of coca as an herbal medicine. This could not be denied by the Peruvian government which caused it to move very cautiously in its treatment of the situation and the potential violent confrontation with the coca growers.

Beginning in the early 1980s, to placate the US government's aspirations to reduce as much as possible and even eliminate coca, the Belaunde government introduced its office of coca control and eradication (CORAH) as well as a special project for legal crop development (PEAH) in the UHV. US funding was forthcoming to reinforce these positive currents which now placed the US anti-drug policy on an operational footing. While this set the course for the US-Peruvian anti-drug efforts for the years to come, there were other factors and effects which came into play to immediately begin to buffet against and generally bog down the joint effort.

Immediately apparent was the effort of the coca farmers and the narcotraffickers to organize themselves in a coherent and unified manner to resist the government's overtures and pressures to cause the coca growers to desist from producing coca and switch to alternate crops. This was not a new phenomenon as it was also taking place at the same time in Bolivia. The Colombian cartels saw the coca grower organizations as a logical step to help protect a highly lucrative business enterprise. In turn, the coca farmers welcomed this organizing initiative as a way to represent their views and lobby the Peruvian government so as to protect their new livelihood and preserve their newly acquired lands (squatters rights). The entrepreneurial spirit was also alive and as the coca industry grew in size so also did its supporting agro-economic infrastructure which provided a livelihood for thousands of more people in this booming cottage industry.

Yet if there was one aspect peculiar to Peru which would loom large and cast a negative shadow over the entire anti-drug effort in Peru, it was the Sendero Luminoso (SL) insurgency which embraced the entire Peruvian nation in one form or another. This insurgency and its competing rival, the Tupac Amaru Revolutionary Movement (MRTA) took advantage of the ever increasing coca boom as a cheap and convenient way to finance their respective revolutionary enterprises.

Through the extortion of money in the form of "taxes", as the guerrillas termed their operations, the coca farmers, coca-cocaine producers, narcotraffickers and even government officials in the contested zones of the UHV were exploited. This exploitation was enough to support the SL and MRTA war chests and yet just bearable enough for most coca farmers to earn sufficiently high profits to remain in business. That the guerrillas were willing to both protect and adjudicate the coca-cocaine business, protecting the growers from government harassment and undue exploitation by the narcotrafficker buyers and trafficking barons, was for many growers a worthwhile, albeit costly necessity to stay in the coca business.

The SL-coca nexus was one that placed the Peruvian government on the horns of a dilemma and in a quandary as to what should be done. This was not fully appreciated by the US anti-drug policy which blithely maintained for the most part of a decade its own single policy focus and related courses of action, attempting to impose its eradication program on Peru as its first and foremost priority. Yet to attack coca and force its eradication through repressive measures would (and did) drive the coca farmers more deeply into the arms of the guerrillas. To successfully engage and root out the guerrillas as a deadly threat to the government would require the general support of the coca growing population whose eyes and ears were the only real source of intelligence that the government's security forces had to bring to bear in support of a counter-insurgency campaign. To do this would require winning the "hearts and minds" of the coca growing population which also meant that the government would have to desist from its coca eradication and narcotrafficking suppression projects.

The Peruvian Army units committed to the UHV to carry out counter-insurgency operations against the SL and MRTA clearly understood the problem and the implications stemming from this situation. The SL had to be defeated first and only then could the coca situation be addressed in an effective manner. If the US government and its Country Team in Lima did understand this situation, they ignored it or refused to admit that the SL guerrillas represented the paramount, first priority problem in the UHV. In any event the US government would countenance nothing more than efforts made within the context of the anti-drug policy's eradication focus. Despite the conflict of policy priorities, there was no getting around the fact that the countervailing SL issue would have to be dealt with effectively or there would be no real progress in the anti-drug effort. Not to defeat or neutralize the insurgency in some manner would merely tend to exacerbate the already complicated situation and prejudice its successful conclusion.

The Country Team opted to ignore the insurgency issue in its extreme and reaped a correspondingly ever more difficult situation to deal with. The SL's presence in the UHV was ubiquitous and especially vindictive against anyone who strayed away from its protective cloak, began working with the government, or failed to pay the stipulated taxes for the revolution. The political violence that occurred and its coercive effect generated enough fear among the coca farmers and the general population to generally keep them in check in terms of seeking government aid in exchange for eradicating coca. Only the presence of a significant military and police force tended to ameliorate the coca farmers' situation. Nonetheless, the effects of the SL/MRTA insurgencies continuously buffeted against the forward progress of the US anti-drug effort in Peru.

Another aspect which created a counter-vailing impact that also undermined the US anti-drug policy was that of the dependency of the Peruvian government on the substantial economic support and input into the economy provided by the coca-dollars. This was particularly evident by the mid-1980s when at least a quarter of the Peruvian export income was estimated to be derived from the coca industry. As the SL insurgency's operations began to hamper the Peruvian economy, foreign investment fell off and the economy began to falter even more, while the government's dependency on the inputs from the coca industry grew ever stronger. This of course affected its will to cut off what was otherwise deemed an important source of general revenue for its economy. The coca industry was also a safety valve for reducing the pressures of the unemployed which in theory meant there would be potentially fewer discontented people available for exploitation by the insurgencies.

A further factor working to undermine the anti-drug policy in Peru was the element of corruption which played upon the endemic overall poverty of the Peruvian people and the low salaries of the government's officials and the security forces. This became a serious issue as they came into contact with the narcotraffickers. With the huge profits that were generated by the trafficking system, the narcotraffickers could always afford to invest hundreds of thousands if not some millions of dollars as part of the cost of doing business to bribe or otherwise buy off sufficient government officials, police and military personnel who might otherwise inhibit trafficking operations. This allowed the traffickers significant freedom of action to continue to engage in their business and to neutralize to a large degree the anti-drug efforts on the part of the US and Peruvian governments.

An economic aspect of the situation confronting the US anti-drug policy in Peru was the relatively large disparity in profits which coca had in its favor compared to other food crops. As the Belaunde government came to an end in the mid-1980s, the coca business was flourishing in Peru as it had never had before. As a result, the coca farmers as a whole were less inclined to embrace any form of alternate crop program offered by the US and Peruvian governments. Only in cases where there was a significant government security presence combined with the threat of eradication did the farmers bend to the pressures of the situation to consider seriously the alternate crop options. In coca's favor was the fact that it could grow and flourish where other crops generally could not. This was always a major detriment to the US anti-drug policy and a key influence for the coca farmers in ultimately deciding on what was in their own best interests.

With the election of President Alan Garcia in 1985, the US anti-drug policy appeared to get a boost. Garcia was outspoken in his castigations of the narcotraffickers and the US Drug Enforcement Administration (DEA) was now able to bring into play its more militant Operation Condor. Nonetheless, over time Garcia himself began to realize that his government too was dependent to a considerable degree on the coca industry. That some thousands of hectares of coca were actually eradicated was off set by the increases in coca crops produced by the ever greater number of people arriving in the UHV every month to grow coca. The coca growers themselves became more militant and, while agitated to a considerable degree by their various coca federations, in conjunction with the traffickers and guerrillas alike, they began to confront the government with strikes, demonstrations and forms of violence. The Peruvian government did take note.

The US Country Team on the other hand had its anti-drug policy in Peru buoyed up by President Reagan's National Security Decision Directive NSDD 221. This imperative for action acted as a positive factor which drove the Country Team forward in a relentless effort to achieve an anti-drug policy success. If nothing else it kept the anti-drug issue at the forefront of the Country Team's agenda well into the 1990s. But national security considerations also affected the Peruvian government's perceptions as to what was happening in the UHV with the result that Alan Garcia ordered the police and military back into the Valley en masse to reassert government control over some of the towns and airports which had fallen under either SL or MRTA control. At the same time the US was able to obtain Peruvian support for a forward operations base (Santa Lucia) deep in the UHV. This initially served very well the DEA's Operation Snowcap and enabled the US sponsored, mobile police field forces (DIPOD) to position themselves favorably to better attack the narcotrafficker laboratory systems and airfields with helicopters. Coinciding with this was the public awareness programs fostered by the Peruvian government and supported to a large degree by US funding. Nonetheless, these efforts had no decisive effect in stemming the overall flow of coca-cocaine products out of Peru.

It was difficult for the Peruvian government to establish and maintain a permanent presence in the UHV. Only token attempts were made to control major towns and the police and government eradication teams were left largely on their own to confront the SL and MRTA guerrillas. That the intended use of herbicides failed to gain acceptance in the face of ecological concerns was a major setback for the US anti-drug policy and dashed any hopes for an easy solution to the eradication problem in the UHV. This meant that the traditional means of manual eradication, either pulling up the coca bushes or cutting them off at the stumps, would have to continue. That the police were often not available in sufficient force meant that the eradicators' lives were often placed in jeopardy when the SL and MRTA guerrillas were around. This slowed eradication down and in some cases brought it to a complete halt.

While the US Congress might have been an inhibiting factor in terms of financing the pursuit of an effective anti-drug policy in Peru due to doubts over the policy's potential for success, President Reagan always intervened and certified the anti-drug program for further funding. This was a positive element which overrode Congressional objections to a large degree and enabled a steady amount of funding to flow in support of the Country Team's efforts. Yet as the US government's support and enthusiasm for the anti-drug policy continued to rise, the government of Alan Garcia began to be more critical.

Garcia, as part of his overall change in policy, began to criticize the US programs in Peru. In addition, as a deliberate policy decision, he decided to only pay about a fifth of the Peruvian national debt service due to the international financial community and world leaders. Since Peru was seriously in arrears, the US Congress had its own reservations about approving more funding for Peru. Even so, the Country Team and US Department of State were able to obtain waivers so that funding continued. These were turbulent times for Peru as its economy was failing, debt and inflation were increasing and the SL insurgency was gradually expanding its operations, extending them into Lima proper.

The MRTA guerrillas were not idle either and their operations complimented to some degree those of the SL. The SL was also expanding its influence over the coca growing regions of southern Peru. That the US had focused in the main on the UHV was that much more of a detriment to its efforts at achieving success in suppressing the growth of coca throughout the remainder of Peru. The coca outside the UHV provided the narcotraffickers with up to a third of the coca paste they required to sustain their production operations.

Even as the US did successfully strike some of the laboratories and eliminate some of the narcotraffickers, the Colombian cartels adjusted their operations accordingly, sending their representatives into Peru to manage and oversee as required the smooth functioning of the cocaine production business. In addition they did not hesitate to use Brazilian territory to consummate their productive enterprises and trafficking. As a response the US pressed for an increased military presence on the part of the Peruvians in the UHV. Yet, when the Army was reintroduced into the region it faced the same dilemma over priorities as did its predecessors - to attack the guerrillas, or the coca growers and narcotraffickers. For national security reasons the natural inclination was to attack the guerrillas. The US was unhappy about this situation and vociferously worked to have the military engage itself more against the narcotraffickers. To this end the military found itself vulnerable and highly susceptible to bribes from the narcotraffickers themselves. In short the US anti-drug effort was once again undermined by the factor of corruption and the conflicts in policy. All the while the narcotraffickers continued to ply their trade.

The administration of President George Bush, while it did through its National Security Directive (NSD) 18 and the Andean Initiative make an effort to provide sufficient funding for its anti-drug programs in Peru, found the US anti-drug effort unable to overcome the multiple social-economic and political obstacles which continuously thwarted its progress. Bush, at both the Cartagena and San Antonio anti-drug summits argued for more intensive military involvement in the Peruvian UHV. The US involvement increased considerably in 1989 with intensified support from the US Southern Command (SOUTHCOM). The use of radars, intelligence gathering platforms, planning and operations teams, military trainers and contracted US personnel in support of the air, ground and riverine anti-drug activities, while innovative and effective as far as they went, still only accomplished a relative modicum of success.

The intransigence of some campesino farmers, the ability of the narcotraffickers to locate to points further north out of range of Santa Lucia and even outside the UHV itself or into neighboring countries (the *balloon effect*), the harassment by the SL, and the corruption of poorly paid police, military and judicial officials all cascaded against the progress of the US anti-drug policy in the early to mid-1990s. These countervailing factors tended to bog it down in a virtual quagmire of crosscurrents which inhibited its chances of realizing success. Likewise the inability to develop a suitable, competitive alternative crop to that of coca and a suitable market infrastructure contrasted starkly with the situation that found the price of coca dropping in late 1989 and early 1990 to the point where no profits could be made on the part of the coca growers. Here the USAID program still could not respond with an appropriate alternate crop in a timely manner to exploit the drop in coca prices. This lent further credence to the coca farmers' perception that it was still worth while to wait until the coca prices and profits eventually recovered. And they did.

The Alberto Fujimori administration's pursuit of an economic solution to the problems of Peru caused the US anti-drug policy to alter somewhat its own intended course or at least place more emphasis on economic alternatives. Fujimori took both a pragmatic and long term view of dire situation facing his country. From his perspective the SL had its roots in and was feeding off of the lack of economic opportunity as a basic pillar supporting the government's claim to legitimacy and the right to rule. For this reason at San Antonio he both reaffirmed his own economic policy and gave support for that portion of the Bush anti-drug policy that provided economic support as a priority over military support. Winning against the SL for Fujimori meant having as many people as possible on the government's side. To this end he decriminalized the growing of coca in an effort to co-opt the allegiance of the coca farmers. In short the Fujimori policy had the premise of turning the economy around so that the Peruvian President could then proceed to eliminate the threat of the SL guerrillas and the narcotraffickers at will. This did not mean that Peruvian anti-drug operations in the UHV would cease.

Despite intensified Peruvian Air Force activity, more active and efficient military and police operations, the declaration of emergency zones, the reorganization of commands and the wholesale purging of corrupted officials, the SL and the narcotraffickers were still able to pursue their flourishing businesses. Even USAID, which continued to find some coca farmers more responsive to alternate crops and development activities, was unable to satisfy all the demands placed upon it. In the meantime the US Congress showed considerable displeasure over the reports of ever increasing violence and human rights violations taking place in Peru on the part of the government's security forces. Citing human rights violations and corruption as factors in its decision, the Congress justifiably reduced US funding for the Peruvian military by almost a third. As time went on Fujimori himself became frustrated and convinced that a lethargic and unresponsive bureaucracy in Peru was holding the nation back in terms of making the required economic and security reforms to bring Peru out of its social-economic morass. He opted for an authoritarian solution to reestablish his authority with sufficient power so that it could effectively pursue his new initiatives for developing incentives and resources.

While Fujimori's actions were controversial and counter- productive in the short run, as the US and the international community suspended aid and financial support, he did garner support internally and consolidated his hold on the government. In addition he intensified operations in the UHV and proceeded to purge more judges and other government officials for corruption. Yet corruption, much like the SL guerrillas, was all pervasive and continuously undermined Fujimori's efforts in the UHV. This situation and the shooting down of the US C-130 aircraft placed a blight on the US military-to-military relationships with the Peruvian military and caused SOUTHCOM and even the ONDCP in Washington, D.C. to reappraise their anti-drug strategy in regards to Peru. Throughout this time the SL became a major distraction for the anti-drug effort in other parts of Peru as it continued its revolutionary campaign and engaged the Peruvian government in its own seat of power - Lima.

For Fujimori the exigencies of the moment dictated that there was no other alternative but to focus on the national security situation in Peru and Lima specifically. Nonetheless, the momentum being built up by the SL and MRTA guerrillas was temporarily stopped with the death or capture of many of the key guerrilla leaders. For the MRTA this proved to be decisive, but for the deeply rooted and well organized SL guerrillas it was a setback only in time. As such Fujimori realized that without a democratic initiative in play and the corresponding support of the international community he would merely contribute to his own failure as a leader. With his economy in decline and isolated from badly needed outside financial help, he had no choice but to begin a process of reestablishing the democratic process if he was to accomplish his original goals for Peru.

For the US anti-drug policy, it now found itself entering the mid-to-late 1990s somewhat in limbo. Despite a coca-killing fungus in play in the UHV and the US government's own attempts to salvage, refurbish and rejuvenate its anti-drug efforts and alternate development programs, the US anti-drug policy in Peru found itself stymied. After more than a decade of trying and apart from some limited aerial interdiction successes, it was not much more better off than when it started in terms of stifling the general flow of cocaine out of Peru. Besides cocaine to deal with, it now also had to deal with heroine producing poppies.

Having reviewed the actors and factors working for and against the US anti-drug policy in Peru, some observations are in order. No matter what can be said about the US anti-drug policy, it failed to come to grips with the reality that is Peru. This includes the Peruvian culture and traditions of the high-Andes population, the depressed social-economic and moral condition of Peruvian society, the tenacity and balloon-like flexibility of the narcotrafficking marketing systems, the fanaticism of the ubiquitous SL guerrillas and the intransigence of the entrepreneurial spirit and nature of the coca farmers who found a new and productive livelihood in the capitalist oriented, coca economy. In addition there were the bureaucracies and policies of both the US and Peruvian governments whose operations in the field often worked at cross purposes with each other. The other factor which may be the most important and most difficult to overcome is the high profitability of the narcotrafficking market system. It is a simple fact that, *if there are profits to be made, there is a market.* Unless the extreme profitability can be taken out of the cocaine market, in all likelihood it will continue to flourish in Peru and continue to trample over all who try to tilt against its profit "windmill."

In theory, the destruction of coca paste and cocaine producing laboratories should raise the risks and costs for narcotraffickers and refiners alike and increase to unreasonable highs the import purchase prices paid by the consumer. Likewise it is assumed that eradication, in conjunction with interdiction, will compound the risk and cost problem to such a degree that the coca grower will become disillusioned and close down his less than profitable business. This premise assumes that all coca profits are made on close margins. Supply and demand, the market logic of production and the social and economic realities of coca production in Peru work to undermine the theory in spades. There are too many *campesino* farmers, refiners, exporters and smugglers working in a loose, yet highly cohesive manner for the eradication-interdiction enforcement effort to stem or otherwise suppress the amount of cocaine being produced for US or European consumption.

While all elements in the drug production and marketing process receive profits based on prices paid, it is *the final price paid by the consumers that supports the whole process* and so badly undermines the anti-drug effort in Peru, as well as other Andean Ridge countries such as Bolivia. In short, narcotrafficking production has not diminished significantly. Even the fragmenting of the Cali and Medellin cartels in Colombia has not reduced narcotrafficking interest in Peru as a source of cocaine. With the Colombian cartels in disarray, narcotraffickers from Mexico have also entered directly into the Peruvian coca markets to ply their trade. (El Nuevo Herald 23 Jul 93) In the end cocaine base and HCl continue to flow into the US and Europe as the narcotraffickers continue to meet the demands of the international market.

What does this mean for both the US and Fujimori initiatives? It is very hard to be optimistic. To wean the coca grower away from his crop will be difficult at best. Unless the alternate crop or work place profit is competitive with the narcotraffickers' ability to pay several times over what he is currently paying for coca leaves, there is little or no incentive for the *campesino* to give up this form of livelihood. As there is no single alternate crop in existence in Peru that can compete with coca as a marketable substitute as long as there is a strong enough demand to keep the coca price above $50 per hundredweight, it appears that the Fujimori initiative, much like its US sponsored predecessors, is ultimately doomed to failure. This is not to say that it will not bring about the badly needed general economic reforms in Peru which will produce an overall financial uplift and generally improve standards of living for the masses. It undoubtedly will do this to some extent, even though it will take years if not decades to accomplish. Nonetheless, the coca economy is not dependent on the success or failure of the Fujimori reforms as its *key center of gravity or commercial momentum is derived from the demand of the consumer.*

Even if the Fujimori reforms should seriously undermine the SL revolutionary movement and bring about its eventual demise, the SL and MRTA guerrillas operating in the financially lucrative coca growing regions such as the Huallaga Valley could become independent and still carry on their operations. They still retain the ability to carry on a contraband-extortion type of operation in exchange for protection and become life-long bandits living off the land and "taxes" in the Latin America tradition. (Miami Herald 13 Jun 93) If the reports of $30 million per year in taxes collected by the SL guerrillas for its revolutionary war chest is correct, the lure of profits to be made would undoubtedly influence the situation in favor of the continuance of some from of the coercive activities that are currently going on in the UHV. Nonetheless, the SL has reorganized with one Maria Jenny Rodriguez Neyra (Comrade "Rita") having taken over the revolutionary effort as its principal director and leader in the field. (El Nuevo Herald 25 Jun 93) This undoubtedly means many more years of conflict for Peru. The MRTA on the other hand appears to be in permanent disarray as a number of its key leaders including Victor Polay Campos surrendered near Tarapoto in mid-1993. (El Nuevo Herald 11 Jun 93 and 22 Feb 94) This situation leaves the SL as the virtual sole contender against the government for control of the UHV and other coca growing areas of Peru.

The author encountered a perspective among some people in the Country Team in Lima in support of the rationale that coca should have a higher priority than the SL based on the argument that, by limiting coca production, one could eventually eliminate the financial support of the SL and MRTA guerrillas. While this has some plausibility and initial appeal, the reality of Peru suggests just the opposite. Only by breaking the SL and resolving the basic causes and appeal of its revolutionary movement can one begin to resolve the anti-drug issues in Peru. To this end the author sees no real progress as yet in resolving the disequilibrium and perverse social injustices on which basis Abimael Guzman was originally able to capture the willing allegiance of a small but fanatical following. (Miami Herald 26 Aug 91)

The Lima core will have to reach out and sincerely embrace and incorporate the high-Andean periphery in a series of fair and meaningful reforms from the point of view of the Indian-mestizo masses; otherwise the situation will remain the same with indeterminate strife continuing as one insurgency after another makes its bid to rectify the continuing socio-economic injustices that abound. To this end the summary executions, arbitrary detention, torture and rape on the part of the government's security forces (Miami Herald 2 and 8 May and 10 Jun 93; and El Nuevo Herald 2 and 7 May 93) will also have to be reformed and brought under control or the government will continue to lose key elements of its legitimacy and provide ample justification for not only the Sendero Luminoso's cause but for other insurgency efforts in the future.

One can not say that the US government has not spent enough money on its programs in Peru in support of its anti-drug policy or that there has not been sufficient support from Washington, D.C. Throughout the history of the US anti-drug effort in Peru and especially since the mid-

1980s, Peru has always received the critical US Presidential certifications as to its importance and status as a cooperating participant in the White House's drug war in the Andes. (House 1992: 300) To this end from 1984 to 1991 the US spent roughly $630 million on economic enhancement, development and food, and $137 million on narcotics and militarily related funding or a total of $768 million in its efforts to stem the tide of cocaine flooding the US. (CRS 1991: Appendix B) From 1991-1995 the US spent roughly $720 million on its anti-drug efforts in Peru as part of the Andean Initiative (Appendix F). Has this had an impact? Even the conservative estimates of coca production by the INM in its 1993 INCSR indicate the implications that the lack of success of the US anti-drug program in Peru means (Appendix E).

As a country, Peru still remains the largest producer of coca. This in itself prejudices the US anti-drug policy in Peru which has had little significant impact in stemming the up to 700 mt of cocaine base and HCl which is produced for the international consumer market every year. (DOS-INM 1993a: 13) Even if one factors in the SOUTHCOM-FAP aerial interdiction campaign, the anti-drug effort in Peru is interdicting or destroying not much more than roughly thirty metric tons of cocaine per year. In short well over 600 mt per year are successfully exported out of Peru each year.

Before embarking on the formulation of a foreign policy, such as the US anti-drug policy that was brought into play in Peru, as a first lesson it is essential that the agencies and personnel involved *review thoroughly the social-economic and political complexities and realities of the country which the policy is to address*. This should be done in as candid a manner as possible in terms of evaluating the chances for a policy to achieve its intended success. An accurate initial assessment of the potential countervailing factors and conditions within a country should reveal both the likely favorable and unfavorable impacts that could be expected. Out of this a judgement as to the policy's chances of success can be rendered. The crafters of the policy must have the courage to acknowledge and face the often complex realities of the host nation's situation. Then too, they must be forthright and candid in their reports and be willing to admit when there are sometimes too many countervailing factors in play to enable a policy to achieve its goals. This is particularly important when a policy is reassessed and evaluated after it has come into play. To pretend that a policy will be successful when it is not or not being willing to admit a policy is failing or has failed, usually means that money, time and resources will continue to be wasted in the pursuit of unattainable goals. That the US anti-drug policy in Peru was initially crafted and applied in what appeared to be a deceptively simple situation is understandable. What does stand out is that the policy was pursued for over a decade despite the fact that it was not achieving its goals. This could have been avoided had proper and candid assessments been made and applied.

Another lesson learned from the Peruvian experience is that a government cannot afford to allow a *single issue* to dominate its foreign policy agenda as the US tended to do in Peru where the host government has a number of national priorities which conflict with the interests of the US. Socio-economic and political factors such as the overall economic condition and a threatening insurgency do have an impact on domestic politics and should not be ignored by the US policy maker. A foreign policy should be crafted and adapted to meet the reality of the host nation's situation. If it is not, it faces the distinct possiblity of clashing with the host nation's own policies and creating otherwise avoidable frictions and even animosities. To not be flexible in the implementation of a policy or not be willing in the short term to subordinate it to a position of secondary importance in the face of other, more pressing priorities from the perspective of the host nation's leaders, means that your foreign policy may not be considered relevant, may never gain acceptance, and in the end may not have the opportunity to accomplish its stated objectives.

A third lesson stemming from this study is that the law of supply and demand - especially demand - is the driving force behind the Peruvian narcotrafficking situation. An anti-drug policy which only addresses the supply side of this issue is *doomed to being less than successful as long as a strong consumer demand is in play*. No matter how much destruction is levied against the narcotraffickers' production infrastructure, as long as sufficiently large profits are to be made from an incessant demand for the drug product, the production apparatus will regenerate itself automatically. This *self-generating aspect* of the drug trade in the current situation in Peru remains as a major countervailing dynamic which in itself prevents the US anti-drug policy from achieving its stated goals. The best that the policy can hope to achieve is merely push the drug enterprises around, temporarily disrupting some of their operations but not enough to keep them from producing the drug product in sufficient quantity to meet the consumers' demand. To this end the narcotraffickers overproduce and adapt their business operations to incorporate anticipated losses so as to compensate for government harassment and repression. In the case of Peru, the narcotraffickers, under attack from the joint airmobile and aerial counter-drug operations of the US and Peruvian governments, merely shifted their operations to other areas within Peru or over the border into Brazil as part of this balloon effect. Until demand reduction is achieved in the consumer nations, the US anti-drug policy in Peru will do little more than harass narcotrafficker operations without diminishing significantly cocaine or other drug production efforts.

A forth lesson learned in regards to Peru is that while a foreign policy may have a *national security imperative* as its basis this *may not be equally aplicable* to the conditions inside the country where the policy is being applied. In the case of Peru, dealing with the Sendero Luminoso and the dire economic situation, over time, became the driving imperatives which established the national priorities for the Peruvian government. As such it did not see narcotrafficking as relatively harmful, especially in light of the boost the proceeds from trafficking were giving the otherwise depressed economy. Neither did it want to seriously attack the coca farmers and destroy their livelihood when there was no other suitable economic alternative available into which they could transition. In short the national security imperative of the US foreign policy was irrelevant in Peru and the anti-drug policy was accepted on its merits as a low priority policy for the Peruvian government.

Foreign policy coherence as it relates to the region is a last lesson learned which is worth while addressing in regards to the US anti-drug policy experience in Peru. In this case the US anti-drug policy in Peru was essentially created and applied in a vacuum in regards to the remaining Andean countries noted in this study. In this sense there was no effort to relate the Peruvian anti-drug policy as part of an integrated strategy being applied throughout the region. This probably took place because there was, throughout the 1980s, no regional strategy in play. As such, what happened in Peru, while critically important in terms of coca paste and cocaine base production to the narcotraffickers, did not have a relevance to the US anti-drug policy elsewhere. Had this been so, the lack of real progress or success in Peru in the face of ever expanding or sustained relatively high levels of coca production should have caused policy makers to rethink the anti-drug problem in terms of their supply-side repression efforts. The possibility of an unsuccessful conclusion to the drug war and alternate solutions which might have better addressed the demand aspects of the problem in its totality, leading ultimately to supply-side success, if they were achievable at all could then have been addressed. In sum, if the end-game can not be achieved in one country which is an integral part of an overall problem, as Peru was for the US anti-drug policy, then the regional implications need to be carefully assessed and the foreign policy radically modified or even terminated.

In conclusion, I would like to point out that the US government badly overestimated its capacity to control and influence the flow of cocaine out of Peru. It pitted an anti-drug policy and strategy against a situation which simply had too many complicating factors and issues which, from the inception of the policy, worked to undermine its success. The US anti-drug policy became caught up in a conflict of interests between its own pursuit of the destruction of the Peruvian cocaine market and that of the Peruvian government which sought to confront both a failing economy and a vicious insurgency as its highest priorities. That the US policy did not address in a sound manner the overwhelming social and economic issues which contended with its success in Peru, indicates that it was a relatively inflexible, single issue foreign policy, attempting to dominate all other possible courses of action open to both it and the Peruvian government. To this end the policy became somewhat irrelevant to the Peruvian government's quest for survival and socio-economic rejuvenation.

Through a steady evolution the US anti-drug policy in the Andes had come full course. The ONDCP virtually admitted US policy failure and was forced to conclude that "illegal drugs continue to pose a significant threat to the country." (ONDCP 1994: 1) Domestic and foreign actors and factors had made their respective marks on the policy's implementation and progress. The significance of this effort is the subject of the final and concluding chapter.

In the end the US policy has failed because it could not effectively address the high demand, capitalist oriented market processes which exploited the abject poverty which is the norm in Peru today or the flexibility and agility of the narcotrafficking organizations which continued to operate despite any and all efforts to obstruct their respective operations. Despite the fact that Peru is the source for approximately two-thirds of the world's cocaine, the US policy, after more than a decade of attempting to turn back the tide, found itself unable to do so and is no better off than when it began. In sum, failure in Peru tends to prejudice the overall future of the US anti-drug policy effort throughout the Andean region.

Chapter 10

Final Observations, Lessons Learned and Conclusions

The US anti-drug policy for the Andean region from its inception was propelled forward by a number of positive factors and actors. Domestic pressures within the US made themselves felt as part of the democratic political process not only with the US Congress, but also during the national elections. Here too, the media highlighted the issue at hand. As the concern grew in the early 1980's, President Reagan declared "war" on drugs and provided the issue with a national focus at the highest levels of government. In addition, political promoters and even those opposed to the President's handling of the situation produced pressures which galvanized the government to further action. As a result anti-drug policy was formulated, monies allocated, and an initial anti-drug policy perspective based on supply side focused eradication in Bolivia and Peru came into play. Albeit disjointed, the policy was well under way by the end of 1984, being implemented by the respective Country Teams.

Nonetheless, by 1985 countervailing aspects primarily in the form of strong international market demand and the often enormous profits to be made in the narcotrafficking industry, as well as the intransigent coca and marijuana growers, were making themselves felt. These all took place in the context of dismal social-economic conditions which afflicted the principal source countries whose abundant, yet poor labor force sought relief through the generally higher standard of living that could be achieved through the wages earned from the production of coca leaves and their derivative coca paste and cocaine products. No other cash crop could compete with the coca leaves growing on the eastern slopes and valleys of the Andes mountains. This was only slowly and grudgingly appreciated by the US government, which after four years of counter-drug activities in the Andes still found that US domestic drug usage was escalating.

With drug policy failure a very distant possibility, President Reagan argued that the root cause of the American population's craving for and alarming use of drugs, especially cocaine, lay inside the source countries themselves. As a result, an essentially domestic issue was elevated to the national security level and on that basis narcotrafficking was declared a threat to the United States. That the threat was largely demand based appeared to be lost on the administration. Over time, the anti-drug policy in the Andes became militarized, beginning with Operation Blast Furnace in 1986. Militarization as a ramification of the national security imperative to "do something" about drugs was an event of considerable consequence. As a legacy, a crusading imperative came into play within the US government which drove the anti-drug policy and its promoting actors ever onward and, if nothing else, justified the additional billions of dollars in funding spent on its behalf.

Still, the government's anti-drug policy lacked coherence and it was not until the US Congress stepped in in the mid-1980s, with a serious legislative effort in the form of a series of anti-drug bills and acts, that a concerted effort was actually made to organize the government's effort in a structurally logical manner. The formation of the Office of National Drug Control Policy (ONDCP) in 1988 gave the Andean anti-drug effort a guiding hand. Through forced federal funding and the oversight of government agency budgets, the ONDCP helped to keep the anti-drug policy in play as a priority agenda item at all levels.

The all-pervasive countervailing effect of strong market demand incentives kept sufficient Andean people so attracted to the narcotrafficking business that the industry continued to flourish and grow as it provided more and more drugs to meet the international (US and Europe) consumer demand, offsetting the operating losses inflicted on it by such counter-drug activities as Operation Snowcap etc. Likewise, host nation governments realized that, while narcotrafficking was an underground economy, it did provide in some cases scores of thousands of jobs for the out of work and was a significant stimulant to their weak economies in the form of foreign exchange which they could not afford to lose. To eliminate the coca economy without some form of viable economic substitute which was equally supportive of the national economies, was essentially to commit economic suicide. Likewise, cultural traditions involving the perceived sacred nature of coca, in particular for much of the Andean Indian population, worked as another countervailing effect, undermining to a considerable degree both US and host country anti-drug endeavors.

President Bush, spurred on by the ever ominous statistics on domestic drug usage, implemented another national security directive in 1989 which once again gave the anti-drug policy a propelling boost in terms of spending. Likewise, the end of the Cold War essentially freed the US military to focus more of its assets in support of the Andean anti-drug policy. To this end Bush promulgated and brought into play the anti-drug strategy known as the Andean Initiative which was the product of a concerted effort on the part of the ONDCP and the US National Security Council. Certainly the policy was not wanting for attention at the highest levels of government. Fully supported by Congress, the Initiative was brought into play. Helping factors in the form of the Colombian government's counter-drug backlashes in response to drug cartel sponsored narco-terrorism gave the anti-drug effort in the Andes a cutting edge that it had not had before. Numerous narcotraffickers were on the run and their operations were being disrupted. Disrupted, temporarily quashed, but not eliminated.

Despite the coordinated focus given the Andean anti-drug policy by the ONDCP, after a mere two years (of a five year program), the now financially enhanced anti-drug policy was being reevaluated and even questioned in terms of its focus by the very office that was in charge of promoting it. A realization had begun to set in that something was not correct in the basic foundation or premise of the supply-sided policy focus. Assisting in this reflection was the economic development emphasis that the Andean countries insisted the US anti-drug policy have in order for it to work effectively.

While the logic of raising the standard of living of the coca farmers and the overall economies of the Andean nations did have considerable validity, it still flew in the face of the ubiquitous strength of the high profits and a strong market demand which enabled the entrepreneurial narcotraffickers to prevail. Only after some ten years of anti-drug effort did the US government (President Bush) begin to acknowledge that demand might be a stronger causal effect after all and that this also needed to be addressed for the supply side anti-drug policy to make any real progress. Yet, efforts to scale back the anti-drug policy in selected cases such as in Peru were immediately met with opposition from other government actors with multiple agendas such as the Department of

State which saw the promotion of democracy as an equal if not more important sustaining element in the general US foreign policy for the Andean region. To this end by the mid-1990s, the anti-drug policy in the Andes was at loggerheads with other US foreign policy interests and here the issue rests today.

While there are dozens of impacting actors and factors, they are not all of equal weight and should be evaluated in this light. The pattern of effects reveals that US anti-drug policy did rather poorly during the 1980s. During the 1990s the policy did have some positive successes in its favor in Bolivia, but in the case of Peru it still remained overwhelmed by countervailing factors. The overriding forces driving the US anti-drug policy forward were the US national security imperative, the US Congress, and bureaucratic momentum. The countervailing factors were the strong market demand for drugs and high profits that could be earned, narcotrafficker resiliency and the balloon effect which continued to inhibit the success of the US anti-drug policy. The reasons why these elements operated in the manner that they did and their implications are worth examining further.

Countervailing actors and factors that undermined the US anti-drug policy have now been enumerated. Deep-rooted and divisive Andean socio-economic problems tended to deflect the US anti-drug policy and neutralize its efforts almost from its inception. The balloon effect of shifting cocaine production across international borders into neighboring countries compensated for and offset the often increasing risks to narcotrafficking operations and the several, narcotrafficking violence-inspired crackdowns by the Colombian government, which was able to temporarily reduce cocaine processing activities, only to see production rebound, stimulated as it was by market demand incentives. There was also a commensurate lack of political will on the part of Andean nations and sometimes an inability to confront the narcotrafficker trade in the face of other, more pressing social-economic issues.

Andean domestic priorities involving the resolution of severe economic and political problems dominated host nation perspectives more often than not and served as distractors undermining the thrust of the US anti-drug policy. This was particularly true in the case of Peru. Institutionalized weaknesses involving corruption, the abuse of power, as well as normal human inefficiency and ineffectiveness all compounded the effects of the factors and actors working against the US anti-drug policy. That poorly paid police, judicial and military personnel were vulnerable to being compromised through corruption and intimidation placed in question their cooperation, loyalty, integrity and efficiency on which the success of an international drug-policy must ultimately depend.

The agility and adaptability of the drug traffickers constantly defied the US anti-drug efforts throughout the Andean region. Even when coca leaf prices dropped due to a glut on the market, the farmers themselves began to process their own leaf into the liquid form of coca past (*agua rica*) which could be stored in jugs and barrels until narcotrafficker buyers eventually arrived to purchase the liquid. Since coca and poppy crops consistently earned higher prices than most other competing cash crops, it was very difficult for US alternate crop and developmental aid programs to compete in a serious manner. Likewise, coca and poppy crops can grow in areas which are generally inhospitable to traditional crops. Steep slopes, acidic jungle soils and torrential tropical rains are conducive to the growing of the drug trades' staple crops.

Professor Bruce M. Bagley of the University of Miami (Coral Gables) has suggested that the perplexing US failure to develop a coherent strategy to stop the ever expanding production and flow of drugs into the US was based on the underlying premise of the anti-drug policy effort which he calls *realism*. (Bagely 1988: 190) To this end the state sensed that it was being threatened by foreign based narcotrafficking interests which were exploiting the American people who were perceived as innocent victims of a vicious, internationally based criminal conspiracy which was making money at the expense of the United States' health and moral values. Since, under the realist paradigm, the state will react out of self-preservation to protect itself by striking back at its adversaries, it was perfectly logical for the US as the hegemonic power in the Western Hemisphere and Andean region to assume the responsibility for enforcing international law and ensuring order and stability. Not to do so was perceived as endangering US national security and the stability of the international system as a whole. Thus the US government's leadership perceived that it had a right and a duty to seek a solution through a supply sided approach, persuading or compelling Bolivia and Peru to cooperate with the US anti-drug policy. (Bagely 1988: 197-198)

Yet the realist position assumed by both the Reagan and Bush administrations ignored or visibly underestimated the resiliency and self-generating aspect of the capitalist system's international market forces in favor of the drug trade which continued to respond to market demand signals as would any other enterprise when great profits were at stake. Strong market signals and the related high profits induced those involved in the drug trade to adapt to the US and Andean countries' anti-drug policy changes by circumventing or overriding the various states' efforts to regulate or suppress the trade. To this end the balloon effect came into play to circumvent any anti-drug policy effort that began to threaten and increase the operating costs and risks of the narcotrafficking business enterprise. In addition, in a market driven, commercial drug production and export situation such as that involving the Andean region, it matters little which type of regime, authoritarian or democratic is in power.

As professor Bagley points out, even authoritarian regimes such as existed in Bolivia and Peru under military rule during the 1970s have been unable or unwilling to control adequately their underground, narcotics supported economies. (Bagley 1988: 198) This is despite the centralizing power structures and relative absence of legal and human rights constraints on government action. In the case of generally more market-oriented and democratic systems, the state is constrained by the need to respect individual privacy and the civil liberties of its citizens. If the US could not permanently dismantle the mafia or eradicate its own multi-billion dollar a year marijuana cash crop, it is unlikely that generally weaker and less than fully institutionalized democracies would be able to disrupt for any length of time or even suppress the agile and wealthy criminal enterprises that have emanated from and are sustained by the drug trade.

It could be considered hypocritical of the US government to insist on eradication measures in the Andes when inside the US by the 1980s the level of domestic US marijuana cultivation had increased from about 2 percent of the world's marijuana trade to about 25 percent by 1986, with US farmers growing an estimated 2,000 mt annually. (GAO 1988: 15-18) That resistance took place within the marijuana growing US population to government countermeasures was indicative of what one could also expect from peasant coca farmers in the Andean region who could not see an advantage in switching to alternate crops for which a market infrastructure did not exist, or even if it did, did not provide a monetary return commensurate to that of coca. In this respect Andean coca farmers and US marijuana farmers had something in common. This begs other questions.

If the anti-drug issue was such a high priority issue that it was of relevance at the national security level for the White House, then why was it allowed to be diluted or even undercut by federal budgetary constraints and competing domestic and foreign policy initiatives and ventures? Why did the White House allow government actors and factors such as the Department of Agriculture or budget crises to deter or diminish its efforts in pursuing its agenda to counter the alleged threat to national security? To this end the ONDCP should have been given the authority to command and enforce its will to ensure that proper coordination was taking place on a national, regional and even local (host country) level in order to effect a sound policy and see it through to a final resolution. If a vital US national security interest really was at stake and society's survival was indeed in jeopardy as the raising of the drug issue to a high priority national security level implied, then an all out war in the classical sense should have been waged and even declared as such by Congress to deal with the problem.

It is my judgement that, since the drug threat's causal roots actually lay in the US domestic society's ever increasing demand and willingness to pay high prices for the stimulants, the supply side anti-drug policy could never really ignore this base aspect or societal fault. The US and Europe's populations' complicity in providing the market incentive for narcotrafficking meant that the US anti-drug policy could never garner the support it needed to overcome the many faceted factors and actors bombarding it as it came into play in the Andes. In sum, the anti-drug problem was a weak national security issue at best and this contributed to the incompatibility of the anti-drug policy's overall objectives with those of other agencies within the US government.

After having spent some $50 billion in anti-drug funding over a ten-year period, the majority of which had been consumed in the supply-side strategy, in terms of reducing the flow of cocaine supplies into the US, the federal government's Andean anti-drug policy was not much better off than when it had started. From 1988 to 1992 cocaine supplies actually increased about 165 percent, going from 400 mt to nearly 1,000 mt (Figure 7). In short, after twelve years of effort, the US anti-drug policy was achieving far less than the anticipated success it was expected to be.

This reflected the increased consumption taking place inside the US (based on emergency room mentions for 1992) which indicated that the demand for cocaine was as strong, if not stronger than in 1988 or well after the Andean Initiative was implemented. Estimated cocaine consumption inside the US for 1992 was 291 mt. This was out of an estimated 430 mt available inside the US or about half of the 955 mt to 1165 mt of cocaine estimated to have been produced in that year by Bolivia, Peru and Colombia together. (ONDCP 1994: 15, 17, and 103) That the US government had intercepted and seized 108 mt in FY 93 inside the US proper and a further 163 mt of cocaine in Mexico, Central

America and the Caribbean transit zones appeared to have no impact on the availability of cocaine HCl on the street. (DOS INM: 1994: 3 and 71) The ONDCP estimated that Americans were spending $49 billion annually on illegal drugs and that 5 percent of the population remained in the drug user category. (ONDCP 1994: 100 and 105)

That the drug crisis in the US was presented as a national security issue tended to exaggerate its actual significance and deflected attention away from its domestic roots to a focus on a false center of gravity in an international arena. It is not the first time that this has happened. During the 1960s President Lyndon Johnson conjured up a national security image that implied if not alleged that an American setback in the face of a communist insurgency in Vietnam was a threat to vital national interests and would place in jeopardy the survival of the US. Based on an actually weak national security interest, the US military was pitted against a false center of gravity in South Vietnam. For ten years the US pursued a policy which, although it achieved numerous tactical successes, in the end was a strategic failure and had no impact on US national security at all. A similar situation has occurred in the Andean region where the US expended up to $8 billion on behalf of its anti-drug policy efforts over the period of a decade, achieving no significant results in stemming the ever rising tide of drugs entering the US consumer market. Here too, numerous tactical success were achieved, but in the end they have been irrelevant in the face of strategic anti-drug policy failure.

Both the Reagan and Bush administrations alleged that the narcotraffickers' production capability was the root cause of the US drug problem. By turning this into a national security issue, they caused the US military to become engaged in a war which had no clearly defined or structured enemy against which it could pit its manpower and firepower to achieve decisive results. The amorphous, regenerative nature of the drug trade's commercial enterprises became readily apparent over time. No sooner was one laboratory seized or destroyed than another surfaced in its place - not to confront the US and host country military or police nemesis, but to meet the overwhelmingly strong international market demand!

In the Andes the US and host nation military and police forces were chasing the illusion of a center of gravity and instead found themselves engaged against a proverbial *hydra's head* in the form of a flourishing industry influenced by huge profits, whereby the more loses that are inflicted on it, the more it redoubles its own efforts to sustain itself. Laboratories, aircraft, production apparatus, narcotrafficking personnel, assets, coca and precursor chemicals could all be seized or destroyed in large quantities, but the system, under the influence of the strong international market demand, simply regenerated itself.

Another point to be made in this regard is that before entering into the promulgation of policy which has international implications and faces any form of potential countervailing actors and factors as obstacles, a government ought to clearly define the problem it confronts before attempting to formulate a solution. Not to do so may bring into play policy initiatives which often work against each other or are overwhelmed by actors and factors which can neutralize the intended outcome of the policy. The US did exactly this by generating a national security imperative without conducting an in depth analysis of the actual roots of the narcotrafficking phenomena and its sustaining market forces. As such it was not until the formation of the ONDCP that a study of this nature was attempted. Here again the national security imperative produced an unintended momentum which, despite the analysis made in 1989, kept the US anti-drug policy focused on the Andean source countries of Bolivia and Peru, distorting the reality of the drug trafficking situation and prejudicing the possibility of an unvarnished appraisal of what the US was actually confronting and what the solution really involved. Improving policy efficiency was the overriding concern and not reappraisal. To this end the government was distracted away from the primary cause of the drug phenomenon - domestic consumer demand, focusing more on the resultant symptoms in the Andean source countries.

Here also, there appears to be a bureaucratic momentum or politics which holds sway over government policies once they come into play. In this sense, despite the fact that over time a number of government actors, including the US government's own General Accounting Office (GAO) in a dozen or more major reports, began to realize that the US anti-drug policy for the Andes was not well conceived and even irrational in not lending itself to a solution to the domestic drug problem, the process of bureaucratic politics took hold to keep the policy in play. Official reports from respected US government agencies such as the GAO, indicating that the anti-drug policy in the Andean region was not achieving its goals, were merely ignored by the White House and other government policy-making agencies since the reports did not support the desired policy in play. From 1988 into the early-1990s US Presidents were formally certifying that Peru and Bolivia were all in compliance with US anti-drug policy goals when in fact there were a myriad of known shortcomings which this study has pointed out. These should have caused the policy to be reevaluated and redirected or curtailed as appropriate. Certification, in this case, merely justified the continued spending of monies often in support of dubious anti-drug policy efforts.

An essentially irrational policy was being driven on by an otherwise rational bureaucratic process which, through its prerogatives, budgets, and survival instinct, was doing everything possible to justify its existence. Professor Eduardo Gamarra of Florida International University contends that this is a typical yet serious negative characteristic of government bureaucratic processes worldwide. Graham Allison discuses this phenomena in his *Essence of Decision* (p. 144-147) and concludes that bureaucratic offices will use their own institutional figures and statistics to justify not only their own existence but also that of a supporting initiative or policy in play. In the case of the US anti-drug policy, the Department of State's Bureau of International Narcotics Matters (INM) did this and increased its budget accordingly. The DEA pursued this in its operations in the Andes as did SOUTHCOM, increasing their budgets accordingly.

Often, "success" is defined by the institution involved in policy development, even as the implementation process occurs. Reams of statistics about the number of traffickers arrested, laboratories destroyed, hectares of coca eradicated, gallons of precursor chemicals and kilograms of coca paste, cocaine base and cocaine HCl captured have been proffered as evidence and proofs that the US anti-drug policy was working and, even if it was not working all that well, that it should still be pursued. When it was obvious that the policy was less than successful as reflected in the statistics, institutional goals were then modified and adapted to the new situation. This tended to mesh policy goals to the results being produced and made the policy "look" better, enhancing its acceptability beyond what it should have been. The ONDCP did this on two occasions with the Andean strategy of the early-1990s.

Had US domestic drug usage and its relationship to market demand and profit incentives, as the driving forces behind the international narcotrafficking, been identified early on or around 1982 and accepted by the US government as a key center of gravity, a more rational approach to dealing with the drug problem might have been achieved. Certainly this was recognized by the RAND corporation and among certain members of the US Congress and the Department of Defense. Nonetheless, this perspective, because it tended to place the American people and their value systems at fault, was not accepted by either

Presidents Reagan or Bush, although the latter was forced to admit in the 1990s at the anti-drug summits that demand was a factor to be considered seriously in the narcotrafficking problem. As it was, the demand aspect was either underestimated or not fully appreciated and, as a result, the government meandered for over a decade promoting an international anti-drug policy which produced impressive statistical results but no real solution to the actual domestic problem facing the US.

The US was not the only demand market for Andean drugs and this also produced an effect which undermined the anti-drug policy more and more over the years. Europe, the Middle East and even Japan were strong alternative markets where their own demands for drugs provided sufficient incentives for traffickers to continue to produce and supply their drug products. This took place even though the US market might decline or even became over saturated. This could be called a market balloon effect which constantly worked to undermine the US anti-drug policy's supply and transhipment interdiction efforts. By the mid-1980s the US government had available to it a cogent study by Peter Reuter of the Rand Corporation which clearly demonstrated the cocaine farm to market price chain (Figure 1).

The Rand study's 1986 data implied quite clearly that with most of the profits from the cocaine industry occurring after the drug enters the US, interdiction in the source countries is not a realistic cost-deterrent to the narcotraffickers. While the price to produce enough coca leaf to make one kilogram (2.2 pounds) of coca is between $65 and $370, the finished product enters the US, is diluted, broken down into smaller increments and then sold at selling prices which garner between $70,000 and $300,000 per kilogram. This meant that there was a tremendous market incentive or demand pull with which to sustain narcotrafficking as a viable commercial enterprise in the Andean region. This was also reflected in the production of coca as the staple cash crop supporting the manufacturing of cocaine.

The amount of coca produced in the Andes has been a seminal indicator and measure of US anti-drug policy progress and success from the perspective of the US Congress and most of the rest of the US government. If one reviews the last five years of Andean coca cultivation, what relatively small successes the US has achieved in eradication was more than offset by coca production in Peru (Appendix E). If eradication was so important to the US government, it would seem fit that Peru would have been made the centerpiece of the US Andean anti-drug effort. That it was not should not belie its importance as a potent source of coca leaves and the resultant coca and cocaine products derived thereof. In short, the world wide coca leaf production which was concentrated for the most part in the Andes consistently increased in metric tonnage from 1987 through 1992. This took place despite two national security imperatives (NSDD 221 and NSD 18) and Operation Snowcap and the Andean Initiative.

The ever increasing narcotrafficking production phenomenon occurred in the face of and paralleled the US government's ever increasing efforts to reduce if not eliminate it. In short, cocaine production went from about 250 mt in the early 1980s to roughly 1,000 mt by 1992 (Figure 7), while US government spending in support of a variety of programs, but most importantly Operation Snowcap and the Andean Initiative, increased significantly (Figure 8).

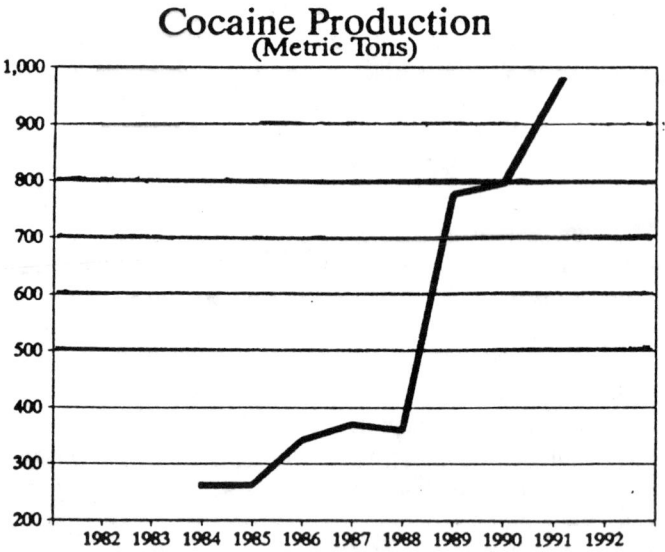

Figure 7

Source: DEA NNICC in House Committee on Foreign Affairs Hearings 3-4 and 11-12 March 1992, p. 13.

Source: DEA NNICC in House Committee on Foreign Affair Hearings 3-4 and 11-12 March 1992, p. 7.

Figure 8

The implication depicted here is that the more the US spent to inhibit or disrupt narcotrafficking, the harder the narcotraffickers worked to expand their production efforts to meet the international market demand and offset the incremental losses that the US anti-drug policy was able to inflict on their production and transhipment operations. Drug supplies consistently entered the US and were available in sufficient quantity to meet the user's needs. Curtailing local, third world support for narcotrafficking may be impossible as long as poverty, inadequate development and debt make drug trafficking economically rational to not only those attempting to improve their livelihood but also the nations which find themselves in deep economic crisis with no immediate solution at hand. One cannot expect a nation dependent on drug-trafficking to any degree or a segment of its population to commit economic suicide when there is no suitable alternative available. Otherwise poor coca and poppy farmers pursue these cash crops because there are few, if any, economic alternatives which are as viable. This will likely remain the case as long as there is a strong market demand for cocaine and heroin. Economically dependent governments will also tend to continue to tolerate narcotrafficking because they know that to reduce it without bringing into play a commensurate economic alternative will merely eliminate a significant source of valuable and badly needed foreign exchange currency. Only economic development can alter this situation to any degree over time.

Serious domestic problems such as drug usage generally tend to have their roots in society at large and the value systems in play. To elevate a serious domestic issue to the level of state national security, as the US did arbitrarily with its domestic drug problem, only clouds the issue and creates more problems and obstacles than it solves, avoiding an open-minded, rational approach to examining the actual causal nature of the societal problem and determining the most appropriate solution. This the US unfortunately did for more than a decade, merely delaying the time of eventual recognition that the educational and treatment process is the basis for a long term solution to the drug problem.

The demand inspired, profit-making incentives of the international drug market tend to overwhelm the supply oriented interdiction solutions and keep narcotrafficking in play. Narcotrafficking infrastructure in this case will merely tend to replace itself and cover its losses due to the activities of an anti-drug policy. This is considered by the traffickers as merely part of their operating expenses. In addition, the more intensively the government pursues the traffickers, increasing their operating risks, the resulting pressures generated will tend to move the trafficking enterprises around (the balloon effect), displacing them rather than stamping them out.

Since the drug industry purchases coca leaf or poppies directly from the farmer and coca paste or gum opium directly from the maturation and processing centers respectively, for any other agricultural alternative to succeed, the marketing and distribution processes and systems of the traffickers must be replicated in terms of ease of production, marketing and relative profits. If this is not done then it is unlikely that any form of alternate corps will be likely to succeed.

It should be remembered that the national security perspective of one nation is not necessarily the same perspective of another. In this case both Bolivia and Peru did not generally accept narcotrafficking as threatening to their societies but looked at economic problems and, in the case of Peru, insurgency situations as far more important, eclipsing the US anti-drug policy imperative. A single issue foreign policy, unless it coincides with host nation interests, is not likely to prevail for long in the face of long-term sustaining interests such as political and economic stability, preserving democracy, respect for human rights and the resolution of dire economic conditions, insurgencies and poverty afflicting the destiny of the nation. In this respect host nation cooperation is critical. Issues of national sovereignty will often surface to plague a policy which is not of consequence to the interests of the host nation's leaders. Policy will also often come into conflict with the host nation's leadership and concepts of national sovereignty when a hegemonic nation such as the US attempts to assert its own policies. This may lead to cool if not bitter relationships.

Finally, a government should pay attention to and be receptive of negative as well as positive feedback and evaluations of its policy initiatives. Here too, if the foreign policy advocates can not see their way clearly, or there are natural countervailing factors intervening to disrupt a policy's progress, then it is well to retrench and reappraise the situation. If you do not know where you are going with a policy or cannot see a clear path leading to policy success, then it is very possible that you should not be embarking on that particular policy effort in the first place. Vietnam in years past and the Andean region today, as well as other situations such as that of Somalia in Africa have appeared to US policy makers as deceptively simple problems, easy to resolve at the onset, but plagued with countervailing actors and factors over the long term. In short, policy makers need to look before they jump.

The reality of US interests in Latin America, involving democratization, regime stabilization, human rights and economic development has tended over the years to mellow the national security imperative of the US anti-drug policy in the Andean region and reduce it to the reality it actually is - a domestic based issue involving considerable social concern. For this reason it was never able to garner the all-out support that it should have merited had it in reality been a threat to the national security of the US.

Short-run domestic political pressures, partisan posturing and electoral cycles all have tended to push the anti-drug imperative onward in uneven thrusts rather than in a steady, relentless manner through the rigorous calculations of costs and benefits for US national interests over the long run. This, in conjunction with a rational, self-serving bureaucratic momentum has tended to make an otherwise irrational policy palatable, giving it a prominence and life which has sustained it far beyond what one would expect from a less than successful policy. The end result of the US anti-drug policy has been that, after more than a decade of effort, more cocaine is being produced and transhipped to the US and the world than ever before. The unintended and adverse consequences of the source or supply-oriented US anti-drug policy have been to actually fuel the continuing expansion and mobility of the coca cultivation and processing activities, not only throughout the Andes but also inside neighboring countries such as Brazil. In effect this process has neutralized the intended effect of the policy for shutting down narcotrafficking operations in general.

As long as the US or international market for narcotics remains highly profitable, traffickers will have an incentive to continue in this type of enterprise and will remain motivated to develop innovative ways to produce and smuggle drugs to supply the demand. To this end they will be able to marshall the resources required to circumvent or override whatever supply oriented enforcement efforts the Andean countries of Bolivia and Peru and the US anti-drug policy are able to undertake. As a result, they will continue to attempt to produce drugs for the US consumer market.

The US Andean anti-drug policy embraced a strategy which was targeted on a false center of gravity - supply. The strategy did not produce the results intended by the anti-drug policy because the demand side of the problem, or the international market pressures generated by millions of drug consuming customers, had not been properly analyzed and suitably addressed. Demand was the driving force behind this fundamentally very commercial, profit making enterprise. Until the US domestic demand issue is seriously addressed through intensive education and proper treatment as the first priority in reducing the consumer market, the supply side or narcotrafficker phenomenon will continue to flourish. In addition, because the cocaine industry in the Andes is demand driven, until the US can reduce consumer demand not only in the US but also other parts of the world, the international drug industry will continue to sustain itself indefinitely.

By promoting strong constitutional and democratic government in the Andean region, along with balanced and sustained economic growth which supports the vast majority of the local populations, the US can, up to a point, reduce the economic dependence of Bolivia and Peru on coca-cocaine products as well as other drugs. Nonetheless, without parallel, fundamental national economic, social and political reforms to address the domestic issues and problems surfaced by this study, it is unlikely that US anti-drug policy efforts in those countries over the long term will garner any lasting success. In the long run, the countervailing actors and factors involving national sovereignty, corruption, bureaucratic politics, base economics, the market demand and its related high profits will continue to impact on any anti-drug policy in the Andes, determining its ultimate course and final destiny for better or worse.

Appendix A

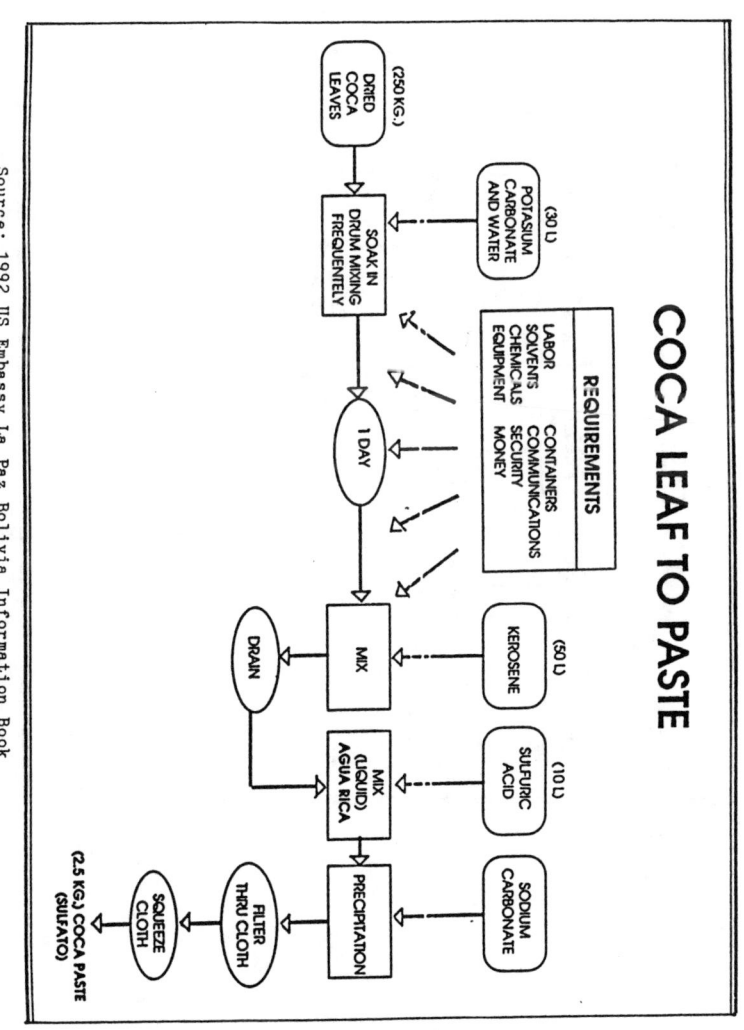

Source: 1992 US Embassy La Paz Bolivia *Information Book*

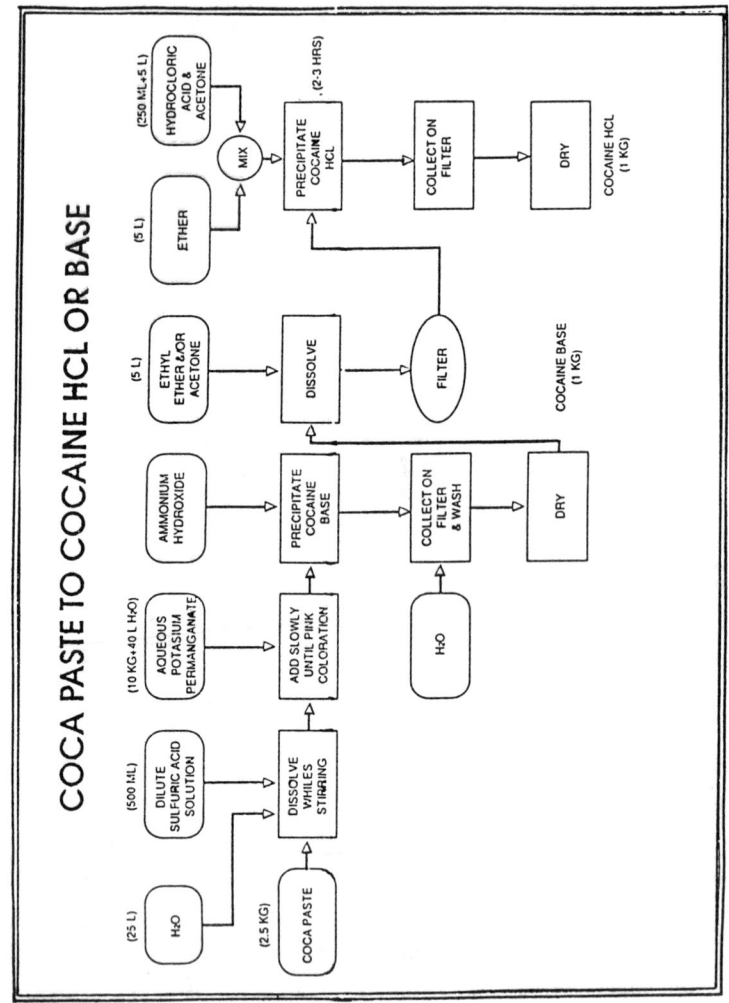

Appendix B

National Drug Control Program Agencies

Office of National Drug Control Policy

Department of Justice
Drug Enforcement Administration
Federal Bureau of Investigation
U.S. Attorneys
Tax Division
Criminal Division
U.S. Marshals Service
Bureau of Prisons
Immigration and Naturalization Serivice
Office of Justice Programs
INTERPOL/U.S. National Central Bureau

Department of the Treasury
U.S. Customs Service
Financial Crimes Enforcement Network
Internal Revenue Service
Bureau of Alcohol, Tobacco and Firearms
Secret Service
Federal Law Enforcement Training Center

Department of Transportation
U.S. Coast Guard
Federal Aviation Administration
National Highway and Traffic Safety
   Administration

Department of Agriculture
Agricultural Research Service
U.S. Forest Service

Department of the Interior
Bureau of Land Management
National Park Service
Bureau of Indian Affairs
Fish and Wildlife Service

Department of State
Bureau of International Narcotics Matters
Bureau of Politico/Military Affairs

Department of Defense

Department of Housing and Urban Development

Department of Labor

Department of Veterans Affairs

U.S. Judiciary

Agency for International Development

U.S. Information Agency

Central Intelligence Agency

In addition, though they are not National Drug Control Program Agencies, the following accounts are part of the National Drug Control Program Budget:

Special Forfeiture Fund (ONDCP)

Asset Forfeiture Fund (Justice)

Organized Crime Drug Enforcement Task Forces (Justice)

Office of Territorial and International
   Affairs

Department of Health and Human Services
Alcohol, Drug Abuse, and Mental Health
   Administration
Indian Health Service
Food and Drug Administration
Office of Human Development Services
Centers for Disease Control
Family Support Administration

Department of Education
Office of the Assistant Secretary
   for Elementary and Secondary Education
Office of the Assistant Secretary
   for Post-Secondary Education
Office of Educational Research and
   Improvement
Office of Special Education and
   Rehabilitative Services

Support for Prisoners (Justice)

Emergencies in the Diplomatic and Consular Service (State)

Appendix C

Andean Strategy Narcotics Related Funding: Bolivia 1990-1994
(in millions of dollars)

Programs	FY 90	FY 91	FY 92	FY 93	FY 94	TOTAL
Military Assistance	$ 33.7	$ 40.9	$ 40.9	$ 40.9	$ 40.9	$197.3
Economic Assistance	95.8	130.8	130.8	130.8	130.8	528.9
Law Enforcement	15.7	15.7	15.7	15.7	15.7	78.5
DEA Support	6.6	6.6	6.6	6.6	6.6	33.0
TOTAL	96.7	159.0	194.0	194.0	194.0	837.7

Source: Office of National Drug Control Policy, June 20, 1990

Appendix D

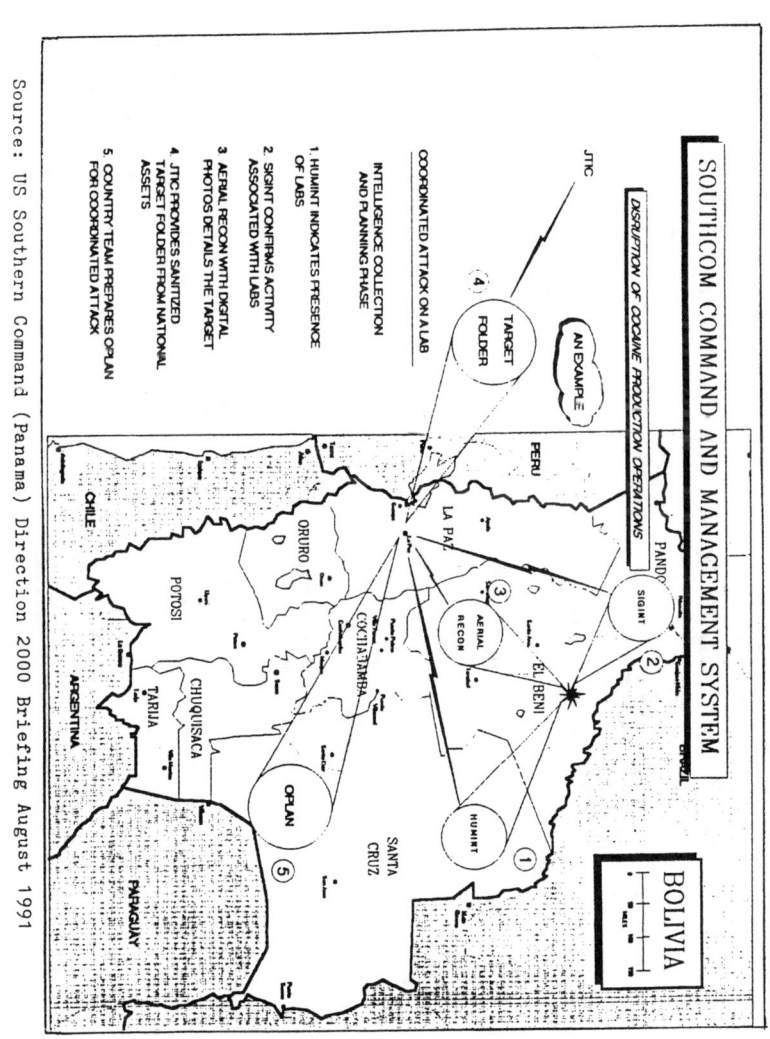

242 Fire in the Andes

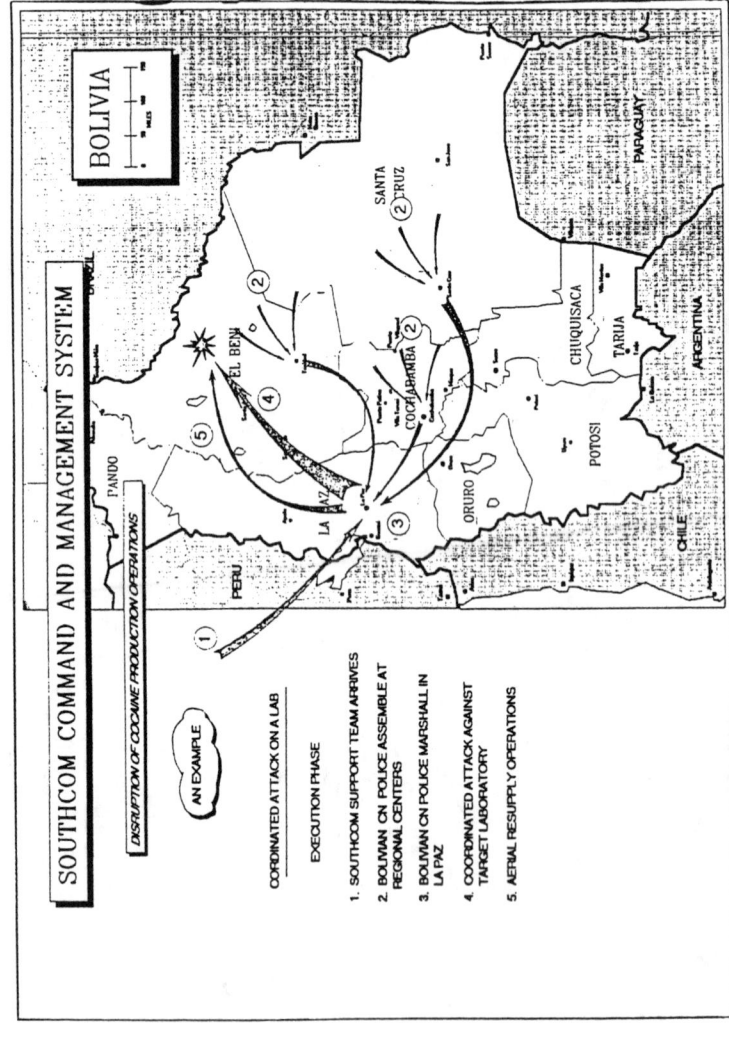

Source: US Southern Command (Panama) Direction 2000 Briefing August 1991

Appendix E

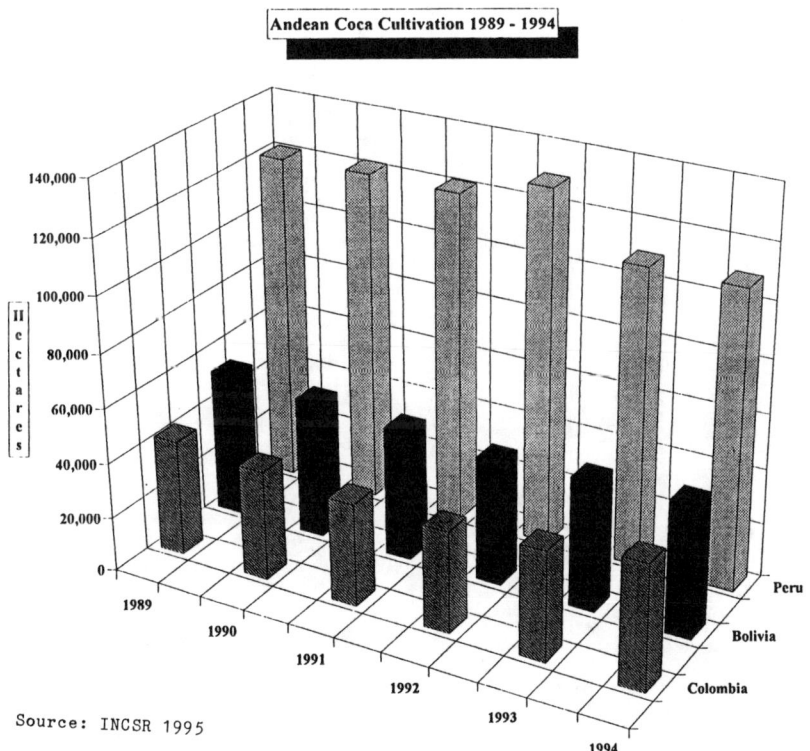

Source: INCSR 1995

Appendix F

Andean Initiative 5-Year Funding For Peru: 1990-1994
(in millions of dollars)

Programs	FY 90	FY 91	FY 92	FY 93	FY 94	TOTAL
Military Assistance	$ 36.5	$ 39.9	$ 39.9	$ 39.9	$ 39.5	$196.1
Economic Assistance	4.3	63.1	103.1	103.1	103.1	376.7
Law Enforcement	19.0	19.0	19.0	19.0	19.0	95.0
DEA Support	6.8	6.8	6.8	6.8	6.8	34.0
TOTAL	66.6	128.8	168.8	168.8	168.8	701.8

Source: Office of National Drug Control Policy, 20 June 1990 in House Report 101-991 (30 November 1990), 17.

Bibliography

Primary Sources

Government/Official Reports

CEDIB (Centro de Documentacion e Informacion - Bolivia). 1992. *Coca - Cronologia Bolivia: 1986 - 1992*. La Paz: CEDIB
Embassy of Peru. 1991. "Executive Summary" in *Peruvian Proposal On Drug Control And Alternative Development* (translated from the Spanish). Washington, D.C.: January.
Inter-American Commission on Human Rights (IACHCR). 1991. *Annual Report of The Inter-American Commission On Human Rights 1990 - 1991*. Washington, D.C.: Organization of American States (OAS).
Inter-American Development Bank (IADB). 1987. *Economic and Social Programs in Latin America: 1987 Report*. Washington, D.C.: Inter-American Development Bank.
_____. 1988. *Economic And Social Programs in Latin America: 1988 Report*. Washington, D.C.: Inter-American Development Bank.
International Monetary Fund. 1990. *International Financial Statistics*. Washington, D.C.: International Monetary Fund.
Ministerio de Asuntos Campesinos y Agropecuario - MACA. 1992. *Resumen de Programas y Projectos de Desarrollo Alternativo y Principales Resultados Alcanzados Hasta 1991*. La Paz, Bolivia. 12 May.
Ministerio de Relaciones Exteriores y Culto - MFRC. 1993. *Analisis del Estado de Nuestras Relaciones Con Los Estados Unidos*. La Paz, Bolivia. March.
National Institute on Drug Abuse (NIDA). 1990-1991. *NIDA Notes*. Washington, D.C.: Department of Health And Human Services.

Office of National Drug Control Policy (ONDCP). 1989. *National Drug Control Strategy*. Washington, D.C.: US Government Printing Office.
_____. 1990. *National Drug Control Strategy*. Washington, D.C.: US Government Printing Office.
_____. 1991. *National Drug Control Strategy*. Washington, D.C.: US Government Printing Office.
_____. 1992. *National Drug Control Strategy: A Nation Responds to Drug Use*. Washington, D.C.: US Government Printing Office.
_____. 1992a. *Selected Seizure Statistics* (fact sheet). Washington, D.C.: ONDCP, April.
_____. 1992b. *1992 National Drug Control Strategy Executive Summary*. Washington, D.C.: US Government Printing Office.
President's Commission on Organized Crime. 1986. *America's Habit: Drug Abuse, Drug Trafficking and Organized Crime. Report to The President and Attorney General*. Washington, D.C.: US Government Printing Office. March.
Seyler, Daniel J. 1991. *A.I.D. and Narcotics Control: An Issue Brief*. Washington, D.C.: Agency for International Development, 3 April.
Shapiro, Charles. 1991. Letter. Bureau of International Narcotics Matters (INM). US Department of State. 4 April.
Taft-Morales, Maureen. 1990. *Peru: Country Background Report* Washington, D.C.: Congressional Research Service.
United Nations (UN). 1990. *Handbook of International Trade and Development Statistics*. New York: United Nations.
_____. 1990a. *Basic Indicators*. New York: United Nations.
_____. Children's Fund (UNICEF). 1989. *State of The World's Children*. New York: United Nations.
U.S. Agency For International Development (USAID). 1986. *A Review of AID's Narcotics Control Development Assistance Program (AID Evaluation Special Study No. 29)*. Washington, D.C.: Agency For International Development.
_____. 1991a. *Alternative Development Strategy (ADS)*. Washington, D.C.: Agency For International Development.
_____. 1991b. *Evaluation Summary* (ES). Washington, D.C.: Agency For International Development. March.

_____. 1991c. *Audit of USAID/Bolivia's Chapare Regional Development Project No. 511-0543* Washington, D.C.: Agency for International Development. 29 August.

_____. 1992. *Andean Counter-Drug Initiative Quarterly Report (January-March 1992).* Washington, D.C.: Agency For International Development. May.

US Department of The Army (DA). 1991. *Bolivia* DA Pam 550-66. Washington D.C.

US Department of Health and Human Services (DHHS). 1987. *Trends in Drug Abuse Related Hosptial Emergency Room Episodes and Medical Examination Cases for Selected Drugs DAWN 1976-1985.* Rockville, Maryland: CSR Incorporated.

_____. 1987a. *Cocaine Client Admissions 1979-1984.* Rockville, MD: CSR Incorporated.

_____. 1991. *Drug Abuse and Drug Abuse Research.* Rockville, MD: CSR Incorporated.

_____. 1991a. *Annual Emergency Room Data 1990.* Maryland: CRS Incorporated.

_____. 1991b. *National Household Survey on Drug Abuse: Highlights 1990.* Rockville, MD: Research Triangle Institute.

US Department of State (DOS). 1992. *International Narcotics Control Foreign Assistance Appropriation Act (INCFAAA) Year 1992 Budget Congressional Submission.* Washington, D.C.: Department of State.

_____. 1992a. *Declaration of San Antonio.* Washington, D.C.: Department of State. 30 July.

_____. 1992b. *Colombia Fact Sheet.* Washington, D.C.: Department of State.

_____. 1993. *The Budget in Brief Fiscal Year 1994.* Washington, D.C.: Department of State.

_____. Bureau of International Narcotics Matters (INM). 1987. "FY 1989-1991 Policy Guidance for Narcotics Control Programs," INM internal document. Washington, D.C.: US Department of State, March.

_____. INM. 1988. "FY 1989-1991 Policy Guidance for Narcotics Control Programs," INM internal document. Washington, D.C.: US Department of State, September.

_____. INM. 1990. *International Narcotics Control Strategy Report (INCSR) 1990.* Washington, D.C.: Department of State.

_____. INM. 1991. *International Narcotics Control Strategy Report (INCSR) 1990*. Washington, D.C.: Department of State.

_____. INM. 1992. *International Narcotics Control Strategy Report (INCSR) 1991*. Washington, D.C.: Department of State.

_____. INM. 1992a. *International Narcotics Control Strategy Report (INCSR) 1991*. Washington, D.C.: Department of State.

_____. INM. 1993a. *International Narcotics Control Strategy Report (INCSR) 1992*. Washington, D.C.: Department of State.

_____. INM. 1993b. *International Narcotics Control Strategy Report Executive Summary (INCSR-ES)* 1992. Washington, D.C.: Department of State.

_____. INM. 1994. *International Narcotics Control Strategy Report (INCSR) 1993*. Washington D.C.: Department of State.

_____. INM. 1995. *International Narcotics Control Strategy Report (INCSR) 1994*. Department of State.

_____. INM. 1996. *International Narcotics Control Strategy Report (INCSR) 1995*. Washington, D.C.: Department of State.

_____. Bureau of Public Affairs. 1992. *Declaration of San Antonio*. Washington, D.C.: Department of State.

_____. Office of Inspector General (IG). 1989. *Report of Audit Memorandum No. 9CI-007*. Washington, D.C.: Department of State.

_____. IG. 1991. *Drug Control Activities in Bolivia: Audit Report 2-CI-001*. Washington, D.C.: Department of State.

US Drug Enforcement Administration (DEA). 1987. National Narcotics Intelligence Consumers Committee (NNICC). *The NNICC Report 1985-1986*. Washington, D.C.: Drug Enforcement Agency.

_____. 1992. National Narcotics Intelligence Consumers Committee (NNICC). *The NNICC Report 1991*. Washington, D.C.: DEA Office of Intelligence, US Department of Justice. September.

_____. 1992a. *Worldwide Cocaine Situation Report 1991*. Washington, D.C.: DEA Office of Intelligence, US Department of Justice. September.

_____. 1992b. *Source to The Street (DEA-92012)* Washington, D.C.: DEA Office of Intelligence, US Department of Justice. October.

Bibliography

_____. 1993. *Source to the Street. Mid-1992 Prices for: Cannabis Cocaine Heroin.* Washington, D.C.: Department of Justice.

US Embassy La Paz, Bolivia (USE-BL). 1988. *Cable 4962.* "Coca Paste Processing." 22 April.

_____. 1988. *Cable 12644.* "Alkaloid Content." 3 October.

_____. 1990. *Cable 15712.* "September 1990 Report of INM-Funded Program Activity." 9 November.

_____. 1990. *Cable 17386.* "October 1990 Report of INM-Funded Program Activity." 11 December.

_____. 1990. *Cable 17982.* "November 1990 Report of INM-Funded Program Activity." 21 December.

_____. 1991a. *Cable 1278.* "December 1990 Report of INM-Funded Program Activity." 30 January.

_____. 1991b. *Cable 1728.* "1990 Bolivian Coca Reduction Statistics." 8 February.

_____. 1991c. *Cable 2932.* "January 1991 Report of INM-Funded Program Activity." 5 March.

_____. 1991d. *Cable 5444.* "March 1991 Report of INM-Funded Program Activity." April.

_____. 1991e. *Cable 7877.* "April 1991 Report of INM-Funded Program Activity." 6 June.

_____. 1991f. *Cable 8905.* "May 1991 Report of INM-Funded Program Activity." July.

_____. 1991g. *Cable 10375.* "INCSR: 1991 Mid-Year Update." 18 July.

_____. 1991h. *Cable 10517.* "Forced Eradication Activities." 19 July.

_____. 1991i. *Cable 12352.* "July 1991 Report of INM-Funded Program Activity." 22 August.

_____. 1991j. *Cable 13952.* "August 1991 Report of INM-Funded Program Activity." 19 September.

_____. 1991k. *Cable 15969.* "September 1991 Report of INM-Funded Program Activity." 22 October.

_____. 1991l. *Cable 17171.* "October 1991 Report of INM-Funded Program Activity. 12 November.

_____. 1992. *Cable 1494.* "December 1991 Report of INM-Funded Program Activity." 28 January.

_____. 1992. *Cable 8710.* "April 1992 Report of INM-Funded Program Activity." May.

———. 1992. *Cable 10382.* "May 1992 Report of INM-Funded Program Activity." June.
———. 1992a. *Welcome to Bolivia* (Briefing Book). La Paz.
———. 1992b. *Information Handbook.* La Paz.
———. 1992c. *Economic Trends Report on Bolivia.* La Paz. May.
———. 1992d. *Investment Climate Statement Bolivia.* October.
———. 1993. *Cable 693.* "Bolivia FY '92 Supply Side Reduction Results." January.
———. 1993. *Cable 1096.* "Bolivia: Coca Prices And Eradication." 26 January.
———. 1993. *Cable 9641.* "Combined Report of INM-Funded Program Activity Part I of II - Bolivia." July.
US Embassy Lima, Peru (USE-PE). 1991. *Agreement On Drug Control and Alternative Development Policy.* 14 May.
———. 1992. *Cable 09548.* "Estimates of Economic Impact of Coca and Coca By-Products Production - Part I." 9 July.
———. 1992. *Agreement Concerning The Project For Control of Narcotics.* 30 July.
———. 1993. *Cable 07416.* "Monthly Report On Narcotics Program Developments In Peru - May 1993." 6 July.
———. 1993a. *Foreign Economic Trends (FET) And Their Implications For The United States Peru.* 15 March.
US General Accounting Office (GAO). 1987. *Status Report On GAO Review of The US International Narcotics Control Program GAO/T-NSIAD-87-40.* Washington, D.C.: General Accounting Office.
———. 1988. *Controlling Drug Abuse: A Status Report.* GAO/NSIAD-88-39. Washington, D.C.: General Accounting Office.
———. 1988a. *Drug Control: Issues Surrounding Increased Use of the Military in Drug Interdiction* GAO/NSIAD-88-156. Washington, D.C.: General Accounting Office.
———. 1988b. *Drug Control River Patrol Craft for the Government of Bolivia* GAO/NSIAD-88-101FS. Washington, D.C.: General Accounting Office.
———. 1988c. *Drug Control US Supported Efforts in Colombia and Bolivia* GAO/NSIAD-89-24. Washington, D.C.: General Accounting Office.

_____. 1991a. *The Drug War: U.S. Programs in Peru Face Serious Obstacles.* GAO/NSIAD/92-36. Washington, D.C.: General Accounting Office.

_____. 1991b. *Drug War: Observations on Counternarcotics Aid to Colombia.* GAO/NSIAD-91-296. Washington, D.C.: General Accounting Office.

_____. 1991c. *Drug Control: Impact of DOD's Detection and Monitoring on Cocaine Flow.* GAO/NSIAD-91-297. Washington, D.C.: General Accounting Office.

_____. 1991d. *Drug Control Status: Status Report on Department of Defense Support to Counternarcotics Activities.* GAO/NSIAD-91-117. Washington, D.C.: General Accounting Office.

_____. 1991e. *Drug Policy And Agriculture* GAO/NSIAD-92-12. Washington, D.C.: General Accounting Office.

_____. 1991f. *The Drug War* GAO/T NSIAD-92-2. Washington, D.C.: General Accounting Office.

_____. 1992a. *The Drug War: Extent of Problems in Brazil, Ecuador, and Venezuela* GAO/NSIAD-92-226. Washington, D.C.: General Accounting Office.

_____. 1992b. *Foreign Aid: Police Training and Assistance* GAO/NSIAD-92-118. Washington, D.C.: General Accounting Office.

_____. 1992c. *Promising Approach to Judicial Reform in Colombia.* GAO/NSIAD-92-269. Washington, D.C.: General Accounting Office.

_____. 1993a. *The Drug War: Colombia Is Undertaking Programs, but Impact Is Uncertain.* GAO/NSIAD-93-220. Washington, D.C.: General Accounting Office.

US Information Agency (USIA). 1992. *Consequences of the Illegal Drug Trade.* Washington, D.C.: US Information Agency.

US Information Service. 1991. *USIS Resource Book.* Lima, Peru: US Embassy.

White House. 1987. *National Security Strategy of The United States.* Washington, D.C.: US government Printing Office.

_____. 1991. *National Security Strategy of The United States.* Washington, D.C.: US Government Printing Office.

World Bank. 1991. *World Trade 1991.* Washington, D.C.: World Bank.

Congressional Hearings And Reports:

US Congress. House Committee On Armed Services. 1989. *Hearing* (H.A.S.C. No. 101-2), 22 February. 101st Congress. 1st Session. Washington, D.C.: US Government Printing Office.

———. House Committee On Foreign Affairs. 1989a. *US Narcotics Control Progress In Peru, Bolivia, Colombia and Mexico: An Update.* 101st Congress. 1st Session. Washington, D.C.: US Government Printing Office.

———. House Committee On The Judiciary and Senate Caucus On International Narcotics Control. 1989-1990. *Joint Hearings.* S. Hrg. 101-1228. 6 November 1989 and 18 January and 27 March 1990. 101st Congress 1st and 2nd Sessions. Washington, D.C.: US Government Printing Office.

———. House Committee On Government Operations. 1990. *The Role of The Department of Defense In The Interdiction Of Drug Smuggling Into The United States.* 101st Congress. 2nd Session. Washington, D.C.: US Government Printing Office.

———. House Committee On Government Operations. 1990a. *The Role of Demand Reduction In The National Drug Control Strategy.* House Report 101-992. Washington, D.C.: US Government Printing Office.

———. House Committee On Government Operations. 1990b. *United States Anti-Narcotics Activities In The Andean Region.* House Report 101-992. (Union Calendar No. 584). 101st Congress. 2nd Session. Washington, D.C.: US Government Printing Office.

———. House Committee On Government Operations. 1990c. *Stopping The Flood of Cocaine With Operation Snowcap: Is It Working?* Report 101-673. 101st Congress. 2nd Session. Washington, D.C.: US Government Printing Office.

———. House Subcommittee On Western Hemisphere Affairs. 1990d. *The Andean Initiative Hearings.* 101st Congress. 2nd Session. 6 and 20 June. Washington, D.C.: US Government Printing Office.

———. House Committee On Armed Services. 1991a. *Fiscal Year 1992 DOD Budget Submission For Drug Interdiction.* H.A.S.C. No.102-19. 102nd Congress. 1st Session. Washington, D.C.: US Government Printing Office.

_____. House Committee on Foreign Affairs. 1991b. *Review of The Presidential Determination on Narcotics Control And Human Rights in Peru*. 12 September. 102 Congress. 1st Session. Washington, D.C.: US Government Printing Office.

_____. House Committee On Foreign Affairs. 1991c. *International Cooperation Act of 1991*. Report: 102-96. 102nd Congress. 1st Session. Washington, D.C.: US Government Printing Office.

_____. House Committee On Foreign Affairs. 1991d. *Hearing*. 10 July. 102nd Congress. 1st Session. Washington, D.C.: US Government Printing Office.

_____. House Committee On Foreign Affairs. 1992. *Hearings - Review of The 1992 International Narcotics Control Strategy Report*. 3, 4, 11 and 12 March. 102nd Congress. 2nd Session. Washington, D.C.: US Government Printing Office.

_____. House Subcommittee on Western Hemisphere Affairs. 1992a. *The Threat of The Shining Path to Democracy in Peru.* Hearings 11-12 March. 102nd Congress. 2nd Session. Washington, D.C.: US Government Printing Office.

_____. House of Subcommittee on Western Hemisphere Affairs and Task Force On International Narcotics Control. 1992b. *The Situation In Peru And The Future of the War On Drugs Joint Hearing*. 7 May. 102d Congress. 2d Session. Washington, D.C.: US Government Printing Office.

_____. House Subcommittee on Western Hemisphere Affairs. 1992c. *The Threat of The Shining Path to Democracy in Peru. Hearing*. 11-12 March. 102d Congress. 2d Session. Washington, D.C.: US Government Printing Office.

_____. House Committee On Foreign Affairs. 1992d. *Joint Hearing*. 7 May. 102d Congress. 2d Session. Washington, D.C.: US Government Printing Office.

_____. House Subcommittee on Western Hemisphere Affairs. 1993. *Hearing*. Mimeo: 10 March.

_____. House Subcommittee on Western Hemisphere Affairs and Task Force on International Narcotics Control. 1993a. *Joint Hearing*. 29 July 1992. 102d Congress, 2d Session. Washington, D.C.: US Government Printing Office.

_____. Senate Caucus on International Narcotics Control. 1987. *The U.N. Draft Convention Against Illicit Traffic In Narcotic Drugs and Psychotropic Substances.* Senate Print 100-64. 100th Congress. 1st Session. Washington, D.C.: US Government Printing Office.

_____. Senate Caucus on International Narcotics Control. 1988. *Hearing.* S. Hrg. 100-1021. 16 March. 100th Congress. 2d Session. Washington D.C.: US Government Printing Office.

_____. Senate Committee On Foreign Affairs. 1988a. *Drugs, Law Enforcement And Foreign Policy.* Senate Print 100-165. Washington, D.C.: US Government Printing Office.

_____. Senate Permanent Subcommittee on Investigations, Committee on Governmental Affairs. 1989. *Hearings.* 26-29 September. 101st Congress. 1st Session. Washington, D.C.: US Government Printing Office.

_____. Senate Caucus on International Narcotics Control. 1989a. *Hearing.* 19 April. 101st Congress. 1st Session. Washington, D.C.: US Government Printing Office.

US Congress. Senate Committee On The Judiciary. 1989b. *Hearing.* 101-591. 101st Congress. 1st Session. Washington, D.C.: US Government Printing Office.

_____. Senate Committee on The Judiciary. 1989-1990. *Drug Policy In The Andean Nations.* Hearing 101-1228. 101st Congress. 1st and 2d Sessions. 6 November and 18 January and 22 March. Washington, D.C.: US Government Printing Office.

_____. Senate Committee on Appropriations. 1990 *Foreign Operations, Export Financing, And Related Programs Appropriations Bill, 1991.* Report 101-519. 101st Congress. 2d Session. Washington, D.C.: US Government Printing Office.

_____. Senate Committee on Governmental Affairs. 1990a. *Cocaine Production, Eradication And The Environment: Policy Impact And Options.* Senate Print 101-110. 101st Congress. 2d Session. Washington, D.C.: US Government Printing Office.

_____. Senate Committee on the Judiciary and Caucus On International Narcotics Control. 1991. *Joint Hearings* 101-1228. 101st Congress. 1st and 2d Sessions. November 6, 1989, January 18 and March 27, 1990. Washington, D.C.: US Government Printing Office.

_____. Senate Judiciary Committee and the International Narcotics Control Caucus. 1991a. *Fighting Drug Abuse*. Washington, D.C.: Judiciary Committee. US Government Printing Office.

_____. Senate Committee On the Judiciary. 1992. *The President's Drug Strategy: Has it Worked?* Washington, D.C.: Senate Committee On the Judiciary. Washington, D.C.: US Government Printing Office.

_____. Senate Committee On Foreign Relations. 1992a. *Hearing 102-652*. 20 February. Washington, D.C.: US Government Printing Office.

_____. Senate Committee on Appropriations. 1992b. *Foreign Operations, Export Financing And Related Programs Appropriation Bill, 1993*. Report 102-419. 102d Congress. 2d Session. Washington, D.C.: US Government Printing Office.

_____. Senate Subcommittee On Terrorism, Narcotics, And International Operations. 1992c. *Andean Drug Initiative Hearing* 102-657. Senate Committee On Foreign Relations. 102d Congress. 2d Session. Washington, D.C.: US Government Printing Office.

Official Statements, Interviews, And Briefings:

Arrieta, Mario. 1992. Interview with the author in La Paz, 10 December. Arrieta is an investigator for the Instituto Latinoamericano de Investigaciones Sociales (ILDIS).

Bailetti MacKee, Jose. 1992. Interview with author in Lima, 30 November. Bailetti is a retired Peruvian Army Colonel and Director of the Instituto de Investigacion de la Defensa Nacional - INIDN.

Baldivieso F., Laura Edith. 1992. Interview with author in La Paz, 9 December. Baldivieso is the Executive Director of Centro Educativo Sobre Estupefacientes (CESE).

Barrion Moron, Raul. 1992. Interview with author in La Paz, 7 December. Barrios is a member of the Facultad Latinoamericano de Ciencias Sociales in Bolivia.

Bedregal Gutierrez, Guillermo. 1987. Minister of Foreign Relations. *Letter*. Dated 24 February to US Ambassador Edward Morgan Rowell. La Paz, Bolivia.

Bolivian Ministry of Defense Official (MD:BL). 1992. Interview with author in La Paz, 9 December.
Cabezas, Hugo. 1992. Interview with author in Lima, 4 December. Dr. Cabezas is a professor of sociology and economics at the University of Lima.
Callahan, Robert. 1993. USIA official interviewed by author in Washington, D.C., 27 April.
Campodonico Sanchez, Humberto. 1992. Interview with author in Lima, 2 December. Campodonico is a member of the Centro de Estudios y Promocion del Desarrollo (DESCO) which is an academic organization devoted to the promotion of development in Peru.
Carlucci, Frank. 1988. *Testimony* before the U.S. Senate and House of Representatives Committee on Armed Forces. 100th Congress, 2d Session. Washington, D.C.: Mimeo of 15 June.
Cheney, Richard B. 1989. *Memorandum*: "Department of Defense Guidance for Implementation of the President's National Drug Control Strategy." dated 18 September. Cited in Colonel William W. Mendel. "Illusive Victory: From Blast Furnace to Green Sweep," *Military Review*. December, 1992.
Clinton, Bill 1993a. *Press Release*: "Remarks by The President In Announcement of Lee Brown as Director, Office of Drug Control Policy." White House: Office of the Press Secretary, 28 April.
––––––. 1993b. *Executive Order 12880*: 16 Nov 1993 in Federal Register, Vol. 58 No. 221 (18 Nov 93), p. 60989.
Corr, Edwin. 1985. US Ambassador to Bolivia. Conversation with author in La Paz, 4 July.
Country Team Official (CT:BL). 1992. Interview with author in La Paz, 8 December.
Country Team (CT:PE) staff/official. 1992. Interview by author in Lima, 2 December.
Cueva, Jose Adan. 1992. Interview with author in San Pedro Sula, Honduras, 27 December. Cueva is an agronomist associated with USAID.
Deering, John S. 1993. Office of Inspector General. US Department of State. Interviewed by author in Washington, D.C.: 27, April
Degregori, Carlos Ivan. 1992. Interview with author in Lima 2 December. Dr. Degregori is a Senderologist and professor of anthropology at the University of St. Marcos and the National University of San Cristobal of Huamanga.

Department of Defense (DOD) official. 1993. Interview by author in Washington, D.C. 28 April.

Department of State (DOS) official. 1993. Interview by author in Washington, D.C. 30 April.

Drug Enforcement Administration. 1991. *Operation Green Ice* (Briefing). San Diego, CA: San Diego Field Division.

_____. Official (DEA:BL). 1992. Interview with author in La Paz, 8 December.

_____. Official (DEA:PE). 1992. Interview with author in Lima, Peru, 1 December.

_____. Official. 1993. Interviewed by author in Washington, D.C., 29 April.

Ferrarone, Don. 1992. Interview by author in La Paz, Bolivia: 1 December. Ferrarone was the Director, DEA in the US Embassy in La Paz 1990-1992.

Funk, Sherman M. 1991. *Statement*. Office of the Inspector General before the House Committee On Government Operations. Washington, D.C., 23 October.

Fujimori, Alberto. 1990 "Estrategia De Lucha Contra El Narcotrafico" *Speech*. 26 April. Lima, Peru: CEDRO.

Gamarra, Dr. Eduardo A. 1990. *Prepared Statement* before House Subcommittee on Western Hemisphere Affairs, Committee on Foreign Affairs. Washington, D.C. 6 June.

_____. 1993. Interview with author in Miami, Florida, 7 February. Dr. Gamarra is an acknowledged expert on Bolivian affairs and a Professor of Political Science at Florida International University.

General Officer Bolivian Armed Forces (BL:MO). 1992. Interview with author in La Paz, 7 December.

Hayes, Edward B. 1988 and 1992. Interview with author in Lima, Peru, 15 October and 4 December respectively. Hayes was the Army-Navy Attache in La Paz, Bolivia (1987-1989) and a key actor in the Country Team anti-drug efforts. He later served as a US Dyn Corporation contract helicopter aviation coordinator and maintenance advisor in Peru (1992-1993).

Hengle, Douglas. 1992. Interview with author in Lima, 1 December. Hengle was the Economics Attache for the Country Team in Lima.

Henson, Sherman. 1992. Interview with Author in Lima, 1 December. Henson was the Country Team's Narcotics Affaris Section (NAS) Director.

International Narcotics Matters (INM), Bureau of, official. 1993. Interviewed by author in Washington, D.C. 28 April.

Joulwan, General George A. 1992. *Briefing*. 1 May 1992 for House Foreign Affairs Committee, in *Joint Hearing*. Subcommittee on Western Hemisphere Affairs and Task force on International Narcotics Control. 102d Congress, 2d Session. Washington, D.C.: US government Printing Office.

———. 1993. *Statement*. Senate Armed Services Committee. Washington, D.C. 21 April.

Lerner Stein, Roberto. 1992. Interview with author in Lima, 4 December. Dr. Lerner is a psychologist with an interest in Peruvian society and anthropology.

Levitsky, Melvyn. 1991. *Statement* of Assistant Secretary of State for International Narcotics Matters before House Legislation and National Security Subcommittee. 23 October.

Lupo Gamarra, Javier. 1992. Interview with author in La Paz, 11 December. Lupo Gamarra is the former Sub-Director of the Bolivian government's Office for Anti-Drug Control Operations (CONALID).

Lupsha, Dr. Peter. 1993. *Letter* to author from Department of Political Science, The University of New Mexico. 26 May.

Martinez, Robert. 1992. *Speech*. 28 October before the Contraband and Cargo Inspection Technology International Symposium. Washington, D.C.: Mimeo of 29 October.

Military official (US). 1992. Interview by author in Lima, Peru, 1 December.

Montalvo, Richard Major (USAF). 1992 and 1993. Interview with author in Miami, Florida, 30 November and 3 July respectively. Montalvo was a former Assistant Air Force Attache with the US Embassy in La Paz, Bolivia.

Narcotics Affairs Section (NAS). 1990. *Briefing Paper*. US Embassy, Lima, Peru.

———. 1991. *Briefing Paper* and *Letter* to author signed by Caesar P. Bernal. US Embassy, Lima, Peru. 2 May.

———. Official (NAS:BL). 1992. Interview with author in La Paz, 10 December.

Narcotics Assistance Unit (NAU) Official. 1988. US Embassy (Country Team), Lima, Peru. Conversation with author.

National Security Council (NSC) official. 1993. Interview by author in Washington, D.C., 30 April.

ONDCP 1. 1993. Key official in Office of National Drug Control Policy (ONDCP) during the 1980s. Interviewed by author in Washington, D.C. 29 April.

ONDCP 2. 1993. Key official in Office of National Drug Control Policy (ONDCP) during the 1980s and 1990s. Interviewed by author in Washington, D.C. 26 April.

Pedraglio, Santiago. 1992. Interview with author in Lima, Peru, 4 December. Pedraglio is the Political Editor for *Si* magazine.

Presidential Advisor (Pres/Adv:BL) and personal friend of President Jaime Paz Zamora. 1992. Interviewed by author in La Paz, 11 December.

Ramirez, Marcel. 1992. Interview with author in La Paz, 8 December. Ramirez is the Director of the Program for Migration Control (PROCON).

Rangel, Honorable Charles B. 1991. *Statement*. House Subcommittee on Legislature and National Security. Washington, D.C.: 23 October.

Reuter, Peter. 1990. "Statement" in Senate Caucus on International Narcotics Control ed. *US International Drug Policy*. Washington, D.C.: US Government Printing Office.

Salinas Castro, Dr. Jose G. 1992. Interview with author in La Paz, 8 December. Salinas Castro was the Under-Secretary for Alternate Development, Ministerio de Asuntos Campesinos y Agropecuarios, government of Bolivia.

Smith, Timothy, 1992. Interview with author in La Paz, 9 December. Smith was the Press Attache (USIS) with the US Embassy in La Paz, Bolivia.

Soberon Garrido, Ricardo. 1992. Interview with author in Lima, Peru, 30 November. Soberon is a member of the Andean Commission of Jourists.

Tanoca, Mary. 1992. Interview with author in La Paz, 9 December. Tanoca was the Economic Attache with the US Embassy in La Paz, Bolivia.

US Agency for International Development official (USAID:BL). 1992. Interview with author in La Paz, Bolivia, 10 December.

US Agency for International Development official (USAID:PE) 1992. Interview with author in Lima, Peru, 1 December.

US General Accounting Office (GAO) official. 1993. Interviewed by author in Washington, D.C. 26 April.

US military mission official (MIL:BL). 1992. Interview with author in La Paz, 9 December.

US military training team official (MTT: BL). 1992. Interview with author in Miami, Florida, 1 October.
US Southern Command (SOUTHCOM) J5. 1989. Author conversations in Panama with several key staff officers working anti-drug issues. April and May.
US Southern Command (SOUTHCOM). 1991. *Direction 2000* (Briefing) Quarry Heights, Panama. August.
_____. 1993. *Command Briefing.* Quarry Heights, Panama: US Southern Command.
SOUTHCOM J3. Briefing for author at Quarry Heights and Howard Air Force Base, Panama. 8 February.
SOUTHCOM Liaison Office Official (LNO). 1993. Interview with author in Arlington, VA., 28 April.
Westrate, David L. 1989. *Statement.* Assistant administrator for Operations, Drug Enforcement Administration (DEA) before the Senate Subcommittee on Terrorism, Narcotics and International Operations. 27 July.
Vassilaqui C., Alejandro. 1992. Interview with author in Lima, Peru, 2 December. Vassilaqui is the Executive Director of CEDRO - Centro de Informacion y Educacion Para La Prevencion del Abuso de Drogas.
Zapata, Eduardo. 1992. Interview with author in Lima, Peru, 2 December. Dr. Zapata is a professor of sociology and political science at the University of Lima.

Polls

APOYO. 1992. Lima, Peru. 500 persons. February and March.
CEDRO (Centro de Informacion y Educacion Para la Prevencion del Abuso de Drogas). 1991. "Encuesta Nacional Opiniones y Actitudes de Los Lideres Peruanos Sobre Drogas." December, 1990.
IPEA (Instituto Peruano de Economia Aplicada. 1992. No. 44. 685 persons. Lima, Peru, 23-27 March.
USIA (US Information Agency). 1991. *Research Memorandum* (RM). Poll conducted in Bolivia 28 June - 12 July. Washington, D.C.: US Information Agency. 6 September.
_____. 1991a. Lima, Peru, 24 June - 14 July.

Bibliography

———. 1993a. *Opinion Research Memorandum* (ORM). Poll conducted in Bolivia 10-25 October 1992. Washington, D.C.: US Information Agency. 19 March.

———. 1993b. *Opinion Research Memorandum* (ORM). Poll conducted in Bolivia 10-25 October 1992. Washington, D.C.: US Information Agency. 19 March.

Secondary Sources

Books:

Alcaraz del Castillo, Franklin. 1989. *Los Eslabones de La Droga*. Bolivia: Editora Atenea S.R.L.

Bagley, Bruce M. 1991. *Myths of Militarization*. Coral Gables: University of Miami North-South Center.

Barsallo Burga, Jose. 1988. *Drogas Responsabilidad Compartida*. Lima, Peru: J.C. Editores S.A.

CEDRO (Centro de Informacion Y Educacion para la Prevencion del abuso de Drogas). 1988. *Legislacion Peruana Sobre Drogas A Partir de 1920*. Lima: CEDRO.

Clawson, Patrick and Lee III, Rensselaer. 1992. *The Negative Economic, Political and Social Effects of Cocaine on Latin America*. Washington, D.C.: US Information Agency.

Clutterbuck, Richard. 1990. *Terrorism and Guerrilla Warfare*. New York: Routledge Press.

Degregori, Carlos Ivan. 1989. *Que Dificil Es Ser Dios*. Lima: El Zorro de Abajo.

Deustua, Alejandro C. 1987. *El Narcotrafico y El Interes Nacional: Un Analisis En La Perspectiva Internacional*. Lima: CEPI.

Dunkerley, James. 1984. *Rebellion in the Veins*. London: Verso.

Eddy, Paul et al. 1988. *The Cocaine Wars*. New York: W.W. Norton.

Gugliotta, Guy and Jeff Leen. 1989. *Kings of Cocaine*. New York: Simon and Schuster.

Lee III, Rensselaer W. 1989. *The White Labyrinth*. New Brunswick, NJ: Transaction Publishers.

MacDonald, Scott B. 1989. *Mountain High*, White Avalanche. New York: Praeger.

Malloy, James M. and Eduardo Gamerra. 1988. *Revolution and Reaction: Bolivia, 1964-1985*. New Brunswick: Transaction Books.

Palmer, David Scott ed. 1992. *The Shining Path of Peru*. New York: St Martin's Press.
SEAMOS. 1991. *Drogas: El Debate Boliviano*. La Paz: Teddy Libros Ediciones S.R.L.
Sheahan, John. 1987. *Patterns of Development in Latin America*. Princeton: Princeton University Press.
Smith, Peter H. ed. 1992. *Drug Policy in The Americas*. Boulder, CO: Westview Press.
Strong Simon. 1992. *Shining Path Terror and Revolution in Peru*. New York: Times Books.
Walker III, William O. 1989. *Drug Control in the Americas*. Albuquerque: University of New Mexico Press.
Washington Office on Latin America (WOLA). 1990. *The War In The Andes: The Military Role in US International Drug Policy*. Washington, D.C.: Washington Office on Latin America.
_____. 1991. *Clear and Present Dangers: The U.S. Military and The War on Drugs in the Andes*. Washington, D.C.: Washington Office on Latin America.
_____. 1991a. *Going To The Source: Results And Prospects For The War On Drugs In The Andes*. Washington, D.C.: Washington Office on Latin America.
_____. 1992. *Peru Under Scrutiny: Human Rights and U.S. Drug Policy*. Washington, D.C.: Washington Office on Latin America.
World Bank. 1992. *World Table 1992*. Baltimore: John Hopkins University Press.
Youngers, Coletta. 1991. A Fundamentally Flawed Strategy: The U.S. "War on Drugs" In Bolivia. Washington, D.C.: Washington Office On Latin America.

Articles/Presentations/Chapters In Books:

Abbott, Michael H. 1988. "The Army and The Drug War: Politics or National Security," *Parameters*. December.
Alverez, Elena. 1992. "Coca Production in Peru" in Peter H. Smith ed. *Drug Policy in the Americas*. Boulder, Co.: Westview Press.
Andreas, Peter R. and Kenneth E. Sharpe. 1991. *"Dead-End Drug Wars"* Foreign Policy. Winter 1991-1992.

_____. 1992. "Cocaine Politics in the Andes" in *Current History*. February.

Aramburu, Carlos E. 1989. "La Economia Parcelaria y El Cultivo De Coca: El Caso del Alto Huallaga" in Federico Leon ed. *Pasţa Basica de Cocaina*. Lima: CEDRO.

Bagley, Bruce M. 1988. "US Foreign Policy And The War On Drugs: Analysis Of A Policy Failure," *Journal of Interamerican Studies*. Vol 30, Summer/Fall.

_____. 1992. "After San Antonio," *Journal of Interamerican Studies*. Vol. 34, Fall.

Briceno, Juan y Martinez, Javier. 1989. "El Ciclo Operativo de Trafico Ilicito de la Coca y Sus Derivados: Implicaciones En La Liquidez del sistema Financero" in Federico Leon ed. *Pasta Basica de Cocaina*. Lima: CEDRO.

Chiri Fernandez, Adolfo. 1992. "Peru" in *North-South*. February-March.

Claudio, Arnaldo. 1991. "Failure Of A Security Strategy," *Military Review*. December.

Collett, Merrill. 1988. "The Myth of The Narcoguerrillas," *The Nation*. 13 August.

Craig, Richard B. 1990. "El Trafico de Drogas: Implicaciones Para Los Paises Suramericanes Productores" in Juan G. Tokatlian and Bruce M. Bagley eds. *Economica y Politica del Narco Trafico*. Bogota: CEI Uniadades Universidad de los Andes.

Dlouhy, David. 1993. "Update On Bolivia: Democracy, Development And Drugs." *Presentation* by Deputy Chief of Mission US Embassy La Paz, Bolivia, at the University of Miami North-South Center. Coral Gables, Florida, 9 March.

Dourojeanni, Marc J. 1989. "Impactos Ambientales del Cultivo de la Coca y La Produccion de Cocaina en la Amazonia Peruana" in Federico R. Leon ed. *Pasta Basica de Cocaina*. Lima: CEDRO.

Dziedzic, Michael J. 1989. "The Transnational Drug Trade And Regional Security," *Survival*. November-December.

Economist Intelligence Unit. 1989. *Country Report No. 2*. London.

_____. 1992. *Bolivian Country Profile 1991-1992*. London: Business International.

Figueroa Buitrago, Mario. 1992. "Mitos Sobre El Poder Benefico de La Hoja de Coca" in *Pantalla*. La Paz: 9 December.

Fishel, John T. 1991. "Lessons From Operation Blast Furnace" in *Military Review*. June.
Fondo Nacional de Desarrollo Alternativo (FONADAL). 1992. Economia and Negocios. La Paz: July.
Gagliano, Joseph A. 1963. "The Coca Debate in Colonial Peru" in *The Americas*. July.
Gaillard, Regina. 1991. "The Case For Separating Civic Action From Military Operations" in *Military Review*. June.
Gamarra, Eduardo A. 1990. "Bush's Andean Initiative" in *Hemisphere*. Fall.
_____. 1991. US Military Assistance, *The Militarization Of The War On Drugs, And The Prospects For Consolidation Of Democracy In Bolivia*. Miami, Florida: Florida International University.
_____. 1992. "Drug Trafficking and Drug Control in Bolivia." *Presentation*. Coral Gables, Florida: University Miami.
Gonzales, Jose E. 1992. "Guerrillas And Coca In The Upper Huallaga Valley" in David Scott Palmer *The Shining Path Peru*. New York: St. Martin's Press.
Gorriti, Gustavo. 1990. "Peru y El Plan Bush" in Diego Garcia-Sayan ed. *Narcotrafico: Realidades y Alternativas*. Lima: Comision Andina de Juristas.
Gros, Christian. 1992. "Los Campesinos de Las Cordilleras Frente A Los Movimientos Guerrilleros y A La Droga: Actores o Victimas, "*Analisis Politico No. 16*. May-August.
Guillermoprieto, Alma. 1993. "Letter From Lima: Down The Shinning Path" in *The New Yorker*. 8 February.
Harmon, Robert E. et. al. 1993. "Counter-Drug Assistance: The Number One Priority" in *Military Review*. March.
Healy, Kevin. 1988. "Coca, The State, And The Peasantry in Bolivia, 1982-1988" in *Journal of Interamerican Studies*. Summer-Fall.
_____. 1991. "Political Ascent of Bolivia's Peasant Coca Leaf Producers" in *Journal of Interamerican Studies*. Spring.
Jennings, Peter. 1992. "The Cocaine War: Lost in Bolivia." ABC-TV: 28 December, as reported in USIS Panama: 4 January 1993.
Larmer, Brook. 1992. "The Newest War." *Newsweek*. 6 January.
Lee III, Rensselaer. 1988. "Dimensions of The South American Cocaine Industry," *Journal of Interamerican Studies*. Vol 30, Summer/Fall.

Leonhard, Ralf. 1993. "Violencia en Peru: El Rincon de los Muertos: in *Pensamiento Propio*. Managua, Nicaragua: February.

Mabry, Donald. 1988. "The US Military And The War on Drugs in Latin America," *Journal of Interamerican Studies*. Vol. 30, Summer/Fall.

Machicado, Flavio. 1992. "Coca Production in Bolivia" in Peter H. Smith ed. *Drug Policy in the Andes*. Boulder (CO): Westview Press.

Maingot, Anthony. 1988. "Laundering Drug Profits: Miami And Caribbean Tax Havens," *Journal of Interamerican Studies*. Summer/Fall.

Masias, Carmen. 1992. "Cocaina: Aspectos Sciologicos de los Paises Productores." Lima: CEDRO

McClintock, Cynthia. 1984. "Why Peasants Rebel: The Case of Peru's Sendero Luminoso" in *World Politics* 37. October.

_____. 1988. "The War on Drugs: The Peruvian Case" in *Assessing The Americas' War On Drugs*. Bruce Bagley ed. *Special Issue of the Journal of International Studies and World Affairs*. Summer-Fall.

_____. 1993. "Peru's Fujimori: A Caudillo Derails Democracy" in *Current History*. March.

Mendel, Colonel William W. 1992. "Illusive Victory: From Blast Furnace to Green Sweep," *Military Review*. December.

Menzel, Sewall H. 1989. "Operation Blast Furnace" in *Army*. November.

NACLA (North American Congress on Latin America). 1989. Report on The Americas in *NACLA*. December/January.

_____. 1990. Report on The Americas in *NACLA*. December/January.

Palmer, David Scott. 1990. "Peru: Democratic Interlude, Authoritarian Heritage, Uncertain Future" in Howard J. Wiarda and Harvey F. Kline eds. *Latin American Politics and Development*. Boulder (CO): Westview Press.

Pearl, Raphael Francis. 1988. "Congress, International Narcotics Policy, And The Anti-Drug Abuse Act of 1988," *Journal of Interamerican Studies*. Vol. 34, Fall.

_____. 1992. "United States Andean Drug Policy: Background And Issues For Decision Makers," *Journal of Interamerican Studies*. Vol. 34, Fall.

Quainton, Anthony. 1990. "Estados Unidos," US Ambassador to Peru presentation for the International Conference on Narcotrafficking in Lima, Peru, 5-7 February 1990 in Garcia Sayan ed. *Narcotrafico: Realidades y Alternativas.* Lima: Comision Andina de Juristas.

Reid, Michael. 1989. "Una Region Amenazada Por El Narcotrafico" in Diego Garcia-Sayan ed. *Coca, Cocaina y Narcotrafico.* Lima, Peru: Comision Andina de Juristas.

Sharpe, Kenneth e. 1988. "The Drug War: Going After Supply" in *Journal of Interamerican Studies.* Summer/Fall.

Smith, Michael L. 1992. "Taking the High Ground: Shining Path and the Andes" in David Scott Palmer ed. *The Shining Path of Peru.* New York: St. Martin's Press.

Soberon Garrido, Ricardo. 1992. "Efectos Juridicos de La Ratificacion de la Convencion de Viena Hecha por El Peru" in *Boletin Comision Andina de Juristas.* Lima, Peru. March.

Stevenson, Sharon. 1989. "In Peru, Coca Plan Succeeds: UN Drug Program Wins" in *Miami Herald* (Florida), 9 October.

Sturm, Linda S. and Frank J. Smith. 1992. "Evaluation of Initial Responses to the Alternate Crops Program by Bolivian Farmers of the Chapare Region." Study prepared for North Carolina State University.

Van Wert, James M. 1988. "The US State Department's Narcotics Control Policy In The Americas," *Journal of Interamerican Studies.* Vol. 30, Summer/Fall.

Walker III, William O. 1992. "International Collaberation in Historical Perspective," Peter H. Smith, ed. *Drug Policy in The Americas.* Boulder, CO: Westview Press.

Werlich, David P. 1987. "Debt, Democracy and Terrorism in Peru" in *Current History.* February.

_____. 1991. "Fujimori and the Disaster in Peru" in *Current History.* February.

White, Peter T. 1989. "Coca - An Ancient Herb Turns Deadly" in *National Geographic.* January.

Wise, Carol. 1989. "Democratization, Crisis, and the APRA's Modernization Project in Peru" in Barbara Stallings and Robert Kaufman eds. *Debt and Democracy in Latin America.* San Fransisco: Westview Press.

Newspapers/Magazines:

Aqui (BL): 30 Jun 90; 3 May, 5 Jul and 4 Oct 91.
Actualidad (PE): 4 Dec 92.
Andean Newsletter (PE): No 21, 1988.
Caretas (PE): 27 Apr and 8 Oct 92.
Christian Science Monitor: 24 May 90; 15 Apr and 22 Jul 91; 3 Jul and 8 Dec 92.
Clarin (AR): 28 Jul 92.
Cuanto (PE): Jun 92.
Diario (BL): 4 and 19 Oct and 12 Dec 89.
Drug Trafficking Update (PE): 13 Oct and 9 Nov 92.
Economist (UK): No 2 1989; and 14-20 and 28 Nov 92; and 30 Jan 93.
El Comercio (PE): 26 and 28 Apr, 27 May and 4 Dec 92; 16 Feb and 3 Mar 93.
El Nuevo Herald (US): 31 Dec 90; 21 Mar, 16 and 17 Apr, 13 and 29 May, 6 Jul, 17 Sep and 31 Dec 91; 6-7 and 21 Jan, 2 Feb, 2 and 11 Apr, 19 May, 29 Jul, 2, 14-15 Aug, 2, 4, and 11 Sep, 4, 8, 10, 21-22 and 31 Oct and 2, 4, 8, 10, 12-14 and 26-27 Nov 92; 4, 8 and 18-21, 23 and 24 Jan, 2, 14, and 23 Feb, 5 and 14 Mar, 17 Apr, 2 and 6-8 May, 16-17 and 25 Jun, 11, 14, 23 and 27 Jul, 2 and 6-7 Aug, 15, 23 and 26 Sep, and 1, 7 and 23 Oct, 22-23, 25, 27 and 29 Nov, 5 Dec 93; 6, 25 and 29 Jan; 4-5, 19, 21-25 Feb; 3, 5, 12, 13-14, 26 and 30 Mar; 8-11, 13, 15-16, 19, 24, 27 and 28 Apr; 3, 5-6 and 18   May 94; 2 Apr, 22 Jul, 3, 20-21 Aug, 1, 4, 8 Oct, 4 and 8   Nov 95; 26 Apr and 5 May 96.
Excelsior (MX): 29 Jan 93.
Expresso (PE): 29 Apr, 27 May and 4 Oct 92; and 18 Apr 94.
Financial Times (UK): 15 Feb 90; and 13 Nov and 11 Dec 92.
Folha de Sao Paulo (BR): 24 Nov 91.
Globe and Mail (CA): 19 Sep 92.
Independent (UK): 21 Jun, 17 Aug, 18 Nov 91; and 27 Feb 92.
INIDEN (PE): Oct 92.
Insight: 2 Apr 90.
Istoe Senhor (BR): 4 Sep 91.
La Epoca (CH): 27 Aug 92.
La Hora (GT): 22 Jun 92.

Las Ultimas Noticias (CH): 29 Oct 92.
Latin American Report (Andean Region): 5 Oct 92.
Latin American Weekly Report (UK): 1 Feb 90; 8 Oct 92; and 7 Jan 93.
Latin American Times (L.A.T.) April/May 91.
Los Angeles Times: 2 Jul 90 and 26 May 91.
Miami Herald: 5 and 14 Aug, 29 Sep, 9 and 31 Oct 90; 11 Feb, 13 and 19 Mar, 14 Jun, 26 and 29 Jul, 26 Aug, 2 Sep, 4 Oct and 21 and 29 Nov, 15 Dec 91; 6 Jan, 2, 9 and 26-27 Feb, 27 Mar, 8, 11, 15, 19, and 25 and 30 Apr, 24 May, 23 Jul, 14 Aug, 20 Sep, 7-8, 12, 28 and 31 Oct, 2, 8, 11, 13-15, 18-19, and 27 Nov and 15 and 21 Dec 92; 10, 14, 19, 21, and 23 Jan, 3, 16-17, 20 and 27 feb, 22 Mar, 5, 10, 16, 19 and 22 Apr, 2 and 8-9 and 24 May, 7, 10-11 and 13 Jun, 1-2, 7 and 13 Aug, 23 and 26 Sep, and 1, 22-23 and 29 Oct, 7 Nov, 3 and 15 Dec 93; 14, 22, 24-25 Jan, 2, 5 and 23 Feb, 5, 13-14 Mar 4, 10, 15-16, 21 and 25 Apr; 7 and 31 May 94; 5 and 15 Jun, 20 Sep, 5 and 27 Oct 95; 1 Apr, 9 and 13 May 96.
Nacional (VE): 25 Jul 92.
New York Review: 22 Dec 88.
New York Times: 13 Jan, 29 Feb and 21 Dec 88; 7 Jan, 20 May and 12 Aug 90; 1, 21, 24 and 27 Sep and 27 Oct 91; 27 Jan; 14 and 17 Feb; 17 Jun, 23 and 29 Jul; 1 Aug; 14-15, and 16 Sep; and 20 Nov 92; and 6 Apr 93.
Newsweek: 19 Feb 90; and 6 and 27 Jan 92.
Nezavisimaya Gazeta (RU): 24 Oct 92.
North-South: Feb-Mar 92.
Oiga: (PE): 19 Oct 92.
Pais: (SP): 28 Sep and 25 Oct 89; 10 and 16 Nov 92; and 3 Mar 93.
Prensa (PN): 16 Feb 93.
Presencia (BL): 25 Oct 89; 3 Jan, 5, 9, and 29 May, 9 Oct, 6 Dec 90; 27 Feb, 2, 5, and 7 Mar, and 1 and 3 Apr, 17 May, 16 Jun, 23 Jul, 14 Sep, and 5-6 and 9 Oct 91; 7 Aug, 6 Sep 92, and 1 Oct 92.
Que Hacer (PE): No 52 May-Jun 88.
Si (PE): 28 Apr 91; and 16-22 Nov 92.
United Press International (UPI): 28 Sep 92.
U.S. News and World Report: 11 Jan and 2 Aug 93.
Vision (PE): 11 Mar 92 and 16 Oct 93.
Wall Street Journal: 31 Jul 92.

Washington Post: 22 and 27 May; and 5 Aug 88; 30 Mar, 17 Apr, 12 Jun, 13 Aug and 4 Sep 90; 18 Jan, 23 Apr, 20-21 Jun 91; 26-27 Jul, and 31 Dec 92; 15 and 24 Feb, 27 Mar, and 16 Apr 93.
Washington Times: 24 Feb 91; and 12 May 92.

Index

Agency for International Development (AID or USAID), 9, 14-15, 20, 23, 46, 53-54, 59-63, 66-67, 73, 79-84, 99-101, 106, 108, 131-132, 135, 137, 139, 142, 154, 164, 168-169, 176, 187, 208
Agricultural Development in The Coca Zones Project, 9
Agro-Yungas Coffee Development Project, 61
AI. *See* Andean Initiative
AID. *See* Agency for International Development
Allison, Graham, 226
Andean Initiative (AI), 46-49, 59, 67, 104, 151, 153, 198, 217, 228
Andean Trade Preference Act, 60
Anez, Lucio, 50, 56
Annex III agreement, 49, 64, 66, 104-105
Anti-Drug Abuse Act, 23, 139
Apolo. *See* Bolivia coca growing areas
Arce Gomez, Luis, 46
Arciniega Hubi, Alberto, 128, 145-146
Bagley, Bruce, 221-222
balloon effect, 75-76, 101, 107, 112, 168, 208, 220, 227, 229
Banzer Suarez, Hugo, 3, 11
Barrios Hermosa, Nicolas, 176
Barthelemy, Fernando, 20
Belaunde Terry, Fernando, 120, 127, 205
Bennet, William, 38
Biggs, Jeffery, 13
Bolivia
    anti-drug policy, 6, 8, 10-12, 16, 24-26, 30, 34-36, 38, 46, 55, 57, 59, 65, 81, 84-85, 88-90, 92, 94-95, 105
    coca
        cultural tradition, 2, 9, 218-219
        eradication, 6, 12-13, 24-26, 34, 53, 59-60, 63, 78, 80, 93, 95, 106
        farmers, 2-3, 5, 8-9, 12, 20-21, 26, 221
        growing areas, 3, 35, 93

production, 2, 24, 34, 75, 78, 93, 99, 213, 218
Congress (Chamber of Deputies), 16, 21, 51
Ministry of Foreign Relations, 90
narcotrafficking, 3, 5, 11, 15, 18-21, 26, 28, 30, 44, 57, 70-71, 73, 78, 92, 108, 112, 219-221
socio-economic conditions, 1, 2, 10-13, 26, 80-82, 91, 94, 98, 108, 218, 228
Supreme Court, 76-77
Bolivian Peasant Workers Sole Confederation (CSUTCB), 58
Brito Roman, Mario, 146
Bureau of International Narcotics Matters (INM), 7-8, 16, 18, 25-26, 29, 33-34, 57, 99, 137, 139, 145, 147, 152, 175, 177, 187-189, 220, 226
Bush, George, 38, 42-43, 46, 51, 66, 91, 104, 151-152, 171-172, 207, 219, 221, 224, 226
Cachique Rivera, 199
Capobianco, Guillermo, 56, 92
Carbajal D'Angelo, Julio, 127, 129
Carlucci, Frank, 41
Cartagena Conference, 46, 151-152
Carvajal, Felipe, 56
Center for Education About Narcotics (CESE), 87
Central Obrera Boliviana (COB), 21
Centro de Informacion y Educaccion para La Prevencion del Abuso de Droga (CEDRO), 135
Chapare. *See* Bolivia coca growing areas
Chapare Regional Development Project, 9
Chavarria Diez de Medina, Isaac ("Oso"), 5, 90
Chavez Penaherrera, Demetrio Limonel, 185, 194-195
Cheney, Richard, 47
COB. *See* Central Obrera Boliviana
Coca. *See* Bolivia and Peru
Coca Reduction Directorate (DIRECO), 11-12, 36, 59, 78-79, 92, 102
Cochabamba Tropic Peasant Workers Special Federation, 64
CONTRADROGAS, 198
Control y Reduccion del Cultivo de la Coca en el Alto Huallaga (CORAH), 120-121, 131-132, 136, 144, 152-153, 166, 195, 202
CORAH. *See* Control y Reduccion del Cultivo de la Coca en el Alto Huallaga
Corr, Edwin, 8, 10, 60
D'Amato, Alfonse, 24
DAO. *See* Defense Attache Office

Index 275

DEA. *See* Drug Enforcement Administration
Decree Law 25444, 175
Defense Attache Office (DAO), 14-15
Department of Agriculture (DOA), 62, 222
Department of Defense (DOD), 39-40, 43
Department of Health and Human Services, 4
Department of Justice, 23
Department of State. *See* Bureau of International Narcotics Matters (INM)
DIPOD. *See* Directorio de la Policia de Drogas
DIRECO. *See* Coca Reduction Directorate
Directorio de la Policia de Drogas (DIPOD), 128, 132, 134, 136, 138, 140-141, 152, 155, 205
DOA. *See* Department of Agriculture
DOD. *See* Department of Defense
Dominguez, Carmelo ("Meco"), 54, 58, 65
DOS. *See* Department of State
Drug Enforcement Administration (DEA), 4-5, 12-13, 16, 18, 25, 29-31, 33-34, 37, 42-43, 52, 57-58, 64, 66, 72-76, 92, 100, 103, 106, 111, 117, 120, 129, 132, 134, 136, 138, 147, 152, 154-155, 205-206, 226
Durand Ramirez, Oscar, 193
Eagleburger, Lawrence S., 47
El Paso Intelligence Center (EPIC), 39
Eli Lilly and Company 139-140, 154
Empresa Nacional de Coca (ENACO), 120, 132, 140
ENACO. *See* Empresa Nacional de Coca
Enterprise for the Americas Act, 60
Eradication. *See* coca eradication in Bolivia and Peru
Estremadoiro, Douglas, 32
Federacion Especial Campesina del Tropico Cochabambino, 21
FEDIP. *See* Frente Para La Defensa de Intereses Populares
FELCN. *See* Fuerzas Especiales para La Lucha Contra Narcotrafico
Ferrarone, Don, 73, 76, 107
Financial Action Task Force (US Treasury Department), 40
Foreign Assistance Act, 4, 10
Frente Para La Defensa de Intereses Populares (FEDIP), 126, 132
Fuerzas Especiales para La Lucha Contra Narcotrafico (FELCN or UMOPAR), 36, 56, 96
Fujimori, Alberto, 158, 160-162, 167, 170-171, 176-177, 182-183, 190, 198, 208, 211
Galvin, John, 17

Gamarra, Eduardo, 226
GAO. *See* General Accounting Office
Garcia, Alan, 46, 129-130, 134, 139, 141, 151-152, 155, 205
Garcia Meza, Luis, 5, 17
Gelbard, Robert, 51, 58, 65
General Accounting Office (GAO), 28, 34, 62, 225
Graham-Rudman Act, 24
Gueiler Tejada, Lydia, 4
Gutierrez, Elias, 56
Guzman, Abimael, 122-124, 180, 193
Guzman-Gonzalez, Erwin, 57, 65, 77
Hayes, Edward, 30-31, 101, 188
Hawkins, Paula, 24
INM. *See* Bureau of International Narcotics Matters
International Narcotics Control Act, 61
Iriarte, Ronald, 77
International Standing Committee (ISC), 7
Iturralde, Carlos, 51
Johnson, Lyndon, 224
Kempff, Noel, 18-19
Klinski, Saenz, 32
Ley 1008. *See* Ley del Regimen de la Coca y Sustancias Controladas - Ley 1008
Levitsky, Melvyn, 146
Ley del Regimen de la Coca y Sustancias Controladas - Ley 1008, 34-36, 45, 67, 80, 84-85, 103
Meese, Edwin, 7, 27, 139
Miller, Dennis, 47
Ministry of Alternate Development (Bolivia), 84
MRTA. *See* Tupac Amaru Revolutionary Movement
Narcotics Assistance Unit (NAU), 27, 30-31, 34, 36-37, 42, 57, 78, 138, 147, 153, 160, 188
NAS. *See* Narcotics Assistance Unit (NAU)
National Commission Against the Improper Use and Illegal Trafficking of Drugs (CONALID), 88
National Drug Policy Board (NDPB), 7, 27
National Directorate of Chemical and Controlled Substances (NDCCS), 67
National Security Decision (NSD) - 18, 151, 207
National Security Decision Directive (NSDD) - 221, 17, 100, 133, 205
National Security Council (NSC), 12-13, 46-47, 219

NAU. *See* Narcotics Assistance Unit
NDCCS. *See* National Directorate of Chemical and Controlled Substances
NDPB. *See* National Drug Policy Board
Noriega, Manuel, 30
NSC. *See* National Security Council
NSD 18. *See* National Security Decision 18
NSDD 221. *See* National Security Decision Directive 221
Nunn, Sam, 4
Office for National Drug Control Policy (ONDCP), 38-41, 46-47, 52, 108, 151, 196, 216, 218-219, 223-226
Omnibus Anti-Drug Abuse Act, 38, 40
ONDCP. *See* Office for National Drug Control Policy
Operation Condor, 129, 131-132, 135
Operation Blast Furnace, 17-21, 26, 101-102, 109, 218
Operation Ghost Zone, 70, 73-74, 107-108
Operation Relampago (Lightning), 134
Operation Safe Haven, 56, 57
Operation Snow Cap, 25, 29, 42-43, 93, 103, 135, 148, 152, 206, 218, 228
Operation Stone Bridge, 55
Operation Support Justice 73, 184
Paz Estenssoro, Victor, 10-11, 16-17, 21, 32, 34, 88, 99-101, 109
Paz Zamora, Jaime, 46, 49, 51, 54-57, 65, 69, 84, 89-91, 104-105
PEAH. *See* Proyecto Especial Alto Huallaga
Peru
  anti-drug policy, 120, 127-129, 135-136, 141, 145-146, 153, 160-161, 163-164, 167, 170-173, 175, 185, 194, 198-199, 203-216
  coca
    cultural tradition, 117, 156, 218-219
    eradication, 154, 166-168, 183, 186, 195
    farmers, 133, 145, 156, 166, 186, 191-193, 199, 205, 221
    growing areas, 118, 143-144
    production, 119, 136, 142, 157, 166, 170, 183, 188, 195, 199-200, 218
  narcotrafficking, 118, 125, 128, 131-133, 137, 144-145, 156-158, 167-168, 185-186, 219-221
  socio-economic conditions, 115-117, 119, 123, 127, 130-132, 137, 143, 145, 157-160, 162, 183, 192-193, 204-205, 218, 228
Proyecto Especial Alto Huallaga (PEAH), 121, 132, 202
RAND Corporation, 28, 112, 226-227

Rangel, Charles, 24
Reagan, Nancy, 6
Reagan, Ronald, 4, 6-8, 12, 17, 23-24, 133, 139, 206, 217-218, 221, 224, 226
Red Dragon, 55
Repentance Decree (*Decreto Supremo 22881*), 65, 77
Rico Toro, Faustino, 56
Rivera Villavicencio, Hugo, 45, 65, 77
Roca Suarez, Asunta, 76
Roca Suarez, Jorge ("Techo de Paja"), 54
Rodriguez, Reynaldo, 145
Rodriguez, Winston, 77
Rowell, Edward 10-11, 15-17, 20-21, 101
San Antonio Conference, 171-172
Sanchez de Lozada, Gonzalo, 92, 94-95
Sasser, Jim, 86
Snowcroft, Brent, 47
SEAMOS (Educational System for Social Mobilization and Anti-drug Addiction), 87
Shining Path. *See* Sendero Luminoso
SL. *See* Sendero Luminoso
Sendero Luminoso (SL), 121-127, 133-134, 140-141, 143, 145-146, 158, 169, 179-181, 185, 189-190, 191-193, 199, 202, 207-208
Shultz, George P., 33
Siles Zuazo, Hernan, 8-12
Single Convention for Narcotics Control, 3
SOUTHCOM. *See* Southern Command, United States
Southern Command, United States (SOUTHCOM), 17, 19, 21, 25, 44-45, 49-50, 55-57, 72-76, 78, 103, 105, 138, 147, 153-154, 165, 176, 184, 207, 209, 226
Special Forces. *See* Southern Command, United States
Spike. *See* Eli Lilly and Company
Suarez Gomez, Roberto, 5, 37, 65
Task Force Janus, 17-19, 25
Taylor, James, 17
Thurman, Maxwell, 49, 105, 153
Torrelio, Celso, 6
Trost, A. H., 41
Tupac Amaru Revolutionary Movement (MRTA), 125-126, 133, 141, 143, 145-146, 158, 178, 180-181, 190, 202, 207, 209
UMOPAR. *See* Unidad Movil Policial Para Areas Rurales

Unidad Movil Policial Para Areas Rurales (UMOPAR), 8, 12, 14-16, 18, 22, 25, 30-31, 33-34, 37, 44-45, 50-52, 54-59, 64-65, 71-72, 74-76, 78-80, 86, 92-93, 95-96, 102-103, 105-106, 111
United Nations Convention of Vienna, 141
United States
   anti-drug policy, 4, 6-14, 16, 23-25, 27, 29, 34, 36, 38, 40-41, 45, 47-49, 51-53, 56-57, 70, 81, 94-95, 98-113, 129, 131-133, 135-136, 139, 142, 152-153, 163-165, 173, 178, 186, 194, 199, 201-233
   Congress, 4, 6, 10, 23, 26, 40, 139, 143-144, 178, 187-188, 206, 209, 217-220
   foreign policy. *See* United States anti-drug policy
USAID. *See* Agency for International Development
US-Bolivia Extradition Treaty, 76, 77
US Information Service (USIS), 86
Velasco Alverado, Juan, 116-117, 123
Walters, John, 47
War on Drugs. *See* United States anti-drug policy
Weinberger, Caspar, 41
Weisman, Marvin, 5
Woerner, Fred, 33
Wroblesky, Ann, 33, 139
Yungas. *See* Bolivia coca growing areas

Author Biographical Sketch

Sewall H. Menzel earned his Ph.D. at the Graduate School of International Studies, University of Miami (Coral Gables). A graduate of The Citadel (B.A., history), he also holds a M.P.A. in public administration from the University of Oklahoma.

Dr. Menzel is a faculty member of Florida International University, where he has taught courses in Latin American politics, U.S. foreign policy, national security affairs and goverment. He spent the better part of the 1980s as a serving U.S. Army lieutenant-colonel foreign area specialist on Latin America, working in Bolivia, Peru and Panama. Other books by the author include *Bullets Versus Ballots: Political Violence and Revolutionary War in El Salvador, 1979-1991* and *The Potosi Mint Scandal And Great Transition of 1652*.